CROSSING BOUNDARIES

CROSSING BOUNDARIES

Tension and Transformation in International Service-Learning

EDITED BY

Patrick M. Green and

Mathew Johnson

Foreword by Robert G. Bringle

STERLING, VIRGINIA

Published by Stylus Publishing, LLC
22883 Quicksilver Drive
Sterling, Virginia 20166-2102

Library of Congress Cataloging-in-Publication Data
Crossing boundaries : tension and transformation in international
service-learning / edited by Patrick Green and Matthew
Johnson. – First edition.
    pages cm
Includes bibliographical references and index.
ISBN 978-1-57922-619-0 (cloth : alk. paper)
ISBN 978-1-57922-620-6 (pbk. : alk. paper)
ISBN 978-1-57922-621-3 (library networkable e-edition)
ISBN 978-1-57922-622-0 (consumer e-edition)
1. Foreign study. 2. Service learning. 3. Education and globalization.
4. World citizenship. I. Green, Patrick (Patrick M.) II. Johnson,
Matthew, (associate professor of sociology)
LB2375.C76 2014
370.116--dc23

                                                    2013048788

13-digit ISBN: 978-1-57922-619-0 (cloth)
13-digit ISBN: 978-1-57922-620-6 (paperback)
13-digit ISBN: 978-1-57922-621-3 (library networkable e-edition)
13-digit ISBN: 978-1-57922-622-0 (consumer e-edition)

Printed in the United States of America

All first editions printed on acid-free paper
that meets the American National Standards Institute
Z39-48 Standard.

Bulk Purchases

Quantity discounts are available for use in workshops and for
staff development.
Call 1-800-232-0223

First Edition, 2014

10   9   8   7   6   5   4   3   2   1

Dedicated to Colleen Mary Green, who has modeled a world of love shared with so many and inspires me daily to extend such love to the larger world. To Maura, Sean, and Bridget Green: May you engage in the world to see its beauty, to make it better, to honor dignity across differences, and to live in the tension that may lead to transformation.

—*Patrick M. Green*

Dedicated to Lura "Peg" Rayburn Elliott and Edward Alfred Elliott, who showed me the world from the picture window of their living room and taught me to dream big. To Savannah and Noah: May you come to know the special places in the world where dignity and humanity are one.

—*Mathew Johnson*

CONTENTS

The Most Powerful Pedagogy

Bringle and Hatcher (2011) posit that international service-learning (ISL) is the most powerful pedagogy in higher education (and invite scholars to prove them wrong). They note that ISL has a more extensive array of desired educational outcomes (versus traditional pedagogies), can attain desired learning objectives across a broader array of conditions and for a wider range of students, can produce deeper and more permanent changes in students' current and future lives, and can produce unique educational outcomes that traditional pedagogies either cannot attain as well or at all.

After analyzing ISL as the intersection of study abroad, service-learning, and international education, they define *ISL* as

> a *structured academic experience in another country* in which students *(a)* participate in an organized service activity that addresses identified community needs; *(b) learn from direct interaction and cross-cultural dialogue with others;* and *(c)* reflect on the *experience* in such a way as to gain further understanding of course content, a deeper understanding of *global and intercultural* issues, a broader appreciation of the *host country* and the discipline, and an enhanced sense of their own responsibilities as citizens, locally and *globally.* (Bringle & Hatcher, 2011, p. 19, italics in original)

The chapters in Bringle, Hatcher, and Jones (2011) explored the possibilities, limitations, and concerns for ISL as well as suggesting ways to document its impact. The chapters explored how ISL has the potential to draw the best qualities of its three constituents (i.e., study abroad, service-learning, and international education) to provide learning opportunities that are consequently extensive, robust, transformational, and distinctive. Clearly, not all ISL programs are exemplary, but anecdotal testimony as well as evidence from case studies, qualitative research, and quantitative research is that ISL can have profound outcomes for students. Unfortunately, most students do not have access to this power pedagogy. Approximately 1–2% of American college students study abroad each year (Blumenthal & Gutierrez, 2009) and an unknown portion of those study-abroad experiences involve ISL (although it must be a small portion).

Numerous chapters in Bringle et al. (2011) explore the ethics of ISL, issues related to neocolonial traps, the centrality of social justice, institutional issues, and community relationships. Our South African colleague, Mabel Erasmus, focused "appropriate attention on the role that the community constituencies (i.e., organizations, residents, clients, consumers) should assume as cocreators of the curriculum, coeducators in the delivery of the curriculum, and coinvestigators in the evaluation of and study of ISL" (Bringle & Hatcher, 2011, p. 21).

Current Volume

Bringle et al.'s (2011) approach to ISL had at least two acknowledged biases: (a) it deliberately had a largely student-centric focus, and (b) it focused on expanding and improving research on ISL. Bringle and Hatcher (2011) conclude with the reflection that "if ISL is the most powerful pedagogy available to higher education, then it deserves a more diligent level of commitment" (p. 23). It is within the context of this scholarship that *Crossing Boundaries: Tension and Transformation in International Service-Learning* is offered. Indeed, this volume has the potential to further the commitment of practitioners and educators to ISL and clearly has a more balanced approach to considering issues for not only students but also faculty, institutions, and community partners within the context of contemporary geopolitical dynamics. Through case studies, critical analysis, and reflection, the authors explore how the commitment to ISL can be implemented, altered, and improved to produce outcomes for students, faculty, and community partners that have higher integrity. The chapters are authored by careful and thoughtful practitioners who are willing to admit the pleasures and perils of ISL. They describe their mistakes, the evolution of ISL programs, and the ways in which they continue to struggle to overcome guiding values, proscriptions, and prescriptions. The case studies that provide a basis for their analysis cover a wide array of institutional types, both graduate and undergraduate curricula, and mostly programs in economically struggling countries. They bear down on many critical issues that surface so clearly in ISL: the challenges of communications and relationships with distant collaborators; the inequalities that are inevitable, challenging, and sometimes irreconcilable (e.g., power, privilege, wealth, education, mobility, charity); students who resist or are unable to broaden their perspective on ISL experiences beyond cross-national voyeuristic orientations; institutional agendas and priorities that do not support or are in conflict with many of the goals and values of ISL; the logistic challenges and unpredictability of ISL; language as an impediment to and a basis for cultural immersion; and the mundane but important question, "Why ISL?" (see Erasmus, 2011; Plater, 2011; Plater, Jones, Bringle, & Clayton, 2009).

This volume is important because it surfaces and discusses critical issues that educators should grapple with in order to design, implement, improve, and evaluate ISL programs. The values, issues, and concerns that are surfaced are not entirely new. Many are them are the same or related to those that guided the early pioneers of service-learning (Stanton, Giles, & Cruz, 1999) and that have been articulated for study abroad (e.g., Hovey & Weinberg, 2009; Reilly & Senders, 2009). They provide one set—a set that is clearly within a critically analytic approach—that is very important to collect and disseminate.

Paralysis Through (Critical) Analysis

Although the proscriptions and prescriptions that are the basis for the critical analysis in this volume are worthy of attention, many are aspirational and some unattainable (e.g., understanding and being sensitive to the nuances of cultures in a country after even years of immersion when ISL involves shorter-term residence). There are some dialectics and challenges in ISL that run the risk of dissuading educators from attempting or continuing with ISL, therefore reducing commitment rather than enhancing it. In some cases, that might be for the best. On the one hand, practitioners, including authors in this volume, readily acknowledge the transformational potential of ISL. ISL is indeed powerful. On the other hand, the authors point out how challenges presented by history, politics, power, status, and the basic interpersonal relationships on which ISL is built all conspire to create potentially negative experiences for someone. Mathew Johnson notes, "Like all powerful human experiences, international service-learning is complex and can injure as easily as transform and can oppress as easily a liberate" (p. 11, this volume). The complexity of ISL needs to be further explored, understood, and appreciated, as the contributions of the authors of these chapters do. However, the gnarled nature of ISL and the potential negative consequences should not stop higher education from continuing to explore the potential for ISL to benefit all constituencies. The chapters in this volume will help educators do a better job of striving to have ISL programs that have integrity. Many of the authors have a perspective, set of presumptions, and collection of learning objectives that some of them admit are not shared by their colleagues, administrators, and students (e.g., social justice, correcting colonial and neocolonial approaches; understanding power and privilege; neoliberalism). In the case of students, this raises an interesting dilemma of largely ignoring the student's lack of interest in those values and learning objectives and what they desire from ISL. For educators to have an agenda with which students are not aligned fits a model of growth in new directions for students. However, it is paternalistic on the part of educators to impose an agenda on students and it ignores self-determination on the students' part as collaborators in the learning experience.

Conclusion

ISL has the virtue that it is a lens through which many of the important issues in study abroad, service-learning, and international education are magnified, sharpened, and clarified. It should be required reading for practitioners in not only those three areas but also the general area of community engagement in higher education. Bringle and Hatcher (2011) suggested the value of a review process for ISL that would "encourage all faculty and staff associated with ISL activities to be conscientious, ethical, and reflective practitioners about their work" (p. 27). The chapters in this volume will also provide a significant basis for helping ISL practitioners reflect on their work, review its nature, and improve its quality for all constituencies.

Robert G. Bringle, PhD, PhilD
July, 2014
Kulynych/Cline Visiting Distinguished Professor of Psychology
Appalachian State University

Chancellor's Professor Emeritus of Psychology and Philanthropic Studies
Senior Scholar, Center of Service and Learning
Indiana University-Purdue University Indianapolis

References

Blumenthal, P., & Gutierrez, R. (Eds.). (2009). *Meeting America's global education challenge: Expanding study abroad capacity at U.S. colleges and universities*. New York, NY: Institute of International Education.

Bringle, R. G., & Hatcher, J. A. (2011). International service learning. In R. G. Bringle, J. A. Hatcher, & S. G. Jones (Eds.), *International service learning: Conceptual frameworks and research* (pp. 3–28). Sterling, VA: Stylus.

Bringle, R. G., Hatcher, J. A., & Jones, S. G. (Eds.). (2011). *International service learning: Conceptual frameworks and research*. Sterling, VA: Stylus.

Erasmus, M. (2011). An international perspective on North American international service learning: Reflections based on South African service learning experiences. In R. G. Bringle, J. A. Hatcher, & S. G. Jones (Eds.), *International service learning: Conceptual frameworks and research* (pp. xx–yy). Sterling, VA: Stylus.

Hovey, R., & Weinberg. A. (2009). Global learning and the making of citizen diplomats. In R. Lewin (Ed.), *Study abroad and the making of global citizens: Higher education and the quest for global citizenship* (pp. 33–48). New York, NY: Routledge.

Plater, W. M. (2011). The context for international service learning. In R. G. Bringle, J. A. Hatcher, & S. G. Jones (Eds.), *International service learning: Conceptual frameworks and research* (pp. 29–56). Sterling, VA: Stylus.

Plater, W. M., Jones, S. G., Bringle, R. G., & Clayton, P. H. (2009). Educating globally competent citizens through international service learning. In R. Lewin (Ed.), *The handbook of practice and research in study abroad: Higher education and the quest for global citizenship* (pp. 485–505). Florence, KY: Taylor and Francis.

Reilly, D., & Senders, S. (2009, Fall). Becoming the change we want to see: Critical study abroad for a tumultuous world. *Frontiers: The Interdisciplinary Journal of Study Abroad, XVIII*, 241–267.

Stanton, T. K., Giles, D. E., Jr., & Cruz, N. I. (1999). *Service-learning: A movement's pioneers reflect on its origins, practice, and future*. San Francisco: Jossey-Bass.

INTRODUCTION

I Came, Reluctantly

Mathew Johnson
Siena College

I don't believe in charity. I believe in solidarity. Charity is so vertical. It goes from the top to the bottom. Solidarity is horizontal. It respects the other person. I have a lot to learn from other people.

—Eduardo Hughes Galeano

On Beginnings and Feelings

I came to service-learning reluctantly, skeptical, and full of doubt. My mentors and teachers were not from the formal service-learning world; they were not Campus Compact luminaries. So, several years ago when Campus Compact chose me, together with my coeditor of this volume, Patrick Green, as a Campus Compact Engaged Scholar, a complicated set of mixed feelings arose in me. The feelings, which ranged from affirmation and pride to guilt and slight embarrassment, echoed the feelings my students have shared with me in their service-learning reflection journals for years. Feelings are instructive.

Feelings are the squishy, ill-defined, subjective, yucky things that most faculty don't like to talk about, never mind see as a resource for learning. This is true even though brain and learning research has unequivocally established the important role of affect in higher level learning. Feelings—affective content of new experiences and information—are the glue that cement the new to the old and weave meaning into what we learn about ourselves and the world around us. And sometimes feelings precede our understanding of the new information in ways that, when we listen to them, can reveal deeper meaning otherwise missed in the new information.

In my case, as is often the case with my students, my feelings were telling me something about my location in a set of power relations. Here I was, an early career American academic, being recognized by the legitimizing

1

institutional power structure for doing work I had come to reluctantly and struggled with for a decade. I struggled because the work of service-learning holds within it the twin potential for liberation and continued oppression. Done as liberatory practice, it is coevolutionary, cocreated colearning. Done as oppressive practice, it is reifying, often humiliating and disempowering, charity. As legitimizing institutions are often interested in reifying current power relations, the recognition called into question my self-perception as an outsider with liberatory praxis.

As the full group of newly chosen Campus Compact Engaged Scholars came together for our first meeting at a retreat center outside Providence, Rhode Island, I came to understand that I was one of many in a new generation of scholar-practitioners who had come to the work of service-learning reluctantly, skeptically, and through many avenues. I learned there too that Campus Compact was struggling to figure out how to foster a new age of service-learning that pushed beyond single episodic course-based projects and sought to rebalance student learning and community outcome priorities. It was in those conversations that the seed of this volume began to germinate. Patrick and I are grateful to those other Campus Compact Engaged Scholars who were then and continue now to be our companions in this exploration.

International service-learning is one of several modes or types of service-learning that highlights this tension between the liberatory and oppressive potentials. As Patrick and I envisioned this volume, we tried to explore that tension. The authors of the chapters that follow struggle with the same tensions and potentials. Some reach temporary resolution, whereas others leave the questions open for the reader. In this introduction, I tried to keep my mentors and teachers in mind and explore the terrain illuminated by discomfort.

In this introduction, I chose not to review the literature on international service-learning. The authors of the chapters herein did that well in many places and in so doing provided the reader with a rich and complete set of textual resources. Instead, I chose to walk the reader through an abridged version of my evolution toward international service-learning and my insights about it. You will see that my evolution is not unique. Indeed in many ways this volume is a more detailed, academic exploration of certain aspects of that evolution. A common theme in every chapter is the developmental nature of this work. It takes multiple attempts, often over years, for an individual or an institution to get this work even nearly right. The challenges of unequal resources, power, and privilege can never be completely erased. As many authors who follow have discovered along the way, however, done well and with an emphasis on reciprocal, sustained relationships, international service-learning comes to possess another kind of power: the potential of transformation.

Discovering the "Other"

At the beginning of my teaching career, I found myself in a small college town in far northern New England. I was a newly minted sociologist and eager to radicalize my students. Little did I realize that my students were already radical. Working-class kids from working-class families get Marx intuitively. They live it. We had lots of fun exploring the nuances of economic exploitation and capitalist power structures. It was too easy. As I looked around for a more challenging teaching project, I discovered late in my first year that the university had in its charter a clause claiming that it was to be about the education of local Native American groups. Still, there were virtually no native students enrolled, and more profound than this was the realization that most of my students, as insightful as they were about class oppression, were blind perpetrators of racial oppression in their own community. Race and racism, on both personal and institutional levels, were the challenge.

For a semester I tried the standard approach. Lecture, seminar, multimedia. My success at inculcating a transferable sociological lens that my students could migrate from class issues to race issues was limited at best. So I focused. I focused in on the issue and designed a new course called Native American Holocaust.

The first day of class, two Wolastoqiyik elders showed up at the door of the classroom. And my learning began. Dan and Carolyn attended every session of that class. They brought to life the readings in ways that were profound for my students. We cried, we laughed, we prayed, we sang, we argued, we shouted, and I learned. In chapter 9 of this volume, "Multidisciplinary Learning: Interdisciplinary Teaching and Community Service-Learning in Jamaica," Mohamed, Loggins, and Floyd illustrate the importance of dialogue across "difference" that is incredibly important to help participants (be they students, faculty, or others) draw the insights and connections that extend learning.

At the end of that semester, Dan asked me to consider working with him to start conversations between the local native communities and the university. A beautiful friendship, a powerful partnership, and an abiding mentorship were born. Over the next several years, Dan and I worked together to build learning experiences that transformed White and native students through dialogue. My students began working in and with the native communities they had come to know in new ways through this dialogue, and at first 3, then 7, then 15, and so on native students enrolled.

Encountering the Other as a cocreator, a colearner, and a coteacher is at the core of good service-learning. In chapter 1, "Power Relations, North and South: Negotiating Meaningful 'Service' in the Context of Imperial History," Mellom and Herrera walk through the struggle to encounter the Other in this way. In their chapter, Mellom and Herrera take the reader through four phases of this process (honeymoon, hostility, humor, home) against the backdrop of the historical context of imperialism and questions about the relationship between the server and the served. Examining the historical and power relations between participants, with participants, as we did with the Wolastoqiyik, is essential to just relations. Mellom and Herrera share their insight about what is necessary (especially for first timers) to help participants move forward through stages of the experience. As students move into an expected hostility phase, some self-segregate. Mellom and Herrera note,

> On the other hand, some preservice students make conscious, daily decisions to fight through the feelings of insecurity and insufficiency and adapt to the new ideas, surroundings, and circumstances. They minimize "self" in order to better understand those with whom they are interacting; students begin to form empathetic relationships with the individuals they encounter. In short, they begin to truly care. They find themselves questioning the long-standing beliefs and attitudes that reflect their prior socialization.

As teachers, designers, and practitioners of these experiences, we can thoughtfully integrate the teachable moments and coaching that are necessary to get students to the next stages.

Reluctance and Zapatistas

Later in my career, in another college town, this time in southern Appalachia (I would later come to realize that where I started was merely the northern extent of the Appalachian belt), the local issue was deep generalized poverty. This college had a Bonner Scholar Program in which students receive a scholarship for long-term, intensive, developmental service commitments to community partner agencies working to alleviate poverty. As Bonner Scholars migrated into my classes, I came to realize that these students were engaged in long-term continuous dialogues with members of the larger community not unlike the ones I had been a part of with my students and the Wolastoqiyik community.

Out of the collective work the Bonner Scholars did in the local community grew a desire among them to explore the challenges faced by communities struggling with poverty abroad. So, egged on by my students (or perhaps I should call them my teachers) and driven to find a just and equitable means to explore these issues abroad, I worked with a colleague working in a human rights NGO to develop a delegation-based travel course that explored indigenous autonomy movements across the semester and then took the class to Chiapas, Mexico, and into Zapatista-controlled territory.

The intensity of dialogue with the "Other" was magnified a hundred-fold. Students spent hours of humble conversation with the Junta of the Caricole followed by community visits in which students and community members shared their stories about family, justice, food, and struggle. On each of these postsemester trips, inevitably at the end of a marathon meeting with the community or the Junta, a student would ask, "How can we help?" and a Zapatista man or woman would respond, "Go home, look around, find the problem in your own community and start there. When you help there, you help here. The challenges we face are symptoms of the same problem that creates the challenges in your community." I am a slow learner. It took six trips over three years for me to hear this lesson, from this teacher, fully.

The Bonner Scholars became my new teachers. Feeling empowered by our Zapatista teachers, Bonner Scholars pushed me to consider the relevance of the sociological theories and the sociological methods for the challenges in the local community. These students challenged me to help them figure out how to move beyond their direct service, and beyond abstract academic journal articles, to build the capacity of their partner agencies and begin thinking about solutions to the underlying causes of community challenges. So I brought community challenges into the classroom, and we began mapping the assets and the needs of the larger community together.

In my last years there, joined by a new colleague, Don Levy, the Bonner Scholars and other students in my class completed a full asset mapping survey of the county and began leveraging those assets to create a community think tank focused on solutions. We also collectively decided to try to connect our newfound ability to link service and academics with our earlier profound cultural immersion experiences abroad. So once again, pushed by the students/teachers, Don Levy and I developed the first true international service-learning offering for our students.

As is illustrated well in several of the chapters in this volume, development, both of individuals and of institutions, is an essential aspect of the work of service-learning. We believed we were ready to move outward and explore more fully our movement toward a just practice. In chapter 2, "Decentering the United States in International Service-Learning: A Comparative Perspective," Espenschied-Reilly and Iverson explore the challenges of moving outward to another culture with an American understanding of service-learning and challenge the reader to consider the motivations for service-learning:

> Morton (1995) believed, "Integrity in service-learning . . . comes not by moving from charity to social change, but from working with increasing depth in a particular paradigm" (p. 19). However, Kendall (1990) posited that service-learning experiences should move students beyond acts of charity to address root causes of systemic social inequality. The poles of

Kendall's continuum—charitable and justice-oriented—are typically identified as competing paradigms within service-learning. Service-learning oriented toward charity is an "exercise in altruism" and emphasizes "character
building and a kind of compensatory justice where the well-off feel obligated to help the less advantaged" (Battistoni, 1997, p. 151). By contrast,
service-learning focused on social change (justice-oriented) helps students
to develop a deeper understanding of social issues, promotes the development of skills necessary to work toward social change, and incorporates an
analysis of power and oppression (Boyle-Baise & Langford, 2004).

In chapter 4, "Asset-Based Community Development and Integral Human
Development: Two Theories Undergirding an International Service-Learning
Program," Morales and Caballero Barrón share their application of asset-based
community development, drawing on the U.S. work of John Kretzmann and
John McKnight. Morales and Caballero Barrón explore a 5-year partnership
between DePaul University (DPU) and residents in Merida, Mexico. In particular, they frame important actions that the university and its programs can
take to set the stage for more reciprocal, open sharing:

> At the outset of the partnership, these institutional differences were miti-
> gated by two factors: (a) DPU staff was bilingual and bicultural, and (b)
> both universities were open to exploring their service-learning pedagogical
> differences. Because the universities shared the same approach to creating
> mutually beneficial partnerships and a common focus on guiding students
> to learn about, generate, and disseminate knowledge that humanizes soci-
> ety and themselves and employing critical reflection to regularly evaluate
> program goals and outcomes, challenges that arose for the partnership were
> mitigated.

As we set out to develop our first international service-learning course,
we would come to know for ourselves the need to actively move students
through resistance as Mellom and Herrera explore; we would come to know
the challenges of translating an American orientation to service-learning in a
new context as Espenschied-Reilly and Iverson explore; and we would come
to know the need for a long-term institutional partnership as Morales and
Caballero Barrón explore.

Bolivia 1.0

I set off for Bolivia in October of that year, spending 10 days there meeting and talking with the community leaders of the three communities on
Isla Del Sol. I set up agreements for us to offer 3 days of intensive English

instruction, together with a human-size container of English games to be left behind in each school for teachers to use. This is what the community leaders had said they most wanted from us. Feelings are instructive. I was conflicted about the request. What did it mean to teach English to Aymara villagers when the colonial Spanish was already slowly replacing the Aymaran language? Was not English merely the language of a more subtle yet more ubiquitous imperialism qua globalization?

In chapter 5, "Partnership Versus Patronage: A Case Study in International Service-Learning From a Community College Perspective," Lori Halverson-Wente and Mark Halverson-Wente explore the struggle to avoid "patronage" and charity and nurture reciprocity as they explain their attempts to work through the Cambodian patron-client relationship dyad. They suggest that a strong counterbalance may lie in the development of a model of assessment that includes program impact on village-partners

In June we returned, 20 students and 5 staff, to Bolivia. We spent 10 days getting to know the country, attending museums, and having meetings with Bolivian academics, NGOs, and indigenous movement groups. Then we were off to Isla Del Sol. Halfway through the island experience, I came to realize that the earlier unease I felt was bubbling up in only half the students. The students, my teachers, who had developed a critical sociological perspective demanded that I offer a few impromptu lessons to the nonsociology students about colonialism, postcolonialism, globalization, neoliberalism, cultural resistance, and indigenismo. The hostel owner allowed me to use the back of the hostel, a dark gray stucco building, and a stone as a chalkboard. By the time we were done, 20 or so other Western travelers had gathered around the fringes of the class, all sitting in a semicircle on the ground. That night my students and I ran impromptu discussion circles late into the night with locals and other travelers, and I knew that my students were grappling with their privileged place in the world and the meaning of the relationships they were engaged in with "Others."

In chapter 3, "Strategic International Service-Learning Partnership: Mitigating the Impact of Rapid Urban Development in Vietnam," Halimi, Kecskes, Ingle, and Phuong echo the need to carefully consider the economic, political, and social context (of Vietnam) in their description of Portland State University's development as a "facilitating institution." They also note several key recommendations that are explored further in the chapter and volume:

- Mutual benefits
- Contextual alignment
- Start small with a collaborative process
- Strategic leadership involvement (university)

- Strategic leadership involvement (local political context)
- Institutional structural investment
- Substantive community involvement
- Scholarly approach
- Disseminate/publicize
- Embrace experimentation/learning/reflective practice

Indeed, Halimi et al. offer the reader important lessons I learned the hard way, from a variety of teachers, across many years of stumbling praxis.

DEEP

Following our attempts in Bolivia, I moved to my current institution, Siena College, which is in the peculiar position of being physically located in a well-off suburb yet is committed through its Catholic and Franciscan mission to "building a world that is more just, peaceable, and humane." At Siena, I relented, fully. Having seen the powerful transformative effects of students working and dialoging with "Others," an effect that not only led to deeper learning but also led to the transformation of "selves" and "Others" more often than not into a "we," I could no longer resist. So I drew together all that I had learned from my teachers over the years—from my students; from Dan, Carolyn, and the Wolastoqiyik; from the Zapatista community and the Junta; from Appalachian coal miners; from Aymaran communities; and from many others along the way—to build a service-learning program.

The Siena College approach to service-learning follows the following core principles of DEEP partnership:

1. *Our partnerships are strategic.* We linked the disciplinary strengths of our college and historical relationships with our community and build around issues we are equipped to tackle to maximize our impact.
2. *Our partnerships are long term.* We build 3- and 5-year partnership plans with communities.
3. *Our partnerships are multifaceted.* We aim to connect with partners in many ways, including through service-learning courses, community-based research projects, coordinated grant applications, internships and multiyear Bonner Scholar placements, postgraduate year-of-service placements, and so on.
4. *Our partnerships are developmental* for students who move from basic direct service to program development and management, for faculty who move from basic service-learning projects to fully community-immersed

courses, and for partners who move from thinking about volunteer maximization to capacity building and networked social change.

5. *Our partnerships are contextualized* through regular attention to historical and cultural understanding for students, community members, and the public at large.

6. *Our partnerships are reciprocal.* The community and its members are coeducators of students and coadministrators of projects, and attention is paid to the costs and benefits of all involved.

7. *Our partnerships are about capacity-building change* and utilizing the academic resources of the academy, together with the wisdom of the community to build the capacity for community change.

Around this set of core principles we have built a robust local service-learning program. Around these core principles we have begun to build our international partnerships. Indeed these principles resonate with several of the principles and best practices discussed throughout this volume. It is important to note that, on the ground, what is often most important for the impact and meaning of these experiences are the micro-level details. As some would say, God (or the devil, depending on your perspective) is in the details.

Core

At its core, all service-learning and especially international service-learning is highly problematic and potentially transformative. As the historical inheritors of privileges grounded in consolidated spoils of colonialism, privilege oft maintained through continuity of shadow colonialism, American students and faculty enter into relationships with "Others" in and through service-learning as wielders of power. Power can distort, it can coerce, it can pervert, it can corrupt. Power can also liberate. Herein lies the core of my original unease, my original resistance, and my residual feelings.

How do we unpack this relationship in a just manner? How do we ensure that in our goal to wed learning and service we are not exploiting the Other for new, or recycled, aims? How do we tilt the scale toward laboratory practice and transformative experience and away from feel-good "voluntourism"? How can we hope to transcend chasms of sociolinguistic, sociocultural, and socioeconomic difference? Should we take such risks with students, with Others? Should the financial costs of such an educational approach be better spent directly addressing the community challenges we hope to address in some small way through our service-learning? Does it really lead to greater learning?

Some of the answers to these questions lie in the values we bring to the work and the values our students form in and through the work. Several of the chapters in this volume are from practitioners from faith-based institutions who draw on the mission and values of their colleges for guidance. See, for example, chapter 11, "International Service-Learning in Faith-Based Contexts" by Kollman and Morgan from the University of Notre Dame. Our own work in the Bonner network and through the National Assessment of Service and Community Engagement (NASCE) suggest that it is indeed values-driven and family-centered experiences that have profound effects on children and youth. Nonetheless, we would be remiss to suggest that these experiences alone create the necessary conditions for the formation of individual values, convictions, and action. Rather, we believe that institutions can indeed shape, in profound ways, their students—be they "students," faculty, or staff. When one pieces apart the pivotal teaching and learning moments of a developmental experience in service-learning and international service-learning, one can ascertain that these experiences are, in fact, replicable and transferable across individual, institutional, and even cultural contexts. See, for example, chapter 10, "Transforming Practice: International Service-Learning as Preparation for Entering Health Care" by Doll, Mu, Jensen, Hoffman, and Goulet. The authors explore international service-learning as a mode of training health care providers with special emphasis on reflective awareness of the differences in power and privilege and the inequities that are embedded in social relationships. Cultivating this reflective awareness is transformational for their students. See also chapter 6, "Building Student and Organizational Capacity: Assignments and Tools" by Gardinier. The author lays out specific assignments and sequencing models to design transformative experiences in international service-learning. We believe more scholarly exploration of just how to tackle the serious, power-laden challenges and the transformative potential of international service-learning is needed.

In my current long-term international project to build DEEP partnerships abroad, I have found useful guidance and significant tensions among colleagues in the world of study abroad. This creative tension is captured well in chapter 8, "When Service-Learning Meets Study Abroad: Locating International Service-Learning Institutionally and Abroad" by Ong and Green. As we move increasingly into an interconnected and smaller world, conversations across international education practices will become more and more necessary and will lead to richer understandings of educational practice, including service-learning, in a global context. In chapter 12, "A Critical Global Citizenship," Hartman and Kiely provide one of the most robust theoretical lenses through which to make sense of the emerging global engagement with which we are all faced. Theirs is a fitting final chapter for readers to delve deeply into the complexities of identity, power, and purpose in international service-learning. Their problematizing of the dominant narratives within international service-learning literature and discourse capture well the terrain from which we have facilitated this volume and out of which we offer suggestions in the conclusion for some steps forward.

I came to service-learning a deep skeptic; I remain a skeptic. I came to service-learning after seeing firsthand the transformative potential for students. Like all powerful human experiences, international service-learning is complex and can injure as easily as transform and can oppress as easily as liberate.

POWER RELATIONS, NORTH AND SOUTH

Negotiating Meaningful "Service" in the Context of Imperial History

Paula J. Mellom
University of Georgia

Socorro Herrera
Kansas State University

If you have come to help me, you are wasting your time. But if you have come because your liberation is bound up with mine, then let us work together.

—Aboriginal sister activist, opendoorcommunity.org

Service: Who Is the "Server" and Who Is the "Served"?

Framing the idea of service-learning without casting those who are participating in the service as the "helpers" and those who are being served as "needing help" is complicated and rife with pitfalls. This problematic is underscored by the fact that although *service-learning* can be defined as "a philosophy, pedagogy, and model for community development that is used as an instructional strategy to meet learning goals and/or content standards" and addresses needs important to the community served (National Youth Leadership Council, n.d.), the concept of "development" is in itself problematic in that it bears with it the idea that the community being served is in need of development, that is to say is "underdeveloped." The "service" then drifts into the realm of "aid," which often has overtones of paternalism (Escobar, 1995; Gelmon & Billig, 2007). The problem is further exacerbated when those who are "serving" come from socioeconomically, ethnically, and linguistically privileged groups (i.e., generally middle-class, monolingual English speakers) and those who are "served" come from peripheral or marginalized groups.

The problematized server-served relationship becomes particularly salient when the service site is a developing country in the "South" and those traveling to serve are from the "North" (Henry, 2005; Kraft, 2002). It is perhaps not irrelevant that many of the communities "served" in Central America are the same communities that once were home to thousands of individuals who have immigrated to the North and now work in the service industry (e.g., hotels, restaurants, landscaping, agriculture) (Hondagneu-Sotelo, 2001). This trend is fueled by Northern desire for inexpensive goods and services and the concomitant need for cheap labor to supply them. This labor has historically been supplied in industrialized nations by the poor and disenfranchised and, in the United States particularly, by successive waves of new immigrants (Cowie, 1999; Sidorick, 2009). However, the larger economic drivers that draw these immigrants North often go unseen by contemporary social reformers who frequently see these populations only as people who need "help" (Gronemeyer, 1992). This only reinforces the persistent attitudes of some service-learning students that they "know what's best" for the communities they are visiting, that is, that they are coming to share their resources and knowledge with those who "need them." These attitudes undermine the idea of service as a reciprocal activity that is conceived of jointly and carried out collaboratively.

North and South: Social and Historical Tensions

Peculiar issues and tensions exist surrounding service-learning, particularly when the service involves the teaching of English as a foreign or second language. Such tensions exaggerate the problems of power discrepancies, reciprocity, and sustainability in the study abroad host communities. Although issues of power often are present in service-learning projects where there are differences of socioeconomic status, ethnicity, and privilege between the students engaged in service and the host community, these issues can be even more exaggerated when there are historical, political, and economic factors that impact host community attitudes toward the country from which the servers come. This study attempts to examine the processes undergone by the student participants in two study abroad experiences, with service-learning components, against their particular cultural and historical backdrops.

These courses took place in two Central American communities in countries that have historically had politically, economically, and socially complex relationships with the United States. One course was a study abroad course held in a rural, mountain Costa Rican community where a large university in the southeastern United States has a campus, a vested interest, and a stated mission to work with the community on projects that are beneficial to both the visiting university students and the community in an integrated way. The service portion of this course, attended by a group of nine participants, was an "English Camp" held during the 2-week, midterm vacation at two small, rural public schools with 35 local students and teachers. The primary goal of this language and culture course was to give pre- and in-service teachers a cultural immersion experience focused on the intersection of language and culture, particularly in diverse classrooms. The second group of 20 participants from a large midwestern university was involved in a study abroad experience in an urban Guatemalan community. The primary goal of this group was completion of a practicum course while teaching English in a high-poverty K–8 school setting.

The issue of language learning and the role of English and monolingual English-speaking service-learning students and teachers is complex and worthy of study, in part because the local children at the service-learning sites in rural Costa Rica and urban Guatemala are learning how to be bilingual in a society that is changing rapidly and is subject to the economic, political, and cultural pressures brought on by the increasing dependence of Central American states on the United States. This dependence strengthens the host communities' perception of English as valuable to their future economic success; however, this perception is a manifestation of increased globalization that challenges local, traditional, cultural, and linguistic norms. Therefore, any study of service or English-language teaching in Central America must be firmly rooted in a framework that considers the social, political, and historical context, because linguistic practices help to construct, reinforce, challenge, and refute social paradigms and structures. As Heller and Martin-Jones (2001) posited, language use and language policy in any given setting in contemporary societies are shaped by colonialism in the 19th and 20th centuries and "new global forms of cultural, economic and social domination" (p. 2).

In the past century, increased globalization has accelerated the process of human migration across political and geographic borders and caused social groups with vastly differing languages and cultures to come into direct and mediated contact with each other at rates and scopes never before seen (Nettle & Romaine, 2000). International commerce fueled by ease of travel and improved communications and media have made it possible for people to either physically cross borders or stay in their own countries and communities and still be in contact with different cultures and languages. Yet the economic and linguistic exchange has tended to be asymmetrical. The influence of the media, tourism, and "service" has tended to flow from industrialized countries or regions toward developing countries or regions, whereas, for the most part, human migration has tended to move in the opposite direction, from developing countries toward industrialized countries or regions (Nettle & Romaine, 2000).

Although Costa Rica and Guatemala were never formally colonies of the United States, their economic solvency has, for more than a century, depended heavily on U.S. aid, international investment, tourism, and now remittances (money sent to home countries by people living and working abroad) from Costa Ricans and Guatemalans in the United States. Although the United States and its citizens are largely respected and admired in Costa Rica and Guatemala, there is, nevertheless, a kind of deep-seated cultural ambivalence toward Americans (and all things "American," including English) that is not exclusive to Central Americans but seen in many countries and territories with an extended political and economic involvement with the United States, such as Mexico, Puerto Rico, and Vietnam.

Historical economic relationships fomented by international companies such as the United Fruit Company have paved the way for more asymmetrical capitalist investment in Central America, which funnels money into Central American businesses but undermines national government protections and efforts by labor organizations to promote fair working conditions and creates deeper divisions between the "haves" and the "have nots." In fact, rather than stemming the flow of immigration by opening new economic opportunities in Central America, the controversial Central American Free Trade Agreement (CAFTA), signed into law in September 2005, has arguably precipitated more economic migration from South to North (Richter, 2009). Despite their decline in 2009 due to the economic crisis, economic analysts published evidence that remittances to several Latin American countries (including Costa Rica and Guatemala) have climbed in national economic importance such that they now represent substantial percentages of the countries' GDP. For example, remittances rank among the three highest sources of foreign currency in Mexico (along with oil exports and tourism) (Villareal, 2012). In Guatemala, remittances now constitute the single largest source of income: fully one-tenth of the GDP (CIA, 2013). This news underscores the economic interdependence between the United States and its neighbors to the South.

But this interdependence goes beyond economics and has far-reaching social and cultural implications for citizens from both the North and the South. A record 2.34 million tourists visited Costa Rica in 2012 (González, 2013), although nearly 2 million visited Guatemala (Instituto Guatemalteco de Turismo–INGUAT, 2013). About half come from the United States, and many of these go as missionaries or study abroad participants engaged in some form of service in communities, schools, orphanages, and so forth. However, this interdependence and economic imbalance muddies the water for those who wish to disentangle the threads of service-learning from a philosophical framework of "aid to the needy" provided by those who know what the host community "needs."

Ethnocentricity and Monolingualism: Impacts on International Service and English-Language Teaching

Much of this biased perception comes from the problems wrought by the imbalance of resources and power, which permit students participating in service-learning experiences to travel to a place where the served are economically and practically bound. These imbalances exacerbate issues of ethnocentric attitudes about culture, language, and social norms that presuppose the superiority of norms in the sending country and color the views of service-learning students toward those who represent the Other (Butin, 2005). Students frequently attempt to superimpose their own cultural framework and paradigms over the practices of the people they are interacting with and judge them as inefficient, insufficient, primitive, or simply wrong (Butin, 2005; Cameron, 2002; Henry, 2005). As Canagarajah (2002) stated, "That cultures are mixed doesn't mean that certain values and practices aren't defined as the cultural capital required for success in mainstream institutions" (p. 135). When service-learning students "mix" with the communities they are serving, they tend to assume that their cultural norms are either the only ones or the "right" ones.

However, although these attitudes are not always shared by the "colonized" or marginalized populations who are so often the "served," those receiving the service often feel conflicted about the resources offered to them by the visiting teachers or service-learning students and at times resist while outwardly demonstrating appreciation for the service. Canagarajah (1993) dealt specifically with the idea of student resistance to English and argued that "attitudes, needs and desires of [the peripheral] communities and students are only partially free from the structures of domination in the larger social system" (p. 603). He found that peripheral students are not necessarily responsive to methods that challenge traditional styles, in part because they are aware of the role English plays in postcolonial society; they feel some ambivalence toward the socioeconomic power English represents. This serves as a backdrop for the examination of the participant attitudes and perceptions as they travel to "serve" and underscores the complexity of the service-learning student-host community panorama within a historical and social context. What is perhaps most salient, however, is the fact that many if not most of the international service-learning participants go into the experience with little or no notion that the host community may have ambivalent feelings about the students being there and what their service represents. As they become immersed in the host culture and get past the initial "honeymoon stage," their realizations can amplify reactions of confusion, shock, and sometimes hostility (see the following discussion of the phases of the U-curve hypothesis).

ISL Courses and Participants

The preservice teachers and humanities students, whose thoughts and reflections are included, participated in study abroad courses whose overarching goal was to prepare the group to teach English-language learners in the United States. Although the students were from two distinct regions of the United States, both had common characteristics including the following:

- Monolingual English speaking
- Preparing to teach ELL students
- Taking courses targeting language and culture
- Coming from large state institutions in areas experiencing unprecedented growth in immigrant populations

One program (nine students) targeted undergraduates and graduate students in any discipline, with approximately half the students coming from education (preservice teachers) and half coming from the humanities. The opportunity to gain professional ESL/EFL teaching experience in a rural community in Central America was an incentive for participants in this program regardless of their career commitment to the field of education. The other program represented 20 preservice teachers enrolled in courses geared at completing requirements for their area of emphasis.

Both programs specifically exposed the students to theories of language acquisition while challenging their assumptions about the intersections between language and culture by examining written and verbal data collected from the community. The courses put a particular emphasis on discussing the global context of human migration that has promoted the increase in immigration to the Southeast and Midwest regions of the United States. Also discussed are ways these shifts in demographics challenge schools. The courses provided students with the opportunity to immerse themselves in the language and culture of another country. Participants gained experience teaching English as a second language to children and adults who are feeling extraordinary social and economic pressure to acquire English. At the same time, the participants felt firsthand what it is like to struggle with acquiring and communicating in a second language. The courses in both programs shared the following common emphases:

- Examination of one's own assumptions, attitudes, and behaviors
- The role of one's socialization in how he or she shapes and responds to new environments
- Connections between language, culture, and education
- Theories of language acquisition
- Work in schools where learners are eager to gain English proficiency

The Phases of the U-Curve Hypothesis and Arriving at "Critical Consciousness"

The journey of preservice students through the various phases of the U-curve hypothesis helps explain their progress, or lack thereof, in acquiring higher levels of "critical consciousness" (Cipolle, 2010) during service-learning experiences (see figure 1.1).

Figure 1.1 Intersections between the U-curve and critical consciousness.

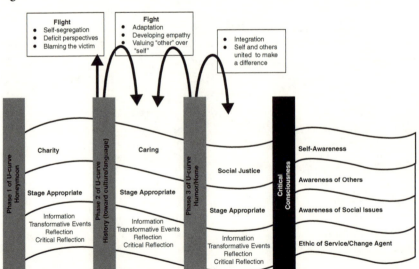

Note: Adapted from Cushner, McClelland, & Safford (2000) and Trifonovitch (1977) [U-curve hypothesis] and Cipolle (2010) [roadmap to critical consciousness]

Phase 1: Honeymoon

Students often embark on university-based study abroad trips at the honeymoon phase of the U-curve, motivated by notions of charity (e.g., approaching marginalized groups and individuals with a "savior" mentality). However, as they become immersed in the culture and language of the new country, they encounter discomforts—physical, linguistic, and psychological—that challenge their sense of efficacy and their desire to remain fully engaged in the service-learning experience. It is at this point that they make a multitude of daily decisions that largely reflect either a flight or a fight response.

At the first stage (caveat: the stages are not necessarily sequential; they can be cyclical and recursive), students immersed in an unfamiliar culture may feel elation and a romantic excitement at everything they see and experience without challenging their reactions. The following quotations taken from the students' reflections are examples of this. Participants' voices were filled with the excitement of "experiencing new cultures" and the many learnings that would result from immersing themselves in a new environment. Assumptions abounded about what life would or should be like once they arrived. They do not, at least initially, express fear, discomfort, or displeasure at the experience because it was new and "exciting." Some may even feel initially that they have found "paradise."

> I was able to experience another culture and find a home away from home at Apoyate en Mi.

> I love this place. I love how everything seems to breathe together; the land, the plants, the animals, and the people. Through this emerges a language that one can't even begin to understand or explain until one is a part of it by joining in with the rhythm.

> In observing the ins and outs of life down here, I hear the song ("Color of the Wind") from the soundtrack of Disney's *Pocahontas*. Everything has a purpose and connection!

The students who wrote these excerpts have a truly romanticized vision of the host country and people. In fact, in the third excerpt, the student even compares the life in the host country to a Disney movie; she has transferred her experience to something so fictionalized that it becomes totally separated from reality. Ironically, her comparison is to the movie *Pocahontas*, which depicts the interactions of English colonists with the indigenous peoples in the Americas and romanticizes the relationship between an indigenous woman, Pocahontas, and an Englishman, John Smith, and does not trouble with the complexities of the colonization at all. This underscores the imbalance in the relationship between the servers and the people being served and illustrates the fact that the servers often have a romanticized and unrealistic view of the people they are serving.

Some students see contrasts from what they are used to or expect, but in the honeymoon phase, they tend to see them in a completely positive noncritical light. Upon students' arrival questions begin to arise regarding the "lifestyles" of the "local people" and the differences that exist between "home" and "the new culture." This student makes sense of what she is observing by writing,

> I am amazed each time we walk down that path to school and home at night. None of the people in the valley are well off by American standards, but they are really happy. Americans in general have so much that we can learn from these people about being happy with the gifts that God gives us each day.

Early in the experiences of the students, a state of "making sense" of the new culture and language exists. Often participants attempted to interpret through their own cultural lens the differences that they observed. Often these observations were attributed to circumstances beyond the control of the families or students. Such factors made the hosts endearing individuals who did much with very little. But again, the students have not arrived at a critical awareness of individuals' lives and how they might feel about "American standards." One participant makes the following observation about the circumstances of the people she had come to know:

> Up until this point, I had no idea how spoiled I was back in the States. I mean I think we all know that we live better than most in other parts of the world, but really, to live with these sweet people and see how they operate and improvise on a day-to-day basis with no complaint or want for more money or material things is so touching—it really makes you check yourself.

In the previous two excerpts, the students are shocked at the contrast between the life they are witnessing and the lives they have led in the United States. Their initial reaction is one of admiration for the host community and the fact that they can "improvise" on a day-to-day basis, "with no complaint." However, these are still couched in infantilizing overtones where they see the host community as "touching" and "sweet." There is little or no reflection on the "better" life that they lead in the United States and how that might be dependent on the relative "poverty" of the people in the host community.

> After seeing how excited the locals were to see us work in the schools or how genuinely happy they were to know we enjoyed living in their homes,

it is difficult to believe that the locals have many negative feelings toward ecotourists. With so many benefits to ecotourism, it is hard to see how it might become a problem within this society.

Similar to the student who compared the host community to a Disney movie without seeing the problematic relationship that the movie portrays but does not trouble, this student cannot see how ecotourism might have negative impacts or that the host community might feel a certain ambivalence toward the visiting students and ecotourism and may not be willing to share their thoughts with them.

At this point in the honeymoon stage, the students face an initial inability to break out of the paradigms that shape the way they see the world.

Phase 2: Hostility

At some point after their initial reactions of romanticized excitement, the students are pushed enough out of their comfort zone by being confronted with different ideas of "what is right" or "normal" that begin to feel threatened. Students who react to these challenges of the hostility phase of the U-curve with a flight response demonstrate, for example, the tendency to self-segregate with others who are most like them. In moderation, this response serves as a coping mechanism to bolster students' confidence as they continue to reach beyond their zones of comfort. When self-segregation with like-minded peers describes the majority of a day, however, little development in critical consciousness can be expected. Individuals are likely to begin deflecting the unsettling confusion they feel by embracing deficit perspectives that place blame on the marginalized community members with whom they interact or the country's larger systems, institutions, and practices.

On the other hand, some preservice students make conscious, daily decisions to fight through the feelings of insecurity and insufficiency and adapt to the new ideas, surroundings, and circumstances. They minimize "self" in order to better understand those with whom they are interacting; students begin to form empathetic relationships with the individuals they encounter. In short, they begin to truly care. They find themselves questioning the long-standing beliefs and attitudes that reflect their prior socialization. Reflection and critical reflection (Herrera & Murry, 2005) related to transformative events are crucial along students' developmental path toward this new level of critical consciousness. Many of them struggle consciously with trying to accommodate these different paradigms for viewing the world.

WOW! I am shocked to see the limited resources these teachers have in their classrooms. How do these teachers teach without a projector, a library full of books, a copy machine, and a computer?!

From the minute I walked into to the classroom I was shocked by what seemed like lack of control. I felt so out of my element because in American classrooms students acting anything near that would be very unacceptable. I could not imagine how any of the students were actually learning anything or how the teacher was holding any of them accountable for their learning.

In these quotations it is clear that the students are trying to make sense of the differences in classroom behavior and setup from what they are used to and their confusion at the fact that they are being confronted with completely different ideas of "normal" and how to negotiate and navigate those structures. In the second excerpt in particular, the student is trying to accommodate her understanding of "learning" and "teacher accountability" within the framework of a scene that was wholly foreign to everything she was used to and had been taught as being conducive to learning. However, in the following excerpt the student is much more hostile to the practices that she sees but is still unsure of how to judge these practices and even questions if her actions have been equally off-putting to the host community. As Americans, the participants often voiced that there were certain essentials that no Americans should be without no matter where in the world they may find themselves at any given point in time. In spite of this, there is little reflection about whether or not these "essentials" are really essential and whether everyone should have or want them. Furthermore, the cultural norms of the host country began to become apparent to the participants, and they questioned how the hosts would "react" if they were in their shoes. Participants in the study became keenly aware of all the differences of the new culture, and the "adjustment" period led them to periods of reflection on self and others. One student describes her experience in the following way:

I noticed this habit of people sucking their teeth to get food out (I guess) after eating. This practice is very loud and completely grossed me out my first day there. This is crude to me. I wonder if I've done anything that caused them to have the same reaction? Has anyone noticed that breastfeeding in public is no big deal here? I've seen it twice.

In other cases, the students' reactions are not just confused but judgmental and even resentful that the host community does not completely embrace their presence and treat them with inordinate respect.

My assumption that people wouldn't be sniffing their chemicals and getting high while we were serving them food was completely wrong. I guess that I assumed that those people would be more grateful and wouldn't do that in front of us, but they did. We encountered at least five people that were sniffing chemicals as we were handing them their food. I guess that they just don't care if we see and know what they are doing.

It seemed as though the students were not paying attention and only had to do the work if they felt like it. Some children spent the whole time playing and messing around rather than taking notes and paying attention.

These students are clearly piqued that the host community is not more "grateful" that they are there and have begun to question their own reasons for coming if they are not appreciated. This also underscores the "savior" mentality and illustrates what happens when the served population does not respond to the "generosity" of the servers as expected. This reaction can also lead to feelings of inefficacy and futility based on a sense of frustration at not being able to do what they are normally able to do. The initial feeling of excitement and willingness to find benefits in what the experience is providing can be short-lived, however, as students find that they are no longer in command linguistically or culturally. For many of the students, feelings of inadequacy began to surface as their inability to communicate in another language became a "frustration" and less "fun" because it created a "barrier" in achieving their original goals of teaching or developing relationships with the host families. One student writes,

> For the first week that we were in Guatemala, I was definitely experiencing frustration because of the language barrier. I would easily get internally upset when I could not communicate with the children and the teachers in the classroom.

The language barrier also led participants to self-isolation, feelings of inadequacy in teaching English, and a need to begin to surround themselves with people who were like them both culturally and linguistically. The students' inability to fully participate linguistically or culturally changed the language they used to describe their needs and the demands they placed on those around them. Unmet needs turned into responses of hostility. One participant described the change that she saw in herself in the following way:

> I became even more uncomfortable with the idea of teaching and being in Guatemala because I felt like I wasn't a good teacher and that everyone thought I was doing a lousy job. When this uncomfortable, frustrating moment happened during my acculturation process, I felt very hostile and just wanted to go home.

> A sense of nervousness and anxiety continually mounts and creates a very insecure and critical version of my normally confident self. This is mainly because I have not been forced to speak the language for extended periods

of time. . . . Therefore, I find myself being debilitated to the point of speaking in the realms of what a young child could produce.

This student expresses the most common of the reactions in the hostility phase of the U-curve, which can lead to a desire to retreat and shut down completely:

I wanted to run out of the mall and hurry back to my hotel room where I could crawl under the covers and hide from the world.

Feelings of appreciation that participants had experienced early on regarding community members' ability to do a lot with a little began to diminish or disappear as participants' feelings of entitlement regarding what they perceived to be basic needs began to enter into the picture. One of them writes,

I feel like I've downgraded the living quarters and am living in poverty. After a couple of days with my family, I am starting not to freak out as much over the insects and spiders (just the small ones). Aggh. I'm definitely in the adjusting phase.

This student's reaction reflects the confusion that often accompanies this phase. The student is aware that her reaction to the conditions in the household illustrate that she needs to "adjust" to the marked difference between what she is used to and what these families are used to; however, the student still views the family with a deficit perspective and clearly values the community members' "living quarters" as less than. There is little self-reflection on why this valuation exists or how it may be altered or revisioned. This type of deficit mentality is also illustrated in student reflections about child care and parental responsibility.

Although each of the students did have some sort of family member that loved and cared for them, the kind of attention and affection that they received was completely different from what I am used to seeing from parents. Most of the students had someone there for them that did their best to get them food to eat, clothes to wear, and a place to sleep, but these children were not necessarily their parents' first priority. So, the fact that a group of people had come from the United States with nothing on their agenda but educating these children and giving them their full attention for a couple of weeks spoke volumes.

This excerpt clearly shows how the student casts the server-served relationship within a dichotomous value frame of good-bad, right-wrong.

Although this student has noticed the difference between what she sees as the parents' priorities and those of the servers, she has not yet begun to question her own assumptions about the "right" way for parents to interact with children and has a nonreflective posture toward the servers' actions and the privilege that has permitted their presence.

The first step toward a more empathetic and self-reflective stance for many of the participants was the realization that although norms differ, this difference does not make another's way of life "wrong." Acceptance of another culture can lead to one's own individual growth. One participant describes this in the following statement:

> Personally, I have learned not to assume things about the norms and ways of other cultures. Just because something is run differently than how I am used to does not make it wrong. This event has helped me be a more accepting person and has shown me that I can get ideas from other cultures and countries.

Critical and conscious reflection of both language and culture and how their own socialization played out in their interpretation of roles and emotional response to the unknown became the catalyst to students' entering the phase of acceptance and humor about the new environment. Participants sought to explore what their role was in the new country and how power relations shifted between groups as relationships were built and a new lens was used to interpret their surroundings.

At this extreme arc of the pendulum, the students have reached a place where they cannot process the differences, and the pressure of dealing with cultural norms that contradict their own paradigms, exacerbated by their inability to adequately express or confront these contradictions, drives them to want to hide from the culture. These reactions are often most prevalent in the homestay situation.

Phase 3: Humor (Acceptance)

After working through the feelings of hostility toward the host culture and inadequacy at attempting to deal with the challenges, the students begin to arrive at an equilibrium where they are able to view with some circumspection the differences of the host country and culture and become less blinded by romantic notions or hostile judgments. Participants continue to be motivated by an ethos of caring as they experience the humor and acceptance phase of the U-curve. Participants reflected, for example, on cultural norms of time and parental involvement. One student reflects on her new perceptions of parental involvement and the limits traditional views often place on families:

> Our family did not leave until 11 o'clock that evening, and our "dad" carried the oven down the hill to our house on his back. If that's not parent involvement, I am not sure what is. The actions of my Costa Rican family support the idea of Latino parents helping out in other ways besides what is the "standard" of the classroom. When discussing parent involvement, I think that it is important to take into account the aspects that make the children who they are, including cultural differences.

The following participant commented on the importance of not limiting our "reference" or "viewpoint" to our "preconstructed ways" of doing things in the United States. This viewpoint is often constructed by our thinking that the way things are done in the United States is the only way it should be done. She states,

> From the interviews, it appears as if the view of parent involvement in San Luís consists of providing time and talents as far as community events to help benefit the school. To this population, parent involvement also seems to be any way that parents are able to help out their students as well. To residents in the United States, I can see how we are dominated by a single viewpoint which forces us to think and behave in preconstructed ways in reference not only to language but also with the ways in which we see parent involvement.

Another student reflects on cultural norms that push people to accumulate "more" for economic gain rather than view life and success as having what is a "sufficient" life:

> For example, one concept which was striking to me was the idea of living a "sufficient" life. The average American is convinced that they need things that are not necessarily true necessities. The people in San Luís have a different way of defining their "needs." They are not controlled by a constant desire for more, and they are content with what some Americans might consider "the basics" such as a modest home, sufficient clothing, and plentiful, healthy food. In this rural community of San Luís, most of the residents were born and raised here, along with their parents and grandparents. However, they are aware of the economic opportunities the city offers them, yet they choose to remain in the valley.

Students even begin to question their own deeply held beliefs about how the world works and what matters. These students were challenged to address the contrast between how most Americans view success and connection to money and how the host community did. The following reflection illustrates this:

> I learned that resources are one of the most unimportant things within a successful school. We have grown to believe that all we need to become better teachers is MORE MONEY. After traveling to Guatemala, I now know that this is completely false.

These excerpts show that the students are beginning to reflect on their own paradigms and the reasons that they are there and if they can "help" the community.

Participants' final reflections were couched around a socialization that had prepared them to see the world through an ethnocentric view that sought to control their surroundings with regard to space, time, and people. The realization that this may not always be true proved liberating in many cultural respects.

> It didn't take long for me to realize that Central America is extremely laid back compared to America. I realized that it was American people that made me the way I was. Always having to be on time to school, work, meetings, and getting in trouble if you were late has been drilled into my head.

> Personally I have grown from this experience by learning that I do not need to be in control of everything, and not one way is always the best way.

This quote summarizes a view many of the participants shared throughout this phase of their acculturation process. A shift in thinking related to the need to control the environment both personally and professionally shifted to one of initial understanding that there is no "one way" of doing business, rather a need to understand culture and build relationships from an equal status. There is also the beginning of a realization that the server can learn from the served.

Phase 3 (part 2): Home

Although participants' arrival at the home phase of the U-curve by the end of the service-learning experience would be the ideal, expectations for their arrival would be unrealistic given the short-term nature of most service-learning experiences. Rather, the progress that students made provides the foundation for subsequent participation in, and critical reflection on, service-learning and other learning experiences. Given sufficient opportunities for interaction with stage-appropriate information, transformative experiences, and critical reflection, students have the potential to attain a social justice perspective that reflects an integrated valuing of self and others in a united effort to make a difference in society. Students become advocates of students and families, working with those who are marginalized to change the realities that make possible inequalities in resources, education, power, and so on.

Conclusions

The challenge for leaders of service-learning programs, especially in international programs where privileged students from the North are serving in peripheral communities in the South, is to cast light on the differences in social and cultural paradigms working through the "server's" unrealistic romantic notions and hostility toward the "served," based on rejection and ethnocentric judgments of the "Other," and to move gently through reflection, discussion, and growing awareness to a posture of social justice. Although we want our students to move to a framework of integration and an ethic of service for social justice, they need to step outside their own norms and see the larger social, economic, and political frames. By viewing with more critical clarity their own assumptions about what is "normal" and learning to accept and understand the paradigms of the Other, they will become more empathetic teachers and advocates for peripheral and marginalized students.

This is going to become more and more critical if current trends in demographic shifts continue and the "face" of students in the United States continues to change, particularly in regions such as the Southeast and Midwest. For example, recent data show that Latinos make up fully 22% of the K–12 population nationwide (Latinos are the majority in four states) (White House, 2010), whereas the vast majority of teachers and those becoming teachers are still White, middle-class women. These classrooms may become more and more akin to the service-learning experience where the teacher/server is "serving" a population of students/served that resembles the Other. International service-learning programs such as those analyzed in this chapter may be a key way to tease out the server-served dichotomy as the borders between South and North become ever more blurred.

Authors' Note

Data for this qualitative study were collected from reflections, lesson plans, narratives, interviews, surveys, and follow-up evaluations (while in the classrooms and upon return to their own institutions) of all participants. The case study was analyzed through a lens of discovery, gained insights, and analysis of the data (Creswell, 2007). Coding was used to initiate data analyses according to the constant comparative method (Strauss, 1987). Ethic codes were guided first by Cushner's (Cushner, McClelland, & Safford, 2006) four phases of the acculturation process; these phases include the honeymoon, hostility, humor, and home phases that individuals go through when experiencing new cultures. We made sense of these experiences by coding them using Cipolle's (2010) framework of critical consciousness in service-learning. Both frameworks guided the explanation of participants' emotional "roller coaster" ride throughout their experiences in their respective projects. Figure 1.1 provides a graphic of the intersection of these two adapted frameworks, as used for interpretation of the participants' experiences. Further analysis of the data from an emic perspective provided the backdrop for discussing participant voice throughout the experience.

References

Butin, D. (2005). *Service-learning in higher education: Critical issues and directions.* New York, NY: Palgrave Macmillan.

Cameron, D. (2002). Globalization and the teaching of "communication skills." In D. Block & D. Cameron (Eds.), *Globalization and language teaching* (pp. 67–82). New York, NY: Routledge.

Canagarajah, S. (1993). Critical ethnography of a Sri Lankan classroom: Ambiguities in student opposition to reproduction through ESOL. *TESOL Quarterly, 27*(4), 601–626.

Canagarajah, S. (2002). Globalization, methods, and practice in periphery classrooms. In D. Block & D. Cameron (Eds.), *Globalization and language teaching* (pp. 134–150). New York, NY: Routledge.

CIA. (2013, December 4). *World factbook: Guatemala.* Retrieved from https://www.cia.gov/library/publications/the-world-factbook/geos/gt.html

Cipolle, S. B. (2010). *Service-learning and social justice: Engaging students in social change.* Lanham, MD: Roman & Littlefield.

Cowie, J. (1999). *Capital moves: RCA's 70-year quest for cheap labor.* Ithaca, NY: Cornell University Press.

Creswell, J. W. (2007). *Qualitative inquiry and research design: Choosing among five approaches.* Thousand Oaks, CA: Sage.

Cushner, K., McClelland, A., & Safford, P. (2006). *Human diversity in education: An integrative approach* (5th ed.). Boston, MA: McGraw-Hill.

Escobar, A. (1995). *Encountering development: Making and unmaking of the third world.* Princeton, NJ: Princeton University Press.

Gelmon, S., & Billig, S. (Eds.). (2007). *From passion to objectivity: International and cross-disciplinary perspectives on service-learning research (PB) (advances in service-learning research).* Charlotte, NC: Information Age Publishing.

González, A. (2013, August 3). Visitas turisticas en el 2012 fueron las más altas de los últimos cinco años. *La Nación*. Retrieved from http://www.nacion.com/archivo/Visitas-turisticas-altas-ultimos-anos_0_1328067181.html

Gronemeyer, M. (1992). Helping. In W. Sachs (Ed.), *Development dictionary*. New York, NY: Palgrave.

Heller, M., & Martin-Jones, M. (2001). *Voices of authority*. Westport, CT: Ablex.

Henry, S. E. (2005). "I can never turn my back on that": Liminality and the impact of class on service-learning experience. In D. W. Butin (Ed.), *Service-learning in higher education: Critical issues and directions*. New York, NY: Palgrave Macmillan.

Herrera, S., & Murry, K. (2005). *Mastering ESL and bilingual methods: Differentiated instruction for culturally and linguistically diverse (CLD) students*. Boston, MA: Allyn and Bacon.

Hondagneu-Sotelo, P. (2001). *Domestica: Immigrant workers cleaning and caring in the shadows of affluence*. Berkeley: University of California Press.

Instituto Guatemalteco de Turismo–INGUAT. (2013). *Boletín anual estadísticas de turismo 2012*. Departamento de Investigacion y Análisis de Mercados Sección de Estadística. Retrieved from http://www.inguat.gob.gt/boletin-anual-2012.pdf

Kraft, R. (2002). International service-learning. In M. Kenny (Ed.), *Learning to serve: Promoting civil society through service-learning* (pp. 297–314). Norwell, MA: Kluwer Academic.

National Youth Leadership Council. (n.d.). *K-12 service-learning standards for quality practice*. Retrieved September 8, 2010, from http://www.nylc.org/k-12-service-learning-standards-quality-practice

Nettle, D., & Romaine, S. (2000). *Vanishing voices: The extinction of the world's languages*. New York, NY: Oxford University Press.

Richter, S. (2009, June 25). *DR-CAFTA and migration in Central America*. Organisation for Economic Cooperation and Development website. Retrieved September 15, 2010, from www.oecd.org

Sidorick, D. (2009). *Condensed capitalism: Campbell soup and the pursuit of cheap production in the twentieth century*. Ithaca, NY: Cornell University Press.

Strauss, A. L. (1987). *Qualitative analysis for social scientists*. Cambridge, UK: Cambridge University Press.

U.S. State Department Consular Services. (2013, August 27). *Costa Rica: Country specific information*. Retrieved September 14, 2010, from http://travel.state.gov/travel/cis_pa_tw/cis/cis_1093.html

Villareal, M. A. (2012). *U.S.-Mexico economic relations: Trends, issues, and implications* (RL32934). Retrieved from http://www.fas.org/sgp/crs/row/RL32934.pdf

White House, White House Initiative on Educational Excellence for Hispanic Americans. (2010). *Improving educational opportunities and outcomes for Latino students*. Washington, DC: Author. Retrieved from http://www.whitehouse.gov/sites/default/files/uploads/improving-educational-opportunities-and-outcomes-for-latino-students.pdf

2

DECENTERING THE UNITED STATES IN INTERNATIONAL SERVICE-LEARNING

A Comparative Perspective

Amanda L. Espenschied-Reilly
Aultman College

Susan V. Iverson
Kent State University

Service-learning emerged in the United States as a grassroots movement in the 1960s and 1970s (Stanton, Giles, & Cruz, 1999) and more recently has been gaining recognition in many regions of the world (Berry & Chisholm, 1999). Early pioneers in the U.S. service-learning movement believed that "action in communities and structured learning could be combined to provide stronger service and leadership in communities and deeper, more relevant education for students" (Stanton et al., 1999, p. 1); because of this, many early mavericks fought hard for this then-revolutionary teaching and learning strategy to become part of the academy. Today, service-learning is almost commonplace in U.S. institutions of higher education, and its practice continues to grow globally.

Yet, this pedagogy is also the subject of much debate about its purposes, which experiences lend themselves to particular learning outcomes, and the directions it will take within the academy (Butin, 2006). As "Americanized" conceptions of service-learning circulate internationally (Silcox & Leek, 1997), educators need to develop clarity about which aspects of service-learning can be adapted to diverse social, cultural, and economic contexts so as not to repeat the mistake of "exporting Western ideas and practice methodologies which may or may not be relevant" (Taylor, 1999, p. 309). Here, findings are presented from an investigation of how culture

and social context shape Irish and U.S. practitioners' perceptions and practices, and discussion is engaged of how successful pedagogical localization
must be accomplished at all three levels of culture—macro, meso, and
micro—in order for the pedagogy to be relevant, effective, and meaningful
within a shared cultural context.

Relevant Literature

Service-Learning in Ireland

The relatively recent development of academic initiatives aimed at promoting civic engagement in Ireland coincides with a widespread national concern about a perceived decline in volunteerism (a common indicator of social
capital) and an increased awareness of the role higher education can play in
supporting civil society (Boland, 2006; Daly, 2007). Boland and McIlrath
(2007) noted a number of national policy initiatives that aim to address
"growing concerns regarding civil society and social capital," including the
establishment, in 2006 by the Irish government, of the Taskforce on Active
Citizenship (2007) to ensure that civic participation grows and continues (p.
91). The Community Knowledge Initiative (CKI) at the National University
of Ireland, Galway (NUIG), was directed to provide leadership for these civic
engagement initiatives and to spearhead collaboration between several Irish
institutions of higher education called Campus Engage, "which will allow civic
engagement activities to grow across the higher education sector in Ireland"
(Taskforce on Active Citizenship, 2007, p. 39). The vision of CKI is to
mainstream service-learning and "to reinvigorate the civic mission of higher
education and instill in students a sense of social responsibility and civic
awareness" (*Service Learning Academy*, 2006).

Impact of Service-Learning: Competing Conceptions

At first glance, service-learning may seem culture neutral (Merrill, 2005);
however, conceptions of service-learning differ from one culture to the next
(Berry & Chisholm, 1999). Just as the "intellectual and philosophical roots"
(Kenny & Gallagher, 2001, p. 18) of service-learning in the United States are
uniquely situated in American higher education and can be traced to "traditions of volunteerism and social activism" (pp. 19–20), so too has service-
learning grown out of other cultural and historical traditions throughout the
world (Berry & Chisholm, 1999).

Research provides clear evidence of the positive impact of service-
learning on "a host of academic, social and cultural variables" (Butin, 2006,
p. 1; Eyler & Giles, 1999). Yet, service-learning scholars differentiate service

experiences and competing conceptions of service-learning as lending themselves to differing outcomes. Morton (1995), for instance, argued that there are three distinct paradigms for service—charity, project, and social change—each with "its own logic, strengths, limitations and visions of a transformed world" (p. 19). Morton (1995) believed, "Integrity in service-learning . . . comes not by moving from charity to social change, but from working with increasing depth in a particular paradigm" (p. 19). However, Kendall (1990) posited that service-learning experiences should move students beyond acts of charity to address root causes of systemic social inequality. The poles of Kendall's continuum—charitable and justice-oriented—are typically identified as competing paradigms within service-learning. Service-learning oriented toward charity is an "exercise in altruism" and emphasizes "character building and a kind of compensatory justice where the well-off feel obligated to help the less advantaged" (Battistoni, 1997, p. 151). By contrast, service-learning focused on social change (justice-oriented) helps students to develop a deeper understanding of social issues, promotes the development of skills necessary to work toward social change, and incorporates an analysis of power and oppression (Boyle-Baise & Langford, 2004).

Service-learning program administrators and educators outside the United States are asking similar questions about the purpose, theories, and best practices of service-learning, with added tensions regarding the real and perceived challenges and frustrations associated with adopting culturally incongruent practices (Iverson & Espenschied-Reilly, 2010). Reflecting on their attendance at an international education conference, Silcox and Leek (1997) wrote, "We were expected to be the experts on service-learning," and they called on practitioners and scholars to reflect on "the impact that [U.S.-based service-learning models] might be having throughout the world," something, they argued, few U.S. practitioners have done because of "isolationist tendencies" (p. 615). Others too have called for thinking about the implications and (unintended) consequences when introducing new pedagogies into a culture. Boland and McIlrath (2007), for instance, advocated for localization, "whereby the philosophy, principles and practices of a particular curriculum innovation are adapted (or even subverted) to reflect and serve local culture, context and conceptions" (p. 83). Shay (2008) concurred, adding that localization needs to take place at varying cultural levels within particular fields, institutions, faculties, and departments.

Culture

Culture can be understood as "the meaning which people create, and which creates people, as members of societies" (Hannerz, 1992, p. 3). Different dimensions of culture exist, reflecting different levels of its visibility (Schein,

1992). The most visible, the micro level, is "concerned with the social processes engendering relations among individuals" (Bevan, 1997, p. 762) and
is evident in behavioral patterns and the constructed physical and social environment. The macro level, the invisible level, represents the structures, or
institutionalized rules, that provide "opportunities for, and constraints on,
individual behavior and interactions" (p. 763). The meso level, representing
the intermediate between macro and micro, arises "either out of micro interaction, or occupying a middle role in the structure of positions" (p. 763).
Related to service-learning, micro interactions (e.g., the attitudes of faculty
about whether to employ service-learning in their classes and students' attitudes toward service-learning) are influenced at the meso and macro levels
(e.g., institutional and national culture, respectively).

Cultural beliefs and dimensions have an impact on service-learning.[1] For
example, the conceptual origins of service-learning are typically attributed to
Dewey's (1966) theories of experiential learning. However, Merrill (2005)
noted that foundational ideas, such as Dewey's,

> resonate in a society that values individualism and self-expression, as the
> U.S. does; on the other hand, they may seem "out of sync" as ways of learn-
> ing in cultures which value the collective and in which elders and authori-
> ties traditionally have been given deference. (p. 180)

Meso and macro dimensions of culture shape micro interactions, and efforts
to develop and implement service-learning programs must attend to all three
levels to reduce cultural tensions and/or invite critical dialogue about cultural
transferability of educational practices. Without cultural congruity, service-
learning practice risks irrelevancy within differing cultural contexts.

As educators are increasingly developing international service-learning
opportunities, scholars are investigating the impact of these experiences.
However, the focal point of this research is largely on the U.S. students'
cultural awareness and intercultural development when learning and serving
in another country. Little attention has been given to the implications of cultural (in)congruence in service-learning practice and possible (unintended)
consequences of deploying pedagogical practices that are taken for granted as
universal and that may not translate, literally or conceptually.

Methods

This investigation was an exploratory pilot interview study designed to compare service-learning in Ireland and in the United States in order to discern
the ways in which culture and social context shape practitioners' perceptions

and practices. More specifically, the research questions that guided this inquiry are as follows:

- How do Irish and U.S. administrators and educators conceptualize and employ service-learning?
- How do culture and social context shape respondents' perceptions and practices regarding service-learning?

The sample for this pilot study consisted of eight participants, four in Ireland and four in the United States. The only criterion for selection was that each participant assumed a role with responsibility for and perspective related to service-learning, volunteerism, or civic engagement. Initial participants were identified using both personal and professional contacts, who were then able to identify potential respondents.[2]

The Irish participants included Nora,[3] a university service-learning coordinator; Aidan, a university service-learning practitioner; Eamon, a college administrator and professor who serves as liaison to numerous student organizations; and Molly, a college international coordinator who aids students with service interests.

Participants from the United States included Robert, the executive director of a Campus Compact state affiliate (in the Midwest); Jessica, program director for the same Campus Compact affiliate; Melinda, a service-learning director at a liberal arts college in the Midwest; and Scott, a professor of psychology at a different private liberal arts college in the Midwest who was instrumental in the creation of the service-learning program on his campus.

Data were collected through in-depth, semistructured interviews (Fontana & Frey, 1994), with an interview protocol set in advance to garner a greater depth of information regarding the participants' perceptions and practices related to service-learning.[4] The text of these 8 interviews was analyzed using established qualitative methods of coding and categorizing to identify broad themes.[5]

Findings

Institutionalization

Service-learning in the United States and Ireland has very different histories. Yet, respondents shared similar challenges related to institutionalization, whether they were involved in a nearly 25-year project in the United States or an initiative in existence for less than a decade in Ireland. For instance, Robert stated that institutionalization of service-learning on U.S. campuses "is the great long-term outcome, but few campuses are there." Furthermore, he noted, one "president could be very supportive and is [then] replaced by someone else with different philosophies. Long-term commitment is a challenge." Robert lamented, "Sometimes it feels like we are spinning our wheels," which he attributed to changes in senior administrators: "As people leave, we have to start all over." Moreover, he cautioned, "because budgets get cut and unfortunately civic work is not as valued as academic work, [service-learning programs are] still on the fringes and in danger of being cut." Nora too shared her frustration with "the rhetoric versus the reality." For instance, she noted, "the [university] president supports service-learning verbally but is still unwilling to embed it across the [Irish] curriculum. . . . If it is to become nationalized, there is the concern of sustainability; will there be enough resources to sustain it?"

In addition to concerns about funding and leadership, respondents shared apprehension about pedagogical consequences to institutionalizing service-learning. Jessica, for instance, observed that it has "become more watered down, more palatable. It's less edgy and experimental." Nora echoed this concern when she shared, "this is a counternormative pedagogy in Ireland, and there is concern that it will lose its excitement and effectiveness if it is to become normalized." Melinda too noted that service-learning, as it "has become institutionalized within [U.S.] curriculum . . . it's become outcomes driven, professionalized." However, she believes there is also space for a "critical voice now because it has been institutionalized. We are free to discuss the problems and tensions." So, although institutionalization (in the United States) or nationalization (in Ireland) appears to be a shared goal, there is also evidence of concern that attainment of this goal could in some ways be detrimental.

Pedagogical Tensions

When asked about their definitions of *service-learning*, respondents all shared a common understanding that resonated with definitions in the literature: a belief that service-learning "has the potential to generate development in the personal, academic, and civic domains" (Aidan); that this "experiential pedagogy brings academic learning objectives to meet community needs and interests in order to further student learning and community growth" (Jessica); and that this "pedagogical methodology allows students to enhance their academic knowledge through community work and possibly allows for community capacity building" (Nora). Furthermore, respondents identified pedagogical challenges that emerged for faculty who were implementing service-learning. Respondents in the United States and Ireland acknowledge that service-learning, like most active learning pedagogies, is unfamiliar to students.

> Student exposure to this pedagogy has been limited so far. I have pitched the idea through presentations to our current second-year students but they have pushed back. . . . Moving from the "sage on the stage" is scary for students as well as faculty because it is the system that they are used to. They both lose their security. The responsibility for the learning is on the student, and that is contradictory to how they've been taught for the previous 14–16 years. (Aidan)

> They [students] resist the experiential form of learning as opposed to the traditional banking model that they are used to. They resist taking more responsibility for their education. These are the same things that we see in institutional resistance. Institutions and faculty resist moving away from the banking model toward active pedagogies that advance the common good. (Jessica)

Respondents also noted that faculty who employ this approach—in the United States and in Ireland—encounter real and perceived risks. Faculty appointments, and more specifically the process by which junior faculty earn tenure, are determined based on teaching and research productivity. Service-learning leaves faculty vulnerable, as there will always be students in their classes who "don't get it" and who will in turn resist by distancing themselves from the "service experience and the in-class learning" (Jones, 2002, p. 11). This resistance can surface in class, at the service site, or on teaching evaluations.

Determinations of good teaching are based on student evaluations of teaching, which, Robert noted, are overwhelmingly "using traditional forms that focus on in-class teaching . . . and may be detrimental to faculty [who use service-learning]." Robert noted the potential risks involved: "The lack of good assessment [of teaching] causes faculty to hesitate to use the pedagogy, especially if they are junior." Melinda, too, indicated her institution considers service-learning an "innovative pedagogy," but "it is not counted under service, which is considered service to the college. However, it can count under scholarship if the faculty member is engaging in community-based research."

Nora noted efforts are under way to get service-learning in Ireland worked into the faculty promotional structure, "but that will take some time." She added that the president would say that service-learning is weighted "under the category of 'other' when considering teaching, research, and other for promotion," but she disagreed, saying that putting it under other "is not clear and not enough." Scott also shared, "I received [resistance] from other faculty that did not think people should get credit for experience. This occurred when I was trying to get the Social Responsibility course approved. They questioned the educational validity of experience. . . . [For one faculty member] learning took place only in a classroom."

Purpose of Service-Learning

Although resistance to its use and questions about its validity circulate, service-learning continues to gain currency in higher education. Yet, as this pedagogy secures a foothold, tensions regarding its purpose resound. Respondents in both countries described service-learning as change oriented, designed to "advance the common good" (Jessica). Robert noted that every campus seeks to develop students who will "become better citizens." Jessica observed that the development of an educated citizenry is foundational to education and that service-learning is a key mechanism for cultivating citizenship: "I believe in an educated citizenry and that an educated citizenry will take better care of each other. It's at the core of education; that there must be something greater than individual development." Melinda also identified "both attitudinal and cognitive" learning objectives, stating that students "grow more appreciative of diversity, increase their cross-cultural awareness, and become more willing to be allies to different others. Their skills in leadership, advocacy, and citizenship increase. They become community problem solvers who understand their social responsibilities." Aidan further asserted that a main objective for using service-learning is "to change the world," and this pedagogy has the potential to create "a generation of change agents." Nora stated that service-learning is important because

> academia . . . [has] a responsibility to share our resources with our neighbors. We are concerned about the decreasing level of student engagement and . . . are worried about the democratic system in Ireland. We need to increase student engagement. . . . This is vital work for the survival of democratic life.

Yet, this view of service-learning as "strengthening civil society [and] supporting democratic practice" is in conflict with the need for the university to maintain a "competitive advantage in an increasingly global marketplace" (Boland & McIlrath, 2007, p. 90). For instance, Nora juxtaposed her earlier comments, regarding a commitment to democracy, with a desire "to make the university more attractive to students in a competitive global higher education market." Aidan, too, observed that "in order to sell it [service-learning] to students you have to show what's in it for them," and he added that because Ireland doesn't have "a history of service, you have to sell it differently here" (Aidan). Robert also noted that administrators have realized students are "coming to campuses with more service experience and are looking to continue that service," adding that campuses have "jumped on this as a marketing tool. Students want to make a difference and contribute more, and campuses have met this need."

Language and Culture

Irish respondents sought distance from the U.S. cultural context and historical origins that have shaped service-learning. Eamon, for instance, drew a distinction between service-learning in Ireland and the United States: "Volunteerism is not ingrained in our culture like it is for Americans [who] grow up volunteering. It seems expected and respected, even enjoyed. It is not as deep in our history." He added that Irish students "want to help those less fortunate, or maybe they are interested in how it might help them professionally. Some are passionate about what they see as injustice." But, he was quick to distinguish his students' efforts from the notion of *social justice*: "That is a term used more by Americans. The idea might be the same, but I doubt our students would use that term."

Nora, too, differentiated between service-learning in Ireland and the United States: "Service-learning is highly contextualized in the U.S. In Ireland the term doesn't mean much, and you'll more often find the use of the term 'civic engagement.' In Ireland, 'service' has a relationship with punishment." Aidan also noted, "The whole concept of serving others seems hierarchical or related to penal servitude." Aidan further indicated, "Anything connected to moral duty or pastoral responsibility is just not language that resonates with current Irish students."

Aidan, citing as an example how Hawaiian educators are using their native language rather than trying to translate new words, argued for drawing on Irish words and concepts. For instance, as an alternative to the U.S. concept of *reciprocity*, Aidan proposed the word *meitheal:* "that means neighbors coming together to work on the land, so a *learning meitheal* is a word Irish people would understand." He and Nora were also critical of the term *reflection*, noting it is "problematic because it can have religious connotations" (Nora). Aidan suggested instead the Irish word *machnamh*, "which means contemplate or contemplative learning."

Discussion

Employing a cultural analysis, the dimensions of culture can be identified and their relationships explained not only at the micro level but also at the meso and macro levels. Although many aspects of service-learning in the United States and Ireland are shared (e.g., pedagogical issues, barriers related to institutionalization), the points of disjuncture (primarily at the macro level) and the relationships between the levels are notable (see table 2.1). Shared barriers to the implementation of service-learning in both countries serve to illustrate how the macro and meso levels influence the micro level. With respect to student resistance (micro level) at the micro-meso and micro-macro interfaces, if service-learning is counternormative to the dominant pedagogical approach (macro level), then institutions base their evaluation process and reward structure (meso level) on what is dominant; students in turn have been socialized to trust what is dominant and question what is alternate. Thus, any meso level lack of trust or confidence in service-learning pedagogy is likely to generate comparable (micro) behaviors from students and faculty.

Although so much appears to be shared at the micro and meso levels (student resistance, leadership, funding, purpose), understanding differences at the macro level is essential to ensure culturally distinct design and implementation at the meso and micro levels. For instance, the U.S. origins of service-learning can be traced to the nation's history of service (Kenny & Gallagher, 2001), whereas Ireland does not have a comparable history. Thus, the term *service-learning* does not resonate with Irish students, and educators instead speak of *civic engagement*. Similarly, in the United States, commonly stated outcomes for service-learning correspond with a stated purpose of education (e.g., civic engagement, good citizenship, and democracy), but this view implies moral duty for the Irish. Aidan noted, "Anything connected to moral duty or pastoral responsibility . . . would almost be scoffed at because of the recent decline of the church due to the scandals in the last 10–15 years." If U.S. service-learning terminology (meso) is culturally incongruent (macro), then civic participation (micro) will be limited.

Conclusion

Issues affecting attitudes toward service (visible at the micro and meso levels) differ from one culture to another, and educators will face challenges in their development and implementation of international service-learning programs and in cultural transfer of pedagogy if they ignore such issues. Although a culturally distinct identification is critical, educators should be cautious to assume a monocultural experience for Ireland or the United States. For instance, although Aidan advocated that "the Irish language must be common to all [service] projects," it is noteworthy that, according to the 2002

TABLE 2.1
Service-Learning and Dimensions of Culture

Country	Macro	Meso	Micro
United States	• National history of service • Role of religious institutions in shaping (positive) conceptions of service (moral duty) • Pedagogically, teaching paradigm (not learning paradigm) dominates • Civic mission of education; higher education, land grant institutions	• Uncertainty about leadership commitment • Funding: risks of budget cuts • Teaching evaluations are not designed to assess experiential learning • Service-learning not counted as service in tenure and promotion guidelines • Outcomes/purpose: develop students who will become better citizens • Market driven: institutional use of service-learning as marketing tool	• Student resistance to experiential form of learning as opposed to the traditional instructor-centered model
Ireland	• Government-endorsed initiative • Negative cultural associations of service with penal servitude and pastoral responsibility • Significance of Irish language • Pedagogically, teaching paradigm (not learning paradigm) dominates	• Uncertainty about leadership commitment • Funding • Service-learning is not in the faculty promotional structure • Outcomes/purpose: create "a generation of change agents" • Market driven: service-learning makes university more attractive to students	• Student resistance: moving from the "sage on the stage" is scary for students and faculty

Irish Census, only 42% of the population of Ireland has the ability to speak Irish, and Irish is the household language for only 3% of the country's population (*Statement on the Irish Language*, 2006), suggesting that translation of U.S. words into Irish may not resonate equally with all Irish students.

Practitioners who do not consider cultural relevancy when implementing "their brand" of service-learning in a new country (i.e., as a visiting scholar) or when traveling with students to perform service in another country may find their efforts "lost in translation." This can lead to issues such as tension, poor student experience, lack of reciprocity, or even complete disintegration of the program and the partnership. Attention to how culture—at all levels—operates and shapes understanding can minimize cultural tensions. Merrill (2005) referred to such a culturally aware approach as "doing *with*":

> Having the intellectual knowledge, the empathetic understanding, and the personal modesty and desire to move *from* one's own certainty about why people act in the ways they do *to* explanations for behavior that are rooted in the cultural context of another society. (p. 191, italics in original)

Such an approach pushes beyond the "traditional" form of reciprocity—making certain that mutuality exists between service providers and service receivers—and instead advocates for an "enriched" form of reciprocity, calling for an examination of the cultural underpinnings of the specific beliefs from which our ideals arise (Henry & Breyfogle, 2006, p. 29).

Cultural conflict cannot be avoided when incorporating new pedagogies; however, a multidimensional cultural analysis may fuel healthy and necessary debate, discourse, and research regarding service-learning's "own blind spots, its own unacknowledged and unexamined assumptions, and its own impositional narratives" (Butin, 2006, p. 1). Critical dialogue about the cultural transfer of service-learning, the centrality of U.S. conceptions on the development and implementation of international service-learning, and the need for multidimensional cultural analysis is necessary and holds potential to strengthen practice.

Endnotes

1. See Merrill (2005) for comprehensive coverage of the ways that culture is embedded in assumptions about teaching and learning, service, and service-learning.

2. This sampling strategy, referred to as snowball sampling, is an acknowledged limitation. Participants were identified using both personal and professional contacts that were geographically convenient in the United States and temporally convenient

during Amanda's travel to Ireland. Our hope is that this pilot will contribute to additional sampling criteria for future research.

3. Pseudonyms are used to refer to the participants.

4. Interview questions covered the following: definition of *service-learning*, institutional support structures for service-learning, assessment, resistance, identification of community issues, and origins of service-learning. Detailed notes were taken during the interviews, and the interview text was shared with participants for their feedback on accuracy and clarity.

5. Findings presented here are the result of careful coding for *central categories*, defined by Strauss and Corbin (1998) as those that "appear frequently in the data." We tagged frequently used words and phrases. A vine of codes grew, as did the need to establish "pattern codes"—a way of grouping "explanatory or inferential codes" into themes, sets, or constructs (Miles & Huberman, 1994, p. 69). We then brought our independent codes together to see how to subsume the "particulars into the general" (Miles & Huberman, 1994, p. 245).

References

Battistoni, R. (1997). Service learning and democratic citizenship. *Theory Into Practice, 36*(3), 150–156.

Berry, H. A., & Chisholm, L. A. (1999). *Service-learning in higher education around the world: An initial look.* New York, NY: International Partnership for Service-Learning.

Bevan, P. (1997). Linking micro and macro research: A sociological perspective. *Journal of International Development, 9*(5), 761–770.

Boland, J. (2006). Pedagogies for civic engagement in Irish higher education: Principles and practices in context. In M. Sanden & A. Zdanevicius (Eds.), *Democracy, citizenship and universities* (pp. 72–87). Kaunuas, Lithuania: Vytautas Magnus University Press.

Boland, J. A., & McIlrath, L. (2007). The process of localizing pedagogies for civic engagement in Ireland: The significance of conceptions, culture and context. In L. McIlrath & I. MacLabhrainn (Eds.), *Higher education and civic engagement: International perspectives* (pp. 83–99). Hampshire, England: Ashgate.

Boyle-Baise, M., & Langford, J. (2004). There are children here: Service learning for social justice. *Equity and Excellence in Education, 37*, 55–66.

Butin, D. (2006). Future directions for service learning in higher education. *International Journal of Teaching and Learning in Higher Education, 18*(1), 1–4.

Daly, S. (2007). Mapping civil society in the Republic of Ireland. *Community Development Journal, 43*(2), 157–176.

Dewey, J. (1966). *Democracy and education.* New York, NY: Free Press.

Eyler, J., & Giles, D. E., Jr. (1999). *Where's the learning in service-learning?* San Francisco, CA: Jossey-Bass.

Fontana, A., & Frey, J. (1994). Interviewing: The art of science. In N. K. Denzin & Y. S. Lincoln (Eds.), *Handbook of qualitative research* (pp. 118–137). Thousand Oaks, CA: Sage.

Hannerz, U. (1992). *Cultural complexity: Studies in the social organization of meaning.* New York, NY: Columbia University Press.

Henry, S. E., & Breyfogle, M. L. (2006). Toward a new framework of "service" and "served": De(and re)constructing reciprocity in service-learning pedagogy. *International Journal of Teaching and Learning in Higher Education, 18*(1), 27–35.

Iverson, S., & Espenschied-Reilly, A. (2010). Made in America? Assumptions about service learning pedagogy as transnational: A comparison between Ireland and the United States. *International Journal for the Scholarship of Teaching and Learning, 4*(2). Retrieved November 22, 2010, from http://academics.georgiasouthern.edu/ijsotl/v4n2/articles/PDFs/_IversonE-R.pdf

Jones, S. (2002). The underside of service learning. *About Campus, 7*(4), 10–15.

Kendall, J. (1990). *Combining service and learning: A resource book for community and public service* (Vol. I). Raleigh, NC: National Society for Internships and Experiential Education.

Kenny, M. E., & Gallagher, L. A. (2001). Service-learning: A history of systems. In M. E. Kenny, L. A. Simon, K. Kiley-Brabeck, & R. M. Lerner (Eds.), *Learning to serve: Promoting civil society through service-learning* (pp. 15–29). Boston, MA: Kluwer Academic.

Merrill, M. C. (2005). The cultural and intercultural contexts of service-learning. In L. A. Chisholm (Ed.), *Knowing and doing: The theory and practice of service-learning* (pp. 177–201). New York, NY: The International Partnership for Service-Learning and Leadership.

Miles, M., & Huberman, A. M. (1994). *Qualitative data analysis: An expanded sourcebook of new methods* (2nd ed.). Newbury Park, CA: Sage.

Morton, K. (1995). The irony of service: Charity, project and social change in service-learning. *Michigan Journal of Community Service Learning, 2,* 19–32.

Schein, E. H. (1992). *Organizational culture and leadership.* San Francisco, CA: Jossey-Bass.

Service Learning Academy. (2006). Galway, Ireland: National University of Ireland, Galway. Retrieved February 20, 2009, from http://www.nuigalwaycki.ie/page.asp?menu=3&page=49

Shay, S. (2008). Assessment at the boundaries: Service learning as case study. *British Educational Research Journal, 34*(4), 525–540.

Silcox, H. C., & Leek, T. E. (1997). International service learning: Its time has come. *Phi Delta Kappan, 78,* 615–618.

Stanton, T. K., Giles, D. E., Jr., & Cruz, N. I. (1999). *Service-learning: A movement's pioneers reflect on its origins, practice and future.* San Francisco, CA: Jossey-Bass.

Statement on the Irish language. (2006). Government of Ireland. Retrieved July 29, 2009, from http://www.pobail.ie/en/IrishLanguage/StatementontheIrishLanguage2006/file,7802,en.pdf

Strauss, A., & Corbin, J. (1998). *Basics of qualitative research: Techniques and procedures for developing grounded theory.* Thousand Oaks, CA: Sage.

Taskforce on Active Citizenship. (2007). *Active citizenship in Ireland: Progress report 2007–2008 and action plan 2008–2009.* Dublin, Ireland: Active Citizenship Office.

Taylor, Z. (1999). Values, theories and methods in social work education: A culturally transferable core? *International Social Work, 42*(3), 309–318.

3

STRATEGIC INTERNATIONAL SERVICE-LEARNING PARTNERSHIP

Mitigating the Impact of Rapid Urban Development in Vietnam

Shpresa Halimi, Kevin Kecskes, and Marcus Ingle
Portland State University

Phung Thuy Phuong
University of Science

Vietnam, a country of 83 million people, is quickly transitioning from a centrally planned to a market-oriented economy. In 1986, Vietnam started a reform program called *Doi Moi* to open its economy to international capital, introduce a market economy, and gradually reduce central control by the state. After 20 years of high growth and economic restructuring, the country has achieved remarkable social and economic progress averaging 8% per annum (USAID, 2007). This economic growth is accompanied by extensive industrialization and urbanization, especially in the major cities. In Ho Chi Minh City (HCMC), with a population of more than 8 million, urban development is placing severe pressures on the city's infrastructure and its environment. Severe water, air, and land pollution is evident throughout the city. To address the severe environmental urbanization challenges in HCMC, the University of Science (UoS) in HCMC and Portland State University (PSU) in Portland, Oregon, United States, formed a partnership in 2005. In the same year the government of Vietnam, through Government Resolution N.14 (November 2005), called for changes in the higher education system and encouraged the institutions of higher education to "improve research, professional, and operational skills within the community."

The partnership emerged as a result of the previous work that PSU had accomplished in Vietnam beginning in 2003. From 2003 to 2005, PSU and its Vietnamese partners (with support from the U.S. Agency for International Development) carried out a 2-year community-based environmental management (CBEM) project in HCMC to engage community stakeholders in restoring the Tan Hao Lo Gom canal (Halimi & Ingle, 2005). Two key lessons emerged from that experience. The first lesson was that urban communities in Vietnam can be engaged to find governance solutions to local problems in collaboration with university, governmental, nonprofit, and business entities. The second lesson was that the engagement process required the "convening action" by an indigenous facilitating institution (Ingle & Halimi, 2007). A local Vietnamese university, specifically the UoS, was well suited to this "facilitating institution" role for two reasons. First, universities and their faculty are highly respected in the Vietnamese cultural context. Second, there is a lack of indigenous nonprofit community-based organizations in Vietnam (Hibbard & Tang, 2004).

Established in 1966, the UoS in HCMC prides itself on its long heritage and tradition of education, fundamental research, and cutting-edge technologies.[1] The university serves more than 16,000 students. Like Vietnam's other research and education universities, UoS uses a traditional pedagogy of teaching that is predominantly theory based. This pedagogy relies heavily on rote learning through lectures and on-campus laboratory work. There are few opportunities for students to link with the urban community as part of their higher education experience, and there is a growing demand among students (and many young faculty members) for "a more relevant educational experience" (Phuong, 2007).

Since 2005, the higher education system of Vietnam has been undergoing a transformation to adopt the new credit-based system. The credit-based system has a diverse set of learning outcomes including specific skills, attitudes, and knowledge that students need to appropriate as part of the degree. As a result, the academic leadership of UoS has been actively seeking innovative teaching methods and working to train faculty in their use.

Bringing Relevance to the Vietnamese Curriculum: A Partnered Approach

PSU's Presidential Initiative on Internationalization, administered by the Office of International Affairs, affirms the value of connecting PSU to communities both locally and globally. The Initiative on Internationalization's mission is stated thusly:

> The integration of teaching, research, and outreach at PSU offers students of a diverse age, ethnicity, and experience the preparation to become responsible citizens attuned to the needs of their own communities as well as those of regional, national, and international communities.

While PSU assists UoS in curricular innovation, especially transferring proven service-learning and sustainability practices, UoS helps PSU internationalize its research initiatives and student body. PSU leadership has identified partnering with diverse stakeholders in Vietnam as a strategic priority. Economically, the Nike and Intel Corporations are important regional partners for PSU; both are located in the Portland metropolitan region and have been heavily investing in Vietnam for years. Academically, students from Vietnam and the United States have enhanced cross-cultural learning opportunities. And, culturally, Vietnam is important to the Portland metropolitan region; Portland is home to more than 20,000 ethnic Vietnamese. Many of these Vietnamese attend PSU while also maintaining their cultural heritage. To address this community need, PSU initiated Vietnamese cultural heritage classes in 2004, among other initiatives.

The UoS-PSU partnership represents an entirely new and innovative approach to enhancing the relevance of educational offerings at UoS; the initiative is also a unique experiment for Vietnamese higher education. UoS fully recognizes the need to build engagement capacity in three areas: the institutional fabric of the university, the general curriculum and specific courses offered at the university, and the surrounding communities where the university is engaged (Phuong, 2007).

PSU is particularly well suited to assist UoS to build capacity for curricular and institutional transformation because of its national and international reputation for curricular innovation and service-learning initiatives (Colby, Beaumont, Ehrlich, & Corngold, 2007; Colby, Ehrlich, Beaumont, & Stephens, 2003; Ehrlich, 2000; Holland, 2001; Zlotkowski, 1998). The Portland, Oregon, region—as Harvard professor Robert Putnam documents in *Better Together* (Putnam & Feldstein, 2003)—is unique because of significantly higher levels of social capital and well-established community engagement processes present, when compared to other metropolitan areas of the United States. PSU's diverse and long-standing community-university partnerships—the ethos of which is captured in the university's motto: "Let Knowledge Serve the City"—operate on the basis of collaboration, reciprocity, and a consensus-building approach for decision making (Kecskes, Kerrigan, & Patton, 2006). Located in Oregon's economic and cultural core, PSU has grown to become a university of distinction that attracts students and faculty from around the globe. PSU is Oregon's largest and most diverse university, enrolling more than 29,000 students. PSU hosts more than 1,300 international students annually.

One of PSU's core values is to create socially responsible, engaged students. Today, PSU offers over 400 community-based service-learning (CB-SL) courses that engage nearly 10,000 students in formal community-learning environments each year (Kecskes & Kerrigan, 2009). PSU's Center for Academic Excellence is the leading entity specialized in faculty and community development for service-learning. Among other colleges, the College of Urban and Public Affairs (CUPA), through its several divisions and institutes, has firsthand knowledge with building capacity in community-based organizations, including the capacity for these organizations to work with university faculty and students.[2]

Best Practice

The overall purpose of the UoS-PSU partnership was to establish an effective and sustainable "community-university engagement program" at UoS that would contribute to the mitigation of environmental challenges resulting from HCMC's rapid urbanization.

The underlying premise was that a program that is coproduced can yield long-lasting results while contributing to mutual learning and sharing of best practices. PSU has embraced the notion of "coproduction," which has become an integral part in the development and implementation of its international strategies. Ostrom (1996, p. 1080) defined *coproduction* as "the process through which inputs used to produce a good or service are contributed by individuals who are not 'in' the same organization." Over the past 20 years of doing leadership development in a variety of organizations and countries and through a process of trial and error, the Mark O. Hatfield School of Government in CUPA has developed a coproduction approach, which at its simplest means joint planning and joint delivery of programs with the organizational partners and with the students (Morgan, 2009).

During the 2004–2005 academic year, the Hatfield School of Government in CUPA hosted a Fulbright Scholar from UoS. In 2005, the Higher Education for Development (HED)/USAID Innovative Development and Engagement Across Sectors (IDEAS) Program issued a request for proposals. PSU and UoS submitted a joint proposal, which was successfully funded in 2006.

The program had three major objectives:

1. establish a community-university engagement facilitation office in the UoS in cooperation with PSU,
2. integrate CB-SL curriculum and guidelines into the UoS's courses on a progressive basis through a series of faculty exchanges and action-research interactions, and

3. collaborate with HCMC's community organizations to undertake a number of community-university engagement projects aimed at strengthening environmental awareness and governance (Halimi, Ingle, Kecskes, &
   Phuong, 2010).

In September 2006, a Start-Up planning session was organized at PSU
where roles and responsibilities for program implementation were formally
assigned. Table 3.1 summarizes the program activities and timelines.

The Institutional Baseline Assessment was conducted at UoS in December
2006 during the first study exchange between PSU and a university in Vietnam. A group of 11 PSU graduate students spent a week in HCMC working
collaboratively with UoS faculty and students.

Furco's *Self-Assessment Rubric for the Institutionalization of Service-
Learning in Higher Education* (2003) served as the foundation for the UoS
baseline assessment exercise. Program leaders adapted the *Rubric* to broaden
the investigation from service-learning to engagement. Questions were used
to assess the stage or level of engagement for each category, ranging from
Stage 1 (which represented a low level of community-university engagement)
to Stage 3 (which represented the sustained institutionalization of engagement). In Vietnam, the information in the original rubric was adapted for
cross-cultural student teams carrying out the assessment. This was the first
time Vietnamese students were given the opportunity to interview UoS
faculty, administrators, and staff. The results of the assessment were presented
in a formal session at UoS in both Vietnamese and English. The session was
well attended by UoS administrators, faculty, and students.

The study exchange and the process of conducting the baseline assessment
was a great learning experience for PSU students. One of the students reflecting
on outcomes from the exchange program wrote, "I learned a lot about leadership and community engagement through our work with the Vietnamese students. The team dynamic between the American and Vietnamese students was
different than what I have been used to in the United States." Another student
noted, "U.S. is good at bridging capital and Vietnam is better at bonding capital. Vietnam is learning to cooperate, U.S. is learning relationship building."

The program was officially launched at UoS in March 2007. The launch
workshop was coproduced and codelivered by the PSU delegation (composed of the program codirector from the Center for Academic Excellence
and a PSU CB-SL expert) and UoS leadership. Over 50 UoS faculty, administrators, staff, and students attended the launch workshop.

The workshop was also attended by one representative from People's
Committee, the director of the HCMC Environmental Protection Agency
and three other agency officials, one representative from the Department of

TABLE 3.1
Program Activities and Timelines in Quarters

Activity	Year 1				Year 2				Year 3
	Q1	Q2	Q3	Q4	Q1	Q2	Q3	Q4	
Conduct program Start-Up session at PSU	x								
Study exchange and baseline assessment at UoS	x								
Launch workshop at UoS		x							
Action-oriented workshop at UoS			x						
CB-SL courses offered at UoS				x					
Study exchange and Year 1 evaluation at UoS					x				
Year 1 evaluation workshops						x			
CEE workshops on the new credit-based system and CB-SL						x	x	x	x
CEE staff technical study exchange at PSU								x	
Final evaluation									x

Note. PSU = Portland State University, UoS = University of Science, CB-SL = community-based service-learning, CEE = Center for Educational Excellence.

Natural Resources and the Environment, one representative from the Institute of Tropical Biology, four representatives from the World Bank's Urban Upgrading Projects, and one representative from Nike, Vietnam. Their participation in the workshop was crucial in increasing their buy-in and leadership commitment.

The fact that PSU delegation intentionally set up an exercise so that students, faculty, administrators, party officials, and other community partners were on a relatively even playing field had a positive impact on most of the participants, especially on the students. This was the first time (according to the student representative) students were invited to interact with lecturers, administrators, and other partners outside the UoS in a more formal educational setting such as a workshop.

After the workshop the PSU delegation met with UoS community-university engagement facilitation leadership team. There were important symbolic outcomes (Kecskes, Collier, & Balshem, 2006) from this meeting. The UoS leadership team learned a lot from simply watching the PSU experts interact with the group, specifically how they shared ideas, brainstormed, modified ideas quickly, and used the full group to help problem solve and creatively approach critical aspects of the program.

Objective 1: Establish a Community-University Engagement Facilitation Office in the UoS in Cooperation With PSU

As a result of the discussions held with the PSU delegation during and after the launch workshop, the UoS leadership made the decision to establish the community engagement office. The director of the Mark O. Hatfield School of Government and the program director from CUPA met with the UoS engagement team in late March 2007 to review the results of the launch workshop and agree on program priorities for the coming months. During a brainstorming session at UoS, facilitated by the PSU program director, the engagement team decided to name the new UoS community engagement office the Center for Educational Excellence (CEE). A proposal for the establishment of the center was developed (in Vietnamese) and sent for approval to the rector of the UoS. In August 2007, the rector issued a formal decree and approved the establishment of the CEE at UoS.[3] The vice rector was appointed as the CEE's director, assisted by two staff members. The former PSU Fulbright Scholar and program codirector was actively involved in the establishment of the CEE.

When first established, the CEE at UoS had three main purposes:

1. apply service-learning teaching and learning methods to enhance university curricula for undergraduate and graduate programs,

2. support teachers and students by providing them with service-learning knowledge and tools, and

3. assess community assets and needs and form partnerships with the community to tailor teaching and learning opportunities toward addressing community and societal issues of concern.

During 2007, the CEE played an important role in facilitating the integration of CB-SL into two courses: Environmental Science and Wastewater Treatment.

In 2008, a new reform started in the Vietnamese university system that required institutions to introduce a credit-based system. The leadership of the UoS requested the departments to rebuild curricula according to the credit-based system and begin implementing the system for incoming freshmen in 2008. Under these new system-wide requirements, the CEE was charged with the task of facilitating the reform by organizing seminars on the credit-based education and teaching methods. During April–May 2008, the center organized four seminars not only for UoS faculty but also for faculty from the nearby Can Tho University. These activities raised the profile of the CEE. During the seminars the CEE also introduced the concept of CB-SL as an innovative teaching methodology.

In the summer of 2008, PSU hosted a one-week technical study exchange for two CEE staff members. During the study exchange, CEE staff increased knowledge and skills associated with service-learning, had access to applied learning activities provided by the Center for Academic Excellence at PSU, and received firsthand exposure to high-quality CB-SL activities with staff from the Center for Academic Excellence, PSU faculty, and their community partners.

CEE staff had the opportunity to attend a Senior Capstone course run by the PSU professor who had delivered the workshop at UoS a few months earlier; the professor's community partner is the City of Portland's Community Watershed Stewardship Program. One of the visiting CEE staff members recalls,

> The Senior Capstone course is structured very differently from the traditional Vietnamese curriculum. Senior Capstone courses are very practical and useful for collaboration with the community. In addition, students are able to work in a team, develop relationships, and collaborate with community members from different fields and specializations.

Upon return to HCMC, the CEE staff applied new insights, implemented selected aspects in the CB-SL courses offered at UoS, and assessed the outcomes.

The establishment of the CEE was an important milestone in the life-time of the program. The center acts as a change agent within the UoS tradi-tional structure and has become a hub for new learning approaches that are being institutionalized in the Vietnamese higher education system.

Objective 2: Integrate CB-SL Curricula and Guidelines Into UoS's Courses

In late August 2007, the CEE hosted an "action-learning" workshop to develop new CB-SL courses and curricula. Over 60 UoS faculty, administra-tors, staff, and students attended the workshop. During the workshop two PSU CB-SL experts worked closely with UoS faculty to review their curricula as part of the development of new UoS courses. UoS faculty developed a set of goals, assignments, activities, and student learning assessment strategies for their courses; explored multiple ways for eliciting and facilitating student reflections; and discussed organizational strategies to engage large classes in CB-SL. As a result of the workshop, three CB-SL courses were planned for initiation in fall 2007 at UoS. The Environmental Science and Wastewater Treatment courses taught by the UoS program codirector from the biology department were hallmarks of accomplishment. The large classes (over 200 students, which are very common for undergraduate courses at UoS) were divided into a smaller section, approximately 20 students who were selected to participate in specific community projects. The process of prescreening students, though time-consuming and requiring more work on the part of the instructor, appeared to be a very important reason for the success of the community projects. Having a smaller group of students to work on the community projects made the management of the projects and the quality control for the work much more feasible.

Despite the successful integration of CB-SL into two pilot courses in the biology department, the CEE realized that the overall institutional environ-ment was not yet ripe for the broad-scale infusion of new approaches into the university's curriculum. More foundational work in terms of faculty develop-ment and curriculum design was needed before the full-scale introduction and institutionalization of the new approach could occur.

Objective 3: Collaborate With HCMC's Community Organizations to Undertake a Number of Community-University Engagement Projects Aimed at Strengthening Environmental Awareness and Governance

The program codirector from the biology department who taught the CB-SL courses established a relationship with the community partner, Dam Sen

Park, a popular amusement and educational park in HCMC. The park administration was faced with the issues of environmental degradation due to water and air pollution, as well as accumulation of solid waste. In the initial steps of the partnership-building process, there was much difficulty in communicating with Dam Sen Park and getting the community partner agreement signed. This resulted in the students having to start their work quite late in the term. Despite considerable challenges, eight student projects were completed, and students gave final presentations at Dam Sen Park.

The day after the presentation, the UoS faculty was interviewed by the local newspaper *Bao Tien Phong*, which published an article titled "When Students Have the Right to Question":

> "Falling leaves and garbage are polluting this lake. . . . Dam Sen Park should pay attention to the treatment method." This statement is not coming from any inspection department but from students of University of Science (National University–HCMC).
>
> This extraordinary class, which has never been applied in Vietnam, was held by the Center for Educational Excellence (CEE). The collaboration between the park and the university allowed the students to carry out the survey on the environment, landscape, and waste treatment at the park. In a small meeting room at Dam Sen Park, with a projector and screen students presented the results of their survey on the water quality of the lakes in the park. After the presentation, another group of students showed a carefully designed physical model of Dam Sen Park.

The establishment of the first community-university partnership, which contributed to the richness of the students learning, was another highlight in the process of UoS institutional transformation of connecting the university with the community and creating opportunities for collaboration and collective learning.

Other Capacity-Building and Assessment Activities

In December 2007, PSU organized the second study exchange. PSU and UoS students formed five cross-cultural teams and conducted the Year 1 assessment of the PSU-UoS engagement program. They organized and conducted focus group interviews with students, faculty, and community partners. Upon completion, the student teams presented on the five different measurement dimensions, including the philosophy of service-learning, faculty, students, community partner, and support structure in the university. The results demonstrated improvements in 12 of 22 categories (see table 3.2). Most significantly, there were major enhancements (labeled "gain" in table 3.2) in four service-learning areas: faculty leadership, student awareness, coordinating entity, and institutional support for staffing. These enhancements were symbolic of UoS conversations about new service-learning concepts, about a deepening of the meaning of service-learning among the faculty and students, and about the advent of a new type of service-based relationship between the university and a community partner.

TABLE 3.2
Year 1 Evaluation Results

Dimension	Baseline Assessment	Year-One Assessment	Difference
1.0 Philosophy and Mission			
1.1 Definition of Service-Learning	1	1	No Change
1.2 Strategic Planning	2	2	No Change
1.3 Alignment With UNS Institutional Mission	1	1+	Progress Toward
1.4 Alignment With Educational Reforms Efforts	2	2	No Change
2.0 Faculty Support and Learning in Service-Learning			
2.1 Faculty Knowledge and Awareness	1	1+	Progress Toward
2.2 Faculty Involvement and Support	1	1+	Progress Toward
2.3 Faculty Leadership	1	2	Gain
2.4 Faculty Incentives and Rewards	1	1	No Change
3.0 Student Support and Involvement in SL			
3.1 Student Awareness	1	2	Gain
3.2 Student Opportunities	1	1+	Progress Toward

(Continues)

TABLE 3.2
Year 1 Evaluation Results (Continued)

3.3 Student Leadership	1	1	No Change
3.4 Student Incentives and Rewards	1	1	No Change
4.0 Community Participation and Partnerships			
4.1 Community Partner Awareness	1	1+	Progress Toward
4.2 Mutual Understanding Between UNS/ Community	1	2	Gain
4.3 Community Partner Voice and Leadership	1	1	No Change
5.0 Institutional Support for Service Learning			
5.1 Coordinating Entity	1	2	Gain
5.2 Policy-Making Entity	1	1+	Progress Toward
5.3 Staffing	1	2	Gain
5.4 Funding	1	1	No Change
5.5 Administrative Support	1	1+	Progress Toward
5.6 Departmental Support	1	1	No Change
5.7 Evaluation and Assessment	1	1	No Change

An important capacity-building activity was the Year 1 Evaluation Workshop organized by the CEE in February 2008. The workshop was attended by 42 faculty, administrators, and students from the UoS, as well as four representatives from Dam Sen Park, including the park manager. The workshop was intended to present the results of the CB-SL courses taught by the faculty in the biology department and to discuss the possibility of expanding the CB-SL courses in the curriculum. In early 2009, the PSU program director visited UoS to conduct the final evaluation.

Successes and Challenges

The PSU-UoS partnership created a mutually beneficial relationship between the two institutions. Yet, this partnership is the story of both successes and challenges resulting from the efforts to institutionalize a new approach to teaching and learning into the Vietnamese higher education context.

One of the major successes was the establishment of the Center for Educational Excellence, the first of its kind in Vietnam. The CEE gained university- and country-wide reputation for pioneering the efforts to introduce the CB-SL and the new credit-based system into the curriculum. This was evidenced by an increasing amount of activity on the CEE website and requests from other universities in Vietnam for information on the CB-SL program. In February 2009, the CEE was contacted by Fullerton State University (under its HED grant) to participate in a region-wide CB-SL workshop in Cambodia in June 2009.

During 2009–2010 the CEE was involved in the following:

- organizing several workshops to introduce CB-SL to every department of UoS;
- developing training courses on soft skills for students (Kecskes & Messer, 2008);
- participating in national conferences on the education system reform in Vietnam, introducing CB-SL, and disseminating the results of implementing CB-SL at UoS;
- participating in an intensive training workshop on service-learning with 13 universities from Laos, Vietnam, the United States, Korea, and Cambodia;
- organizing training courses on active teaching methods and CB-SL for junior faculty of UoS and other universities in HCMC; and
- creating of Student Leaders for Service, a group modeled after PSU's award-winning student civic leadership development program.[4]

The sustainability of the center depends on its ability to expand its services. The CEE is thinking strategically about future directions and is planning to provide training on active learning and CB-SL to faculty and students from other universities on a fee-for-service basis, as well as applying for external funding from local and international foundations.

CB-SL courses were successfully introduced into the UoS curriculum. The courses taught by the program codirector were well organized, and students experienced an enhanced learning environment that combined working on real-life projects and theoretical perspectives. Students developed their analytical thinking, teamwork, communication, and presentation skills and raised their civic mindfulness. In addition, faculty and students had the opportunity to interact with each other, which rarely happens in the traditional classes. According to one junior, he gained experience when working at Dam Sen Park; the course offered the opportunity for him to apply theory into practice.

A senior found the CB-SL course very interesting and useful: "This way of teaching and learning helps students to develop their autonomous thinking, to apply theory to solve real problems. Compared to the traditional teaching and learning method, this method is more interesting." However, according to her, there were some limitations that had to be overcome: only some students could participate in CB-SL projects, it was an overload for the professor to supervise 20 students at the park, the curriculum of biology was too heavy, and it was very difficult to arrange time for the CB-SL project.

The PSU-UoS partnership has also experienced a number of challenges. "A real challenge is figuring out how to adapt the CB-SL curricula for our local context," said the program codirector, who teaches classes packed with 200 or more students. Initially, she selected the top 20 students in both courses to participate in the CB-SL projects. The applied research projects with Dam Sen Park proved so popular that she opened the CB-SL opportunity to all students in her next two classes.

According to her, CB-SL demanded a lot of extra effort and was time-consuming for both faculty and students. Students were required to devote their time to reading materials, conducting research, discussing, and making presentations on proposed topics. The amount of time they spent during the self-study process does not count toward the earned credit hours that go into their transcripts.

Collaborating with community partners and getting agreements completed were the most challenging aspects of the program. Communities in Vietnam are not familiar with working with students. At the beginning of the PSU-UoS project in 2007, the CEE organized a workshop to introduce CB-SL to UoS faculty members, communities, and students. At the workshop, there was skepticism voiced by selected local community members who announced that they "do not believe in the work of students; students seem to create more problems than to solve problems." Long-established beliefs about students such as these made it difficult to build relationships in the community. Despite noteworthy and well-publicized successes such as collaborative UoS work with Dam Sen Park, community members did not seem to consider CB-SL projects as a mutually beneficial activity. Moreover, it is difficult to sustain long-term relationships when there is a high turnover in community leadership.

The course that was taught by another faculty member was not completed as a CB-SL class. This appeared to be the case because a formal agreement with the community partner was not finalized. Even though the professor and the community partner appeared to have some informal plans and agreements for the community service projects, the fact that there was not a more formal agreement was seen to be a problem that resulted in a discontinuation of the course as a CB-SL course.

In the Vietnamese context, there is a considerable need for more "formal contractual agreements" between the university and community partners that have to be approved by the top administrators. As the program codirector expressed it, they were learning how to do CB-SL the "Vietnamese way." The Vietnamese university context is very hierarchical in nature with minimal autonomy and discretion provided to the faculty and individual faculty members. In this case, adjustments are sometimes needed in the beginning of the partnership to allow for the partner to become comfortable and capable of working with the CB-SL courses. Obtaining up-front agreements from senior university administrators requires taking extra time to organize the community component for the CB-SL.

Culture and Context Matter

In the U.S. context, service-learning has been slowly gaining legitimacy over the past quarter century. Resistance to this pedagogical approach was substantial in the mid-1980s and is still strong on some universities and in some academic departments on U.S. campuses today. Thus, the high level of resistance to new pedagogies, and indeed to an expanded mission of universities in entirely new contexts such as Vietnam, should not come as a surprise to the students of social movements.

Substantively, the PSU-UoS initiative identifies three clear areas of challenge:

1. Individual faculty members' challenges associated with being the earliest adopter of a new strategy cause them to feel overwhelmed and to sense a lack of understanding and support on the part of departmental colleagues.
2. Internal structural challenges do not recognize or honor the significant amount of extra time needed and different learning attained within the service-learning context. This is seen in the fact that the self-study process outlined earlier did not "count" toward students' earned credit hours.
3. External structural challenges make it difficult for faculty to work with community partners because there is no precedent for these types of student-driven, faculty-supervised, community-based collaborations in the national context. Community partners do not have any basis for trusting students' work and feel low, if any, motivation for investing time in student-based projects.

As was the case in the U.S. context, it is assumed that it will take many years for service-learning to become more understood and established in the Vietnamese context. Cultural theory applied to campus-community partnership-building efforts (Kecskes, 2006) may provide a theoretical lens through which to view the challenges and possibilities of service-learning establishment in Vietnam. As mentioned earlier, the Vietnamese political system, and by association its higher education system, is built with a largely "hierarchical" structural approach. Thus, the view of leadership tends to be more centralized and positional, potentially making it more structurally challenging for students to assume informal leadership roles in communities as part of their learning and for faculty members to view themselves as egalitarian colearners alongside their community partners and students. This theoretical proposition is largely untested and is ripe for further research.

Transferable Insights

There is an important role for higher education in the global society, but the exact nature

> of that engagement is contested. Higher education's failure and best self can be found by engaging community partners in mutually transformative work that allows us to reimagine, in ways both creative and practical, sustainable communities. Our choice of partners and our visions of what may be accomplished together create opportunities for us to become members of communities and of a world of which we would like to be part. (Enos & Morton, 2003, p. 40)

As a result of the PSU-UoS partnership, a process of transformation was initiated and furthered in both institutions. In Vietnam, the UoS became the first institution of higher education to apply CB-SL, a methodology that shifted the focus from "teaching" to "learning." Faculty expressed their willingness to try community-oriented pedagogies, as evidenced by the work in Dam Sen Park.

UoS high-level administrators were actively involved during program design, implementation, and evaluation. The vice rector served as the program codirector, and even though at the inception of the project she had more of a titular role, she played a more direct leadership role in the later stages when power relationships shifted between PSU and UoS. Initially, PSU was playing the leadership role with the input from UoS. During the second year of the program, through meetings that the PSU codirector had with UoS codirectors, it was decided that in order to do things the "Vietnamese way" and make the program work, the relationship needed to be reversed; specifically UoS assumed the larger share of control and power over what was going on with the program.

At PSU, transformation occurred at different levels from higher administrators to PSU faculty and students. As a result of PSU's growing and formal engagement in Vietnam through the community-university engagement program, three additional programs were initiated:

1. The Advanced Training Program sponsored by the Ministry of Education and Training (MOET) aims at achieving academic advancement through a twinning program with foreign universities. The vice rector of the UoS and program codirector was the head of the computer science department, and she proposed to collaborate with PSU to reform the computer science curriculum of the UoS. The program received funding from the MOET; it serves 50 students who enter the academic program annually as a cohort. The overall goal is to educate Vietnamese students with PSU's computer science curriculum, in English, and to transfer to Vietnam an American standard, world-class computer science curriculum. According to PSU's contacts at the MOET, the PSU/U.S. Advanced Training Program is ranked among the best in Vietnam.

2. Unveiled at the end of 2008, the Intel Vietnam Scholar (IVS) Program is a partnership with Intel that brings up to 40 fully funded Vietnamese engineering students to PSU. These students are funded for 2 years of study, leading to completion of their PSU undergraduate degree in mechanical engineering, electrical engineering, or computer engineering. The IVS program is a comprehensive approach to study abroad and includes specialized bridging courses in engineering and English, with a total investment of approximately $80,000 per student (an investment that is unique both in the university's history and in Intel's). According to PSU's vice provost for international affairs,

> This private initiative recognizes the workforce needs of an important, emerging economic sector in Vietnam. In its ongoing work with Intel Vietnam, Portland State has taken the position that the evolving landscape resulting from new global connections requires higher education to adapt in ways that are flexible, bold, and nimble. In an era of rapid change and many daunting new challenges, the university as a public institution has a responsibility and an obligation to identify opportunities and pursue relationships that will prepare students, both in Vietnam and in the United States, for successful citizenship, careers, and lifelong learning after gradu-

ation. Intel could have chosen any school, anywhere in the world to work on the IVS program; we are especially proud of our effort to develop a critically important engineering education program for Vietnamese and Portland State students and faculty, one that sets the foundation for expanding international collaboration and increasing international recognition.

3. The collaborative PSU-UoS project in HCMC contributed to another major and ongoing transformation in the Mark O. Hatfield School of Government at PSU in the area of public leadership. With Ford Foundation support, in 2007 the Hatfield School began to develop a collaborative public leadership research relationship with the Ho Chi Minh National Academy of Politics and Public Administration (HCMA) in Hanoi. This relationship led to development of an innovative and coproduced "public leadership for sustainable development" framework and curriculum. The new framework, labeled EMERGE, is systems centered and solutions based. The EMERGE leadership framework has a strong "theory to practice" orientation as described in the "Foundations of Public Service" publication (Morgan, Green, Shinn, & Robinson, 2008). The Hatfield School and the HCMA are both transforming their public leadership educational offerings based on the EMERGE framework.

As evidence of continued institutional transformation at PSU, in the summer of 2010, the university launched the Faculty Vietnam Immersion Program on Urban Sustainability. In collaboration with UoS and other community partners in Vietnam, the program sought to strengthen the sustainability dimension of PSU teaching faculty and curricula by immersing a diverse group of PSU faculty from multiple disciplines in an engaged 2-week learning experience in Vietnam. The faculty participated in an intensive and interactive program with Vietnamese stakeholders and served as a living laboratory for thinking and acting creatively around several urban sustainability projects. The CEE at UoS hosted PSU faculty; UoS faculty and PSU faculty worked on cross-cultural teams to develop new approaches to incorporating CB-SL and sustainability into the UoS curriculum.

Future Directions

Through its interaction with the UoS and the higher educational sector in Vietnam, PSU has learned that the development of educational collaborations needs time and quality relationships built on mutual trust and infused with patience and persistence. To be successful, CB-SL approaches need to be carefully tailored to the special requirements of the Vietnamese context. High degrees of collaboration are required to ensure that this tailoring is attended to throughout the project, and this requires substantial financial resources (Latz, Ingle, & Fisher, 2009).

When PSU first established its University Studies undergraduate general education program in 1994—in particular its mandatory six-credit, interdisciplinary, community-based Senior Capstone course requirement—it did so with three guiding principles in mind:

1. Taking a scholarly approach toward innovation,
2. Transforming from a teaching to a learning focus that intentionally expanded the learning environment to incorporate multiple sources of wisdom and knowledge, and
3. Working with community partners in a spirit of reciprocity. (Kecskes, Kerrigan, et al., 2006)

To a large extent, these principles have informed the PSU-UoS collaboration since 2005. Indeed, analysis relevant to this international, institutional partnership suggests the following key recommendations when building future international partnerships in support of service-learning:

- *Mutual benefits:* Strategic partnerships like the one between PSU and UoS need to be grounded in a clear commitment to ongoing, valuable academic benefits for both institutions.
- *Contextual alignment:* Successful introduction of the CB-SL approach in a different context requires paying close attention to the approach's core ingredients to ensure that these features are closely aligned with the political, economic, cultural, social, and organizational characteristics of the local context.
- *Start small with a collaborative process:* Start small, seek early "wins" and promote them, and build consensus at all steps along the way. A coproduction and codelivery approach is well suited as a foundational guiding principle to establish CB-SL in a different context.
- *Strategic leadership involvement (university):* Intentionally designing pathways for high-level administrators and senior opinion leaders among the faculty to participate from the outset of the process is key to ensuring a successful CB-SL process design and implementation.
- *Strategic leadership involvement (local political context):* Involve local political leaders early on in the process by inviting them to attend CB-SL planning meetings, events, and activities, and create opportunities for them to demonstrate support and leadership by having a say in the process design, implementation, and public gatherings.

- *Institutional structural investment:* Establish a facilitating entity—with sufficient administrative, senior faculty, and financial support—to become the hub for teaching, research, and community partnerships in CB-SL, and to provide leadership and needed support at critical junctures.
- *Substantive community involvement:* Identify, intentionally select, and closely collaborate with community partners to leverage their myriad assets and design systems to address their needs in a spirit of reciprocity. This is essential to building long-term, sustainable partnerships for community-engaged teaching and research.
- *Scholarly approach:* Share lessons learned in an atmosphere of scholarship, in particular by participating in conferences, preparing joint publications, and so on.
- *Disseminate/publicize:* Attract the attention of the media, tell stories, and disseminate results early, often, and broadly.
- *Embrace experimentation/learning/reflective practice:* Expect fallout and learn from both challenges and successes in a collaborative spirit that honors multiple perspectives. Collaboratively assess programmatic progress in a systematic way that honors local wisdom and knowledge, as well as traditional metrics in a spirit of continuous improvement and transparency.
- *Share power/build trust:* Don't underestimate the need to share power and build trust. Listen carefully to all key stakeholders.

The PSU-UoS partnership is well established now as evidenced by the events of the past 5 years. And the journey continues, driven by a clear sense of mutual benefits and professional relationships. As the partnership becomes institutionalized, many new collaborative opportunities are emerging on a regular basis. For example, discussions are under way for a PSU Fulbright Scholar now residing in Thailand to travel to Vietnam to work on a collaborative service-learning program with the CEE. Concurrently, UoS has an interest in hosting one of PSU's EMERGE seminars on "Leadership for Sustainable Development." Both institutions remain committed to further exploring the untapped potential of using the community-engaged service-learning approach to mitigate the impact of Vietnam's rapid urban development.

Endnotes

1. In 1996 the University of Natural Sciences was officially founded as an affiliate with the Vietnam National University–Ho Chi Minh City. In 2007 the name was revised as University of Science (UoS) to mark a new stage of the teaching knowledge about sophisticated sciences and computer technology.

2. Of special note is the School of Urban and Regional Planning's Community Watershed Stewardship Program. This innovative program, implemented in cooperation with community partners and the City of Portland's Bureau of Environmental Services, represented an excellent capacity-building model for UoS. On June 3, 2008, the Jimmy and Rosalynn Carter Partner Foundation designated PSU as the recipient of the Jimmy and Rosalynn Carter Partnership Award for Campus-Community Collaboration for its Watershed Stewardship Program.

3. www.cee.hcmus.edu.vn/vi/welcome

4. www.pdx.edu/student-leadership/student-leaders-for-service-members

References

Colby, A., Beaumont, E., Ehrlich, T., & Corngold, J. (2007). *Educating for democracy: Preparing undergraduates for responsible political engagement.* San Francisco, CA: Jossey-Bass.

Colby, A., Ehrlich, T., Beaumont, E., & Stephens, J. (2003). *Educating citizens: Preparing America's undergraduates for lives of moral and civic responsibility.* San Francisco, CA: Jossey-Bass.

Ehrlich, T. (2000). *Civic responsibility and higher education.* Phoenix, AZ: Oryx Press.

Enos, S., & Morton, K. (2003). Developing a theory and practice of campus-community partnerships. In B. Jacoby (Ed.), *Building partnerships for service-learning* (pp. 20–41). San Francisco, CA: Jossey-Bass.

Furco, A. (2003). *Self-assessment rubric for the institutionalization of service-learning in higher education.* Providence, RI: Campus Compact.

Halimi, S., & Ingle, M. (2005). *The community based environmental management toolkit for Vietnam.* Portland, OR: Portland State University.

Halimi, S., Ingle, M., Kecskes, K., & Phuong, P. T. (2010). *Community-university engagement: Mitigating the impact of rapid urban development in Vietnam.* Retrieved from http://www.cee.hcmus.edu.vn/uploadtemp/Material/Prospectus%20SH%20March2010.pdf

Hibbard, M., & Tang, C. C. (2004). Sustainable community development: A social approach from Vietnam. *Journal of the Community Development Society, 35*(2), 87–104.

Holland, B. A. (2001). Toward a definition and characterization of the engaged campus: Six cases. *Metropolitan University: An International Forum, 12*(3), 63–72.

Ingle, M., & Halimi, S. (2007). Community-based environmental management in Vietnam: The challenge of sharing power in a politically guided society. *Public Administration and Development, 27*(2), 95–109.

Kecskes, K. (2006). Behind the rhetoric: Applying a cultural theory lens to community-campus partnership development. *Michigan Journal of Community Service Learning, 12*(2), 5–14.

Kecskes, K., Collier, P., & Balshem, M. (2006). Engaging scholars in the scholarship of engagement. In K. McKnight Casey, G. Davidson, S. Billig, & N. Springer

(Eds.), *Advancing knowledge in service-learning: Research to transform the field* (pp. 159–181). Greenwich, CT: Information Age Publishing.

Kecskes, K., & Kerrigan, S. (2009). Capstone experiences: Integrating education for civic engagement. In B. Jacoby (Ed.), *Civic engagement in higher education*. San Francisco, CA: Jossey-Bass.

Kecskes, K., Kerrigan, S., & Patton, J. (2006). The heart of the matter: Aligning curriculum, pedagogy and engagement in higher education [Special issue on "Indicators of Engagement"]. *Metropolitan Universities, 17*(1), 51–61.

Kecskes, K., & Messer, W. (2008). *The new "hard skills": Connecting social sustainability and partnerships to update what really "counts" in 21st century learning*. Paper presented at the 11th Annual Western Region Campus Compact Consortium "Continuums of Service" Conference, Portland, OR.

Latz, G., Ingle, M., & Fisher, M. (2009). *Cross-border capacity building: Selected examples of Portland State University's involvement in tertiary level educational reform in Vietnam*. Paper presented in the PICMET Conference, Portland, OR.

Morgan, D. F. (2009). *Co-production: A leadership development techniques for higher performance*. Paper presented at the First International Conference on Government Performance Management and Public Governance, Lanzhou University, China.

Morgan, D. F., Green, R., Shinn, C. W., & Robinson, K. S. (2008). *Foundations of public service*. Armonk, NY: M.E. Sharpe.

Ostrom, E. (1996). Crossing the great divide: Coproduction, synergy and development. *World Development, 24*(6), 1073–1087.

Phuong, T. P. (2007). Community involvement in urban watershed management: From the US Pacific Northwest to Ho Chi Minh City, Vietnam. *Journal of Environment Development, 16*, 307–332.

Putnam, R., & Feldstein, L. (2003). *Better together: Restoring the American community*. New York, NY: Simon and Schuster.

USAID. (2007). *Vietnam country report*. Retrieved August 23, 2010, from http://usaid.eco-asia.org/programs/cdcp/reports/Ideas-to-Action/annexes/Annex06_Vietnam.pdf

Zlotkowski, E. (Ed.). (1998). *Successful service-learning programs: New models of excellence in higher education*. Bolton, MA: Anker.

4

ASSET-BASED COMMUNITY DEVELOPMENT AND INTEGRAL HUMAN DEVELOPMENT

Two Theories Undergirding an International Service-Learning Program

Marisol Morales
University of La Verne
Arturo Caballero Barrón
Marist University

In 2005, after almost 20 years of DePaul University (DPU) operating a winter quarter study abroad program in Mérida, Mexico, a fortuitous introduction to the Universidad Marista de Mérida (hereafter referred to as Marist University or UMM) transformed a traditional study abroad program into a two-quarter international service-learning (ISL) program. The case study presented in this chapter showcases an ISL program coordinated by two Catholic-inspired universities, UMM in Mérida, Yucatán, Mexico, and DPU in Chicago, Illinois, United States. The program between the universities, which has operated since 2005, utilizes the conceptual frameworks of asset-based community development (ABCD) and integral human development (IHD) as the theoretical and practical philosophies for engagement, partnership, and reflection. The success of this program can be attributed to (a) the involvement of service-learning professionals from DPU who are bilingual and bicultural and understand the culture and language of the community receiving the service and the service-learning professionals from UMM who have the trust and relationships with the local community,

(b) a shared philosophy on community engagement, and (c) the incorporation of participatory processes of reflection throughout different program development stages that enabled improvements each year and led to the development of sustainable service-learning projects. In addition, the case study demonstrates that continual analysis and incorporation of lessons learned can result in transformative benefits for ISL programs such as in the case of this program that eventually came to incorporate participatory action research (Gabarrón & Hernández, 1994; Izcara, 2009). This example clearly demonstrates how academic service-learning and international education can be connected to create a transformative ISL experience for all parties.

DePaul University and Marist University: Missions of Service

> A Catholic university must prioritize issues which are not always emphasized by other lay institutions, especially those related to the study of "serious current problems" such as the dignity of human life, the promotion of justice for all, personal and family quality of life, protection of the environment, the search for peace and political stability, a more equitable distribution of the world's resources and a new economic and political order which will better serve the human community at the national and international level. (Pope John Paul II, 1990, p. 8)

DPU and UMM share a commitment to service derived from their founding Catholic orders, the Vincentians and Marists, respectively. Engagement of students with marginalized communities as part of their studies is one way that both universities realize this commitment. Service-learning is a key instrument by which they bridge their teaching and service missions.

Founded in 1898, DPU is the largest Catholic university in the United States. Enrollment in 2009–2010 exceeded 25,000 students. The university was founded on the values of the 17th-century priest Vincent de Paul and incorporates a mission of service to the poor, with special emphasis on providing opportunities for first-generation college students (DePaul University, 1991). At DPU the office spearheading service-learning and ISL is the Irwin W. Steans Center for Community-based Service-Learning and Community Service Studies. DPU began incorporating service-learning in 1998 as part of the university's strategic plan, and in 2001, Harrison Steans (a philanthropist, banker, and DPU trustee) and his family provided a $5 million endowment for the creation of the Irwin W. Steans Center, named after their late father, making it one of the few endowed service-learning programs in the nation. This endowment, as well as generous university support, helped to make the Steans Center one of the strongest service-learning programs in the country, consistently ranking among the top 25 in *U.S. News and World Report*, sending out close to 3,000 DPU students to over 250 community-based organizations in the Chicago area and nationally. In the Steans Center model, students electing service-learning are directed to various communities. The Steans Center has become an engine for connecting the university's teaching and service mission.

The Marist Brothers are a community of Catholic brothers who conduct their ministry through the "education of children and young people, with a preference for those who are the most neglected. St. Marcellin Champagnat, a priest from France, founded the Congregation of the Marist Teaching Brothers in 1817" (Clisby, 2006). They have had a presence in Mérida since 1899. Most of their work focuses on supporting primary and secondary education (Instituto de los Hermanos Maristas, 2003). In 1996, UMM was founded to offer higher education in the Marist tradition. UMM is a small university with approximately 1,200 students. Upon its founding, the Marist Provincial Superior, Antonio Cavazos Bueno, gave the university a mandate to "challenge the economic model which has generated such an unequal structure" (Cavazos Bueno, 1996) and established an evaluation parameter: "The thermometer shall be when our poor, our Mayan people, the legitimate inhabitants of these lands, show signs of social and economic improvement, when they have solid evidence based upon fact that they have emerged from their plight, due to the efforts of students, faculty, citizens and government in favor of social justice. Then, our university will truly be useful" (Cavazos Bueno, 1996).

At UMM the execution of service-learning occurs through the Programa de Aprender Sirviendo, or Service-Learning Program. This model has service-learning incorporated throughout students' academic career and executed in developmental stages to prepare students for successful community engagement. UMM focuses its service-learning resources and efforts in the community of Emiliano Zapata Sur (EZS) through CEMADE el Centro Marista de Desarrollo, or Marist Development Center.

International Service-Learning

In her article "Theoretical Frameworks of International Service-Learning," Robbin Crabtree referred to ISL as "a variety of experiences common in U.S. higher education today: faculty/staff-led co-curricular 'mission' and service trips, academic courses with international immersion that include service experiences, study-abroad programs with service components, and international programs with formal service-learning curricula" (Crabtree, 2008,

p. 18). DPU has a variety of these types of programs, such as alternative spring and winter breaks led by University Ministry, but the programs that are considered ISL for DPU are those operated through the Steans Center in coordination with the Office of Study Abroad. The ISL programming ranges from short-term programs, which utilize the "Bringing It Home" model where students do minimal service in another country but conduct service in the United States on an issue or at an organization related to what they learned about in the host country, all the way to study abroad programs that include a service component. The program that DPU developed in Mérida initially began as a study abroad program with a service component, but it evolved into a two-term experience that integrated formal service-learning curricula and linked to the community service studies (CSS) academic minor at DPU. The importance given to this program and partnership facilitated the first formal ISL memorandum of understanding that DPU developed with an international university, although prior to 2008 the partnership operated without a formal university agreement.

In 2005, UMM's vice rector and service-learning director were introduced to the assistant director for community development from the Steans Center by DPU's in-country Mérida coordinator, who coordinated the homestays, field trips, and course placements for DPU students and was familiar with UMM's Programa de Aprender Sirviendo and with DPU's service-learning program. This fortuitous introduction allowed both universities to draw on their shared missions to develop an international partnership to support service-learning as a component of the DPU study abroad program. Both institutions had a history of integrating service-learning as pedagogy into their curriculum, but each had differing models for integration, given their size and broader curricular, cultural, linguistic, and pedagogical differences.

The UMM model requires service-learning for all students and focuses the university's efforts in one community of Mérida, EZS. The DPU model utilizes service-learning as one of four options for students to fulfill the university's junior-year experiential learning requirement, and the Steans Center works with various communities across the Chicago area. The dialogue that took place regarding differing models of implementation enabled learning between the institutions, and over time they collectively came to an agreement on which ISL model would be most beneficial for this particular ISL program. The DPU program was able to make use of the long-standing relationship that UMM had developed in the community and focus students' experiences in one community.

At the outset of the partnership, these institutional differences were mitigated by two factors: (a) DPU staff was bilingual and bicultural, and (b) both universities were open to exploring their service-learning pedagogical differences. Because the universities shared the same approach to creating mutually beneficial partnerships and a common focus on guiding students to learn about, generate, and disseminate knowledge that humanizes society and themselves and employing critical reflection to regularly evaluate program goals and outcomes, challenges that arose for the partnership were mitigated.

ISL has the potential to be a transformative experience within the study abroad context, but it also has the potential, as local service-learning does, to replicate stereotypes and perpetuate paternalism. These challenges are evident in the service-learning literature (Crabtree, 2008; Cruz & Giles, 2000; Kiely, 2004; Simonelli, Earle, & Story, 2004). The key to confronting those conflicts, as we have found in the execution of the Mérida ISL program, is based on the models we chose around which to embed the program. The social justice orientation of the service-learning programs at both universities allows and demands the ongoing consideration of mutually beneficial relationships, with emphasis on the benefit for the community. Although other ISL programs focus on global citizenship or world peace (Crabtree, 2008), in our program we have other aims. For students, we seek to challenge students' perceptions of poverty by taking them out of the middle-class homestays they are housed in during their time in Mérida and placing them with a resilient community. This allows them to see the multiple layers of society that exist in Mérida and to understand the broader forces of globalization that have been the impetus for the development of a community like EZS. This exposure and connection to globalization assists them in connecting with broader economic and social policies and seeing how the latter impact communities locally and internationally, as well as their impact on the current immigration debate in the United States. For the community, the program seeks to have students participate in the programs they have created, provide support especially in relation to working with local children, and link them to university resources. For the universities, the program provides opportunities for collaboration around the mission-driven work of both.

Although some have promoted community service and service-learning around the idea of civic participation or citizenship in a democratic society (Barber, 1992; Boyer & Hechinger, 1981; Commission on National Community Service, 1993; Crabtree, 2008; Kraft & Dwyer, 2000; Rutter & Newman, 1989), at DPU and UMM the Catholic orientation of both has been the catalyst by which service-learning and community service have been promoted, reflected in their respective mission statements:

> The Steans Center for Community-based Service Learning provides educational opportunities grounded in Vincentian community values to

DePaul students. The Center seeks to develop mutually beneficial, reciprocal relationships with community organizations in order to develop a sense of social agency in our students through enrollment in CbSL courses, community internships and placements, and community-based student employment. (Steans Center, 2001)

The Service-Learning Program materializes and brings to life the mission that we share. The "PAS" [Programa de Aprender Sirviendo] involves the Marist university community, who, by taking on every service learning Project, prepare themselves to contribute to the creation of a world that is more socially and economically just and in solidarity. This commitment should translate into a professional and human attitude of "be, to serve." (Red Marista Internacional de Instituciones de Educación Superior, 2010)

This grounding in the university's mission allows service-learning to be supported and promoted as part of what it means to receive a Vincentian or Marist education. In addition, the international orientation of both Catholic orders supports the premise of ISL as an extension of the universities' work.

During the past 5 years, DPU and UMM have participated in an ongoing dialogue about how best to structure their ISL partnership. Their common goal was to guide DPU students toward a transformative educational experience that afforded them the opportunity to better understand the concept of human dignity through constructive and reciprocal forms of engagement with residents of EZS. UMM was committed to this partnership not only for the benefits it brought to the community but also because of its commitment to partnership in general. The partnership allowed for both universities to learn from each other through engagement and reflection.

UMM representatives introduced Steans Center staff from DPU to EZS in 2005. The observation of the impactful service-learning work taking place in EZS, as well as the common philosophy around community engagement, convinced DPU representatives that as opposed to having students engage in separate service experiences, they could engage collectively with a community process and have a more meaningful and impactful service and learning experience. UMM had years of prior experience building trust in the community, a factor allowing DPU staff and eventually students to engage quickly with residents in a way that respected the community's role as equal partners in the service-learning project development.

EZS, located in Santa Rosa Urban District No. 5 to the south of Mérida in the state of Yucatán, is a group of settlements that has greatly expanded over the past three decades. The development of such neighborhoods as EZS, which are so underresourced they generally lack public services, was the product of migration from rural to urban areas resulting from changes in the Mexican economy that undermined the peasant economy of the Yucatán and neighboring states (Baklanoff & Moseley, 2008; Boltvinik & Damián, 2005; Villoro, 2007). Like many in Mérida, the settlements reflect a crisis in access to affordable urban housing to serve the demand of families arriving from rural Mayan communities throughout the region of southeast Mexico (Alonso, 2006). Families arrived in the city in search of employment opportunities following, for example, the crisis faced by single-crop agave cultivators in the region (Caballero, 2001). During the 1980s, urban sprawl in Mérida covered 8,321 hectares. By 1990, the urban sector had grown to 13,522 hectares, and by 2000, it had grown to 18,284 hectares (Secretaria de Desarrollo Social, 2003). EZS is a neighborhood of informal housing, a community of settlers making their homes from discarded materials. Recognizing both the resilience and the needs of this community, the Marist Brothers and eventually UMM sought to work with this community.

Program Design

Since 1987, DPU has hosted a study abroad program in Mérida during DPU's 10-week winter quarter (January–March). The program staff included a DPU faculty director and on-site coordinator. DPU students would take an anthropology course and Spanish-language courses at the Universidad Autónoma de Yucatán (a public university) and a course with the DPU faculty director. Starting in 2004, the program integrated ISL during a spring quarter (April–June) extension for five students interested in continuing their Spanish studies and participating in a community internship. These students were interviewed and selected to participate in a 100-hour internship at a local Mérida nongovernmental organization (NGO). They also enrolled in a community internship class, one of three foundation courses in DPU's CSS minor. Students were hosted by a variety of organizations throughout Mérida. During the 2005 spring quarter, UMM's site at EZS became one of three internship placements for the internship course (CSS 395). The following year, UMM's sites became the only sites for the course. In 2007, DPU introduced a second-foundation course in the CSS minor sequence (CSS 201: Perspectives in Community Service), which was integrated into the winter-quarter program and required all students to participate in 30 hours of service in EZS. A local professor, contracted by UMM, taught the CSS 201 course. Those students selected to remain in the spring extension program were also given the opportunity to extend their stay into the summer for an additional 100-hour paid internship. The stipend for the spring and summer internships allowed these students to offset the cost of staying an additional quarter or more to participate in the program. In turn, community partners and families in EZS had additional assistance for their respective community projects.

Conceptual Frameworks for the Mérida ISL Partnership

Jacoby and associates (1996, p. 5) defined *service-learning* as "a form of education in which students engage in activities that address human and community needs together with structured opportunities intentionally designed to promote student learning and development. Reflection and reciprocity are key concepts of service-learning." Over the years, DPU and UMM sought to integrate these basic concepts of service-learning and experiential education (Dewey, 1933; Díaz Barriga, 2006) with concepts drawn from ABCD (Kretzmann & McKnight, 1993) and IHD (Pope John Paul II, 1988) theories.

Asset-Based Community Development

ABCD is a community development model that challenges the needs-based approach to which many capital-poor, but resilient, communities are subjected. Through the Institute of Policy Research at Northwestern University (Evanston, Illinois, United States), John Kretzmann and John McKnight developed the principles of ABCD in their 1993 book *Building Communities from the Inside Out: A Path Toward Finding and Mobilizing a Community's Assets*. In their model, all members of the community are perceived as capable of contributing to the community's development. The premise is that members of the community must be protagonists in their own community's development, and institutions such as government, universities, and businesses are assets that the community itself can tap (Kretzmann & McKnight, 1993). It seeks to look at underresourced communities from the perspective that the glass is half full as opposed to half empty; this approach challenges the labels often ascribed to marginalized communities, which often are communities of color.

The Steans Center began incorporating the ABCD model in 2005 as its basis for university-community engagement. This model was integrated into all aspects of the center's functions, from how students are placed in the communities to how work is performed and relationships are formed with the community partners. The ABCD approach calls for resilient communities to be viewed as intellectual spaces that have knowledge and assets with the capacity to be coeducators of our students. Over the years, staff, student workers, faculty, and community partners have been trained in this model, and it has become the foundation for the CSS minor program. There are two key components of this approach: seeing that the community has assets, and understanding structural explanations for communities facing extreme obstacles such as poverty. As such, this model was employed at the early stages of relationship development between DPU and UMM.

Integration of ABCD into the Mérida ISL program occurred through the CSS foundation courses CSS 395: Community Internship, offered during the spring quarter since 2005, and CSS 201: Perspectives in Community Service, offered during the winter quarter since 2008. This permitted students who elected to stay winter and spring to complete two of the three foundation courses for the CSS minor. Kretzmann and McKnight's book became the course textbook, and the learning objectives included development of "a critical understanding of the ABCD model and the role of community based organizations and nonprofits in community building" (Morales, 2005). This focus allowed students to interpret the challenges they were experiencing in Mérida and more specifically in the community where they did service, not as result of residents' deficiencies but as a product of the community's resiliency in the face of global policies that led to the creation of communities like EZS (Mathie & Cunningham, 2003).

Integral Human Development

IHD is a concept first introduced by Pope Paul VI in the 1967 encyclical *Populorum Progressio*:

> Development cannot be limited to mere economic growth. In order to be authentic, it must be complete: integral, that is, it has to promote the good of every man and of the whole man.

This type of development, as stated by Pope John Paul II in 1987, is a "duty of all for all, and must be shared by the four parts of the world: East and West, North and South." The four guiding principles of Marist's IHD framework are as follows: (a) human dignity: a person's assets/need to love, work, and transcend; (b) solidarity: the community's assets/need to generate social progress; (c) self-actualization: the continuing development of a person's assets/needs; and (d) prosperity: economic growth/changes that improve the standard of living of the poor (Boltvinik & Damián, 2005; Fontana, 2005). It is a conceptual framework that promotes collaboration (Pope John Paul II, 1988), peace, and sustainability (Pope Benedict XVI, 2009).

According to the IHD framework, the path for the elimination of marginalization and poverty is a high priority for the individual and the community (Burpee, Heinrich, & Zemanek, 2008). Analysis and efforts by social actors switch from the vocational and transcendental aspect of the person (e.g., love of God and neighbor, faith, Christian hope) to community action for social justice and the common good. This community action includes solidarity, charity, assistance, communication, and political action to generate social mobility and leisure time, guaranteeing the conditions for the continuing development of basic human strengths nurtured by love and work, education, philosophical and theological reflection, science, and truth applied in the community with well-defined IHD goals (Sen, 1996, 2001). Once this personal-communal-personal process is implemented, technological and economic development efforts can be directed toward bettering the standard of living for people in certain localities and cultures (PNUD, 2004). This theoretical framework utilized by the Marists in their community engagement work is taught to the DPU students as a foundation theory and guide to their service-learning work. IHD assisted students in developing a lens to guide their work, but, parallel to the ABCD model at DPU, it was also employed as a philosophical foundation for community engagement.

Integration of ABCD and IHD

The Mérida-based CSS 395 course was developed as a bilingual, online hybrid class that included readings in English and Spanish with in-person reflection sessions conducted on-site by UMM's service-learning director.[1] As a coeducator of the course, the UMM service-learning director integrated the model of IHD in reflection sessions with students, because it was a model already being implemented at UMM.

ABCD and IHD are very compatible underlying frameworks for guiding the development and implementation of a service-learning or ISL program. Both understand that community development is central to service-learning and ISL. ABCD focuses on mobilizing a community's assets. IHD challenges the traditional models of international development that promote external forces and strategies as the only legitimate model of development for marginalized communities (Crabtree, 2008; McMichael, 2004) and that lead to urbanization, the feminization of poverty, and outward migration (Briggs, 2002; Middlebrook & Zepeda, 2003; Pearce, 1978). Instead, with both an ABCD and an IHD perspective, development is linked to the common good: the material, cognitive, institutional, moral, and spiritual goods people need to fulfill their humanity (Pope Benedict XVI, 2010) and to assist people "to lead full and productive lives, meeting their basic physical needs and living their lives in an atmosphere of peace, social justice and human dignity" (Heinrich, Leege, & Miller, 2008, p. 5). It is a framework based on asset maximization that assists households to leave poverty and reduce vulnerability (Heinrich et al., 2008). The combination of the ABCD and

IHD underlying philosophies is the foundation by which this ISL program developed. The integration of these frameworks—both of which honor local knowledge and assets and support mechanisms for understanding oppression and poverty and internalizing solidarity, self-actualization, and human dignity—not only serves as the undergirding philosophy of the program but also is an important area of learning for students. Examples of this are presented in the following student reflections:

> When I arrived in Mérida and I saw Emiliano Zapata Sur for the first time, I could see that many of my assumptions were wrong. The influence of the Marist religious order was very visible in the place of worship, which had an image of Saint Guadalupe, and church-like pews. This was reflected in the community as well, because many homes have church artifacts. I was also able to see that I didn't need to make a program, but rather to follow a program. I learned that it's not my place to say to the community or the women what they need, but to be here and freely support what the community wants. Many problems in the community are the result of globalization and poverty, perhaps the result of poverty from a history of globalization through colonization. With globalization and this migration, there are discrimination and stereotypes in the minds of many people from the city. Surely the Yucatecos see town and city folks as different. Stereotypes have a negative effect on people. (A. Doc.1)

> Every time that I commit to a community service project, I find myself completely concerned with issues such as poverty, health or lack of organization affecting the community. As I already explained, this is natural because these are the problems that catch our attention. Of course, issues such as poor health, poverty, or illiteracy are what most threaten people's daily life and need to be resolved. However, these matters are not the most important issues in my work, and should not be overemphasized. These are questions that come from the problems caused by oppression, which create injustice in our society. I learned this little by little as I worked with the food group in Emiliano Zapata Sur. I consider these situations superficial problems because not only do they not appear out of the blue, but also they are manifestations of very profound problems in society caused by our prejudices such as religion, racism, sexism, and elitism. It's difficult to see at first glance that superficial problems such as poverty come from a system of oppression that has very deep roots in our culture, society, and history. During my time working with the EZS women, I learned that changing the level of awareness was the most important thing. It is this process of educating each other to achieve simple human interaction that I consider to be social service. We teach each other that we have the power to change ourselves, our lives, and the lives around us. In the process of doing this, it's possible also to have an effect on the world situation. (M. Doc.2)

Reflection on the Program's Development

Arriving at a place where a sustainable ISL partnership based in ABCD and IHD frameworks could be nurtured and developed was not easy. Its success was due in large part to reflective practices involving students, community members, and faculty and staff. At the student level, reflections not only contributed to assisting students to process and understand how their service related to the two conceptual frameworks and other theories presented in the courses but also contributed to informing program improvements. At the community level, reflection involved regular communication on the progress of students and the projects they conducted, and this, too, helped to inform program improvements. At the faculty and staff level, representatives from the two higher education institutions reviewed the reflections of students and community members, considered staffing and policy changes on a yearly basis, and adapted to institutional policy changes. Therefore, reflection undertaken each cycle incorporated feedback from multiple stakeholders and allowed for establishing and reviewing the program goals for the subsequent cycle.[2]

The reflective practices also led to the development of a participatory action research project that included DPU students, community members, and professors from both universities during the spring quarter in 2009. Drawing on the results of the research project, a UMM professor has been working since August 2009 to develop an action plan and framework for understanding marginalization and poverty in EZS.[3] This framework is allowing for a better understanding of behaviors observed in the community, such as spirituality, popular religiosity, cultural traditions, solidarity among residents, their vision for education, their work skills, and, at the same time, an inability to complete projects because of lack of leadership, consistent participation by residents, and leisure time (Mounier, 1976).

Lessons Learned

The sustainable partnership that applied ABCD and IHD between DPU and UMM successfully expanded and adapted over 5 years because staff from both institutions were committed to reflection on their practice and incorporating community, student, and faculty input as part of ongoing program review. Through the reflection process several lessons were learned that contributed to the success of the ISL program and partnership.

The first lesson learned was the importance of the bilingual and bicultural staff representatives from DPU who had the capacity to develop and maintain the partnership in general and in particular when navigating cross-cultural misunderstandings that arose between the institutions. As an example, the overly legal nature of DPU's memorandum of understanding (which was insensitively originally prepared only in English) seemed to contrast sharply with UMM's refusal to receive payment for the placement support it provided to DPU students (although payment was made to support the UMM faculty teaching CSS 201). UMM perceived the partnership as a natural affiliation between two Catholic universities committed to service as an integral part of their respective missions, and so exchanging money didn't make sense. The bilingual and bicultural DPU representatives were able to manage the misunderstandings in these situations and prevent the misunderstandings from undermining the program.

The second lesson learned involved the importance of having a shared philosophy of community engagement. Although DPU's model of engagement is based in ABCD and UMM's is IHD, both models share as their foundation a profound belief in the community's ability to transform itself. This shared perception and belief in community empowerment created a synergy in the work that allowed for quick problem-solving and adaptive practices that have been key in sustaining a quality program. This shared philosophy also contributed to the development of trust between the parties. This trust then facilitated the third lesson learned: participatory reflective practices.

Participatory reflective practices allowed DPU and UMM to critically reflect on each other's roles, support the growth of the program, and incorporate input from students and community partners every year. What facilitated this practice was a shared understanding of the critical nature of reflection in successful service-learning, not only for the students involved but also for those, like university faculty and staff, who promote service-learning. The partnership was able to successfully manage challenges that arose through the years, such as changes in administrative structures and personnel, challenges with students, or unsuccessful community projects. The issues were discussed honestly and openly and allowed for quick resolution. It also created sustainable community projects and helped the program evolve to include participatory action research.

The adaptability and flexibility demonstrated over the past 5 years by program administrators offer a solid foundation for program continuation. It offers a model for how two faith-based institutions can draw on their common missions and program philosophies to educate students to become more socially engaged in ways respecting the capabilities of those marginalized so as to develop creative solutions to challenges the latter face in their daily lives. In doing so, the students begin to understand better their service role as one that supports asset building. They also develop a greater sense of respect for the dignity of residents living in communities where education and literacy are weak, such as EZS. Most important, through reflection, students begin to see human development not as a one-way process but as a process that engages all participants in a greater understanding of their own and others' humanity.

Endnotes

1. A hybrid class is one that takes place both online (e.g., via Skype and Blackboard) and through in-person reflection sessions.

2. *Reflection upon action* is defined as "thinking retrospectively as to what we have done to discover how our knowledge in the act possibly contributed to unexpected results" (Schön, 1987, p. 26, cited in Pacheco, 2005).

3. This professor is also the coauthor of this case. He is an economist with a master's in education and has worked in the ISL program resulting from the partnership at DPU and UMM since 2005. He was responsible for the establishment of the CEMADE in Emiliano Zapata Sur, work that he started in 2002.

References

Alonso, J. F. (2006). Posibles escenarios económicos para nuestro estado en los próximos años. *Boletín Economía Hoy, 12*(69) 2–17.

Baklanoff, E. N., & Moseley, E. H. (Eds.). (2008). Yucatan in an era of globalization. *The Latin Americanist, 52*(3), 79–81.

Barber, B. R. (1992). *An aristocracy of everyone: The politics of education and the future of America*. New York, NY: Ballantine. Boltvinik, J. (2005). Ampliar la Mirada. Un nuevo enfoque de la pobreza y el florecimiento humano. *Papeles de Población, 11*, 9–43.

Boltvinik, J., & Damián, A. (2005). *La pobreza en México y el mundo*. México: Siglo XXI Editores.

Boyer, E. L., & Hechinger, F. M. (1981). *Higher learning in the nation's service*. Washington, DC: Carnegie Foundation.

Briggs, L. (2002). *Reproducing empire: Race, sex, science, and US imperialism in Puerto Rico*. Berkeley: University of California Press.

Burpee, G., Heinrich, G., & Zemanek, R. (2008). *Integral human development (IHD): The concept and the framework*. Retrieved from www.crs.org

Caballero, A. (Coord.). (2001). *Los Mayas en la ciudad* [testimonial video]. Producer F. Chan. Editor "Compartimos Bienestar y Salud para los niños Mayas," I.A.P. Executed by the community of San Antonio Xluch, Mérida.

Cavazos Bueno, A. (1996, September 2). Inaugural speech at the Marist University Founding, Marist Brothers, Mérida.

Clisby, E. (2006, April 17). *Who we are*. Retrieved from http://www.champagnat.org/en/220100000.htm

Commission on National Community Service. (1993). *What you can do for your country*. Washington, DC: Government Printing Office.

Crabtree, R. D. (2008). Theoretical foundations of international service-learning. *Michigan Journal of Community Service Learning, 15*(1), 18–36.

Cruz, N. L., & Giles, D. E. (2000). Where's the community in service-learning research? *Michigan Journal of Community Service Learning, 7*, 28–34.

DePaul University. (1991, November). *DePaul.* Retrieved from http://www.depaul.edu/about/mission/index.asp

Dewey, J. (1933). *How we think: A restatement of the relation of reflective thinking to the educative process* (Rev. ed.). Boston, MA: D. C. Heath.

Díaz Barriga, F. (2006). *Enseñanza situada: Vinculo entre la escuela y la vida*. México: McGraw-Hill.

Fontana, S. (2005). *Naturaleza de la Doctrina Social de la Iglesia* (2nd. ed.) México: Instituto Mexicano de Doctrina Social Cristiana.

Gabarrón, L., & Hernández, L. (1994). *Investigación participativa*. Madrid: Centro de Investigaciones Sociológicas, Cuadernos Metodológicos No. 10.

Heinrich, G., Leege, D., & Miller, C. (2008). *A user's guide to integral human development: Practical guidance for CRS staff and partners*. Baltimore, MD: Catholic Relief Services.

Instituto de los Hermanos Maristas. (2003). *Misión Educativa Marista* (Progreso 2nd. Edición, 1st. Reimpresión, pp. 33–36). México.

Izcara, S. P. (2009). *La praxis de la investigación cualitativa; guía para elaborar tesis*. México: Plaza y Valdés.

Jacoby, B., & associates. (1996). *Service-learning in higher education: Concepts and practices*. San Francisco, CA: Jossey-Bass.

Kiely, R. (2004). A chameleon with a complex: Searching for transformation in international service-learning. *Michigan Journal of Community Service Learning, 10*(2), 5–20.

Kraft, R. J., & Dwyer, J. F. (2000). Service and outreach: A multicultural and international dimension. *Journal of Higher Education Outreach and Engagement, 6*(1), 41–47.

Kretzmann, J., & McKnight, J. (1993). *Building communities from the inside out: A path toward finding and mobilizing a community's assets*. Chicago, IL: ACTA Publications.

Mathie, A., & Cunningham, G. (2003). *Who is driving development? Reflections on the transformative potential of asset-based community development*. Antigonish, Nova Scotia: Coady International Institute.

McMichael, P. (2004). *Development and social change: A global perspective*. Thousand Oaks, CA: Pine Forge.

Middlebrook, K. J., & Zepeda, E. (Eds.). (2003). *Confronting development: Assessing Mexico's economic and social policy challenges*. Stanford, CA: Stanford University Press.

Morales, M. (2005). *CSS 395: Community internship* (Syllabus, Community Service Studies). Chicago, IL: DePaul University.

Mounier, E. (1976). *Manifiesto al servicio del personalismo* (4th ed.). Madrid: Taurus.

Pacheco, D. (2005). *Pensamiento critica y responsabilidad social y personal en un programa aprender-sirviendo en educación superior* (Tesis para obtener el grado de Doctor en Educación Superior). Facultad de Educación, Universidad Autónoma de Yucatán, Mérida, México.

Paul VI. (1967). Carta Enciclica. *Populorum progression*. Vaticano.

Pearce, D. (1978). The feminization of poverty: Women, work and welfare. *Urban and Social Change Review, 11*, 28–36.

PNUD. (2004). *Informe de Desarrollo Humano*. Retrieved from http://www.undp.org.mx/desarrollohumano/informes/index.html

Pope Benedict XVI. (2009). *Carta Enciclica Caritas in veritate*. Vaticano: Libreria Editrice.

Pope Benedict XVI. (2010, May 22). *Development, progress and the common good*. Retrieved from http://www.fides.org/en/news/26726-VATICAN_The_concept_of_integral_human_development_requires_precise_coordination_such_as_subsidiarity_and_solidarity_as_well_as_the_interdependence_among_the_State_society_and_the_market#.Ut_iaPbTn-Y

Pope John Paul II. (1988). *Encyclical Letter Sollicitudo Rei Socialis* (30 December 1987), 6–7: AAS 80, 517–519.

Pope John Paul II. (1990). *Constitucion apostolic Ex Corde Ecclesiac*. Vaticano: Libreria Editrice.

Red Marista Internacional de Instituciones de Educación Superior. (2010). *Misión Marista en la Educación Superior*. Roma: Instituto de los Hermanos Maristas.

Rutter, R., & Newman, F. (1989). The potential of community service to enhance civic responsibility. *Social Education, 53*, 371–374.

Secretaria de Desarrollo Social. (2003). *Estudios Urbanísticos y Ambientales en 75 barrios correspondientes a 31 ciudades del Sistema Urbano Nacional*. Mérida Integrado, México: SEDESOL.

Sen, A. (1996). Capacidad y bienestar. In M. Nussbaum & A. Sen (Eds.), *La calidad de vida* (pp. 54–83). México: Fondo de Cultura Económica.

Sen, A. (2001). *Development as freedom*. Oxford, UK: Oxford University Press.

Simonelli, J., Earle, D., & Story, E. (2004). Acompañar obedeciendo: Learning to help in collaboration with Zapatista communities. *Michigan Journal of Community Service Learning, 10*(3), 43–56.

Steans Center. (2001). Home. Retrieved from http://steans.deapul.edu

UNESCO. (1998). Declaración mundial sobre la educación superior en el siglo XXI Versión aprobada por la Conferencia Mundial sobre Educación Superior. *Revista Perfiles Educativos, XX*(79–80), 126–148.

Van Dijk, T. (2005). Discurso, conocimiento e ideología. Reformulación de Viejas cuestiones y propuesta de algunas soluciones nuevas. *Cuadernos de Información y Comunicación*, No. 10, 285–318.

Villoro, L. (2007). *Los retos de la sociedad por venir*. México: Fondo de Cultura Económica.

5

PARTNERSHIP VERSUS PATRONAGE

A Case Study in International Service-Learning From a Community College Perspective

Lori Halverson-Wente and Mark Halverson-Wente
Rochester Community and Technical College

*We have experienced, time and again, that the teacher becomes the
learner and the learner becomes the teacher.*

—Paulo Freire

The egalitarian, open-enrollment mission of community colleges embraces service to the local community (American Association of Community Colleges [AACC], 2010). Community colleges have a long history imbued with the substance and meaning of concepts such as "service-learning" or "experiential learning," rooted in their mission-based, programmatic practice of learning through service to their respective communities (Milliron & de los Santos, 2004; Raby & Valeau, 2007; M. L. Smith, 2008; Zieren & Stoddard, 2004). This mission is reflective of a philosophy regarding community colleges as "not just *in*, they were *of*, *by*, and *for* the people in their surrounding area" (Zlotkowski et al., 2004, p. 14).

Despite their historic mission of local service, community colleges have limited international service-learning (ISL) experience (Raby & Valeau, 2007), instead regarding ISL as outside of their mission proper (Boggs & Irwin, 2007; Green, 2007). This perception is changing. Sparked by a shift in the understanding of the concept of "community," many community colleges have expanded their mission to include explicitly international study and service. Indeed, because of globalization and its economic, technological, ecological, and social consequences, the context of "community" itself has expanded to include the global community (Richards, 2005). As Bell-Rose and Desai (2005) remarked, "Today's students will be working in a global marketplace and living in a global society. . . . They must be prepared to trade with, work alongside, and communicate with persons from radically different backgrounds than their own" (p. 2). Two-year institutions, with their emphasis on "direct learning experiences to teach cognitive and social skills" (Raby, 2008, p. 8), must explicitly commit to "the globally educated learner and to building the global community" (AACC & Association of Community College Trustees [ACCT], 2006). Political impetus was given to global education and ISL by President Obama's "Community College Initiative" (n.d.), noting that "in an ever increasingly competitive world economy, America's economic strength depends upon the education and skills of its workers [and] in the coming years, jobs requiring at least an associate degree are projected to grow twice as fast as those requiring no experience." Tougher economic times have moved American colleges and universities toward developing shorter term programs in poorer, less costly nations, thus rendering ISL more accessible to 2-year institutions (Rooney, 2002).

ISL in Cambodian Culture

The core of service-learning, for Rochester Community and Technical College (RCTC), was well stated by Jacoby and associates (1996, p. 5):

> Service-learning is a form of experiential education in which students engage in activities that address human and community needs together with structured opportunities intentionally designed to promote student learning and development. Reflection and reciprocity are the key components of service-learning.

Jacoby's definition features three areas of service-learning, all applicable to ISL: First, the needs addressed through service-learning are defined by the community itself; second, "reciprocity" is emphasized, that is, a reciprocal service-learning relationship with mutual respect in a context in which participants are simultaneously teachers and learners with everyone benefiting in the process (Cone & Payne, 2002; Freire, 2005); and last is reflection, which makes clear the crucial connection between the service relationship to the courses and programs studied (Eyler & Giles, 1999; Hutchinson, 2005; Jacoby & associates, 1996; Kozeracki, 2000).

ISL is more than the application of service-learning methodology in an international context. With ISL, cultural differences and unfamiliarity both enrich the experience and pose challenges and complexities, often unforeseen. The International Partnership for Service-Learning and Leadership (IPSL) (Eisenhardt & Ninassi, 2010) noted that ISL involves work and communication across different cultures, often with different languages, thus offering a more diverse and, generally, more challenging experience (Annette, 2001; Jay, 2008; Seponski & Lewis, 2010; Tonkin, 2004). ISL provides additional positive student outcomes over simple domestic service-learning. For example, ISL offers students the opportunity of experiencing cultural immersion and a corresponding intercultural competency and respect. Ideally, ISL provides a deep relationship between "server" (faculty and students) and "served" ("host country" community partners) wherein all involved become "mutual learners" (Kraft, 2002; Miller & Gonzalez, 2009), forming the basis of a sustainable reciprocal service partnership, what Sheffield (2005) termed a "two-way service ethic" (p. 48).

As a basis for its ISL, RCTC aims to adopt what Porter and Monard (2001) termed a *philosophy of reciprocity* with CFO (Cambodian Family Organization), RCTC's NGO partner, and rural village-partners. This philosophy is an "expression of values—service to others, community development and empowerment, and reciprocal learning" (Stanton, 1990, p. 67). Moreover, this philosophy determines the nature and process of social and educational exchange between the ISL program (with its individual student experiential learning) and its host-village(s) and NGO partners—taking into due account the articulated needs of the NGO and villages. Reciprocity-based ISL features a mutual partnership involving students, faculty, educational institutions, NGOs, and rural villages in which student reflection and the needs of rural villages have primacy. Complications stemming from cultural factors render reciprocity difficult to implement and sustain by preventing open communication between all participants. Two complications immediately stand out. First, ISL itself is a product of Western culture and promotes the values of tolerance and multiculturalism as necessary to its enterprise; however, the values of tolerance and multiculturalism, usually understood in the West as grounded in individual or group rights, are not necessarily regarded as such in Cambodian culture (Asma, 2005; Butin, 2010; Fish, 1999). Second, ISL is characterized by basic structural inequities in power. This power differential is evident semantically (Foucault, 1973): Phrases such as "Third World" versus "First World," "developing" nations versus "developed" nations, "servers" versus "served," or even the notion of ISL as a "response to a need" (Eby, 1998), and so on, demonstrate a linguistic dominance and power differential that exaggerates the importance of the person who "serves." Such dominance impedes the forming of authentic, mutually satisfying partnerships. Indeed, in an intercultural relationship initiated and directed by the more powerful of the two, the stronger always "runs the risk of reducing the weaker to the canvas upon which the stronger represents itself and its power" (Crabtree, 2008, p. 22).

If an ISL program, intentionally or unintentionally, adopts the "dominant" role of a "provider" in Cambodia, an unhealthy, disempowering "patron-client relationship" is created, with the ISL program assuming the character of a "patron" rather than "mutual learner" or reciprocal service partner (Nee & Healy, 2003; Nee & McCallum, 2009; Seponski & Lewis, 2010). The Khmer patron-client relationship exists within a hierarchical society void of individual rights based on equality. In the family, hierarchy is based on birth order and sex; outside of the family, hierarchy is based on a number of factors, sometimes interrelated: age, sex, race, wealth or access to sources of wealth, education, religious status, and political and governmental ties and associations (Ledgerwood, 2010; Ovesen, Trankell, & Öjendal, 1996). The patron-client relationship, noted Scott (1972), involves an

> exchange between roles—[that] may be defined as a special case of dyadic ties involving a largely instrumental friendship in which an individual of higher socioeconomic status (patron) uses his own influence and resources to provide protection or benefits, or both, for a person of lower status (client) who, for his part, reciprocates by offering general support and assistance, including personal services, to the patron. (p. 92)

The cultural tendency of Cambodians to view RCTC as "patrons," coupled with the inherent power differential of the ISL enterprise, has challenged the program's guiding philosophy of reciprocity. It repeatedly appears in the process of establishing and nurturing reciprocal partnerships and, correspondingly, in the creation, implementation, and sustainability of the program. This tendency is particularly vexing because it encourages the program to adopt a patronage role even while engaging in its ISL "best practices" (Eisenhardt & Ninassi, 2010). Cambodians, culturally, tend to look for answers and change from the top—any person or organization with greater power, prestige, and resources qualifies (Hinton, 2005; Nee & Healy, 2003). When patronage is a cultural norm and expectation, and, as such, assuming the role of a patron is often convenient and seemingly facilitates the success of a project, RCTC program leaders found that an ISL program may resort to patronage. O'Leary and Nee (2001) remarked,

> When or if development practitioners are unconscious of the power dynamics [i.e., patronage] in their relationship with villagers, or perceive

these to be the norm, they tend to assume that their project activities are participatory and empowering regardless of the actual level of engagement of villagers in decision-making processes and the nature of the relationships formed. . . . The power imbalance in the donor-partner relationships is an immediate and direct consequence of the donor having the funds and the right to decide whether or not the "partner" receives funding and whether they will continue to receive funding. The imbalance inherent in donor/grantee relationships makes them particularly difficult relationships, even when the donor [NGO, ISL program, etc.] . . . is trying to be supportive and is sensitive to this. (pp. v, vii)

If legitimate ISL is to occur, the patronage mind-set in the fabric of Cambodian culture, and the manner in which the ISL program responds to it, must be recognized, openly discussed, and critically examined by all program participants: faculty, students, Cambodian NGO service partners, and Cambodian host-villages.

Starting From Scratch: Initiating an ISL Program

From the outset, RCTC's Cambodia program encountered cultural complications. Reflecting tendencies of a Western cultural mind-set, RCTC was eager, if not impatient, to make a positive difference in a nation of extreme poverty. However, a sincere, yet naive, desire to quickly "do good" likely results in a failure to form honest relationships that enable programs to see and learn the "dilemmas of poverty," resulting in "students and professors intruding into poor people's lives often trying to fix things they do not understand" (Ver Beek, 2002, pp. 55–56). Furthermore, the Khmer Rouge genocide and, later, the flood of foreign NGOs infused a lack of "trust" into the social fabric of Cambodia toward the motives and consistency of the aid of the "outsider" in Cambodian development (Nee & Healy, 2003; Nee & McCallum, 2009).

Time and nurture are necessary to quality ISL partnerships. Much ISL literature, then, counsels "steps that must be followed in establishing a credible program" (Kozeracki, 2000, p. 3), including choosing a site that will facilitate sound student-learning outcomes through planned service (Eisenhardt & Ninassi, 2010; Eyler & Giles, 1999; Raby, 2007; Urraca, Ledoux, & Harris, 2009). RCTC's program's inception—how its leaders were brought together toward a common goal of ISL—was due less to ISL "best practice" than to good "karma." As Kim Sin, a program founder, put it, "I was looking for some way to give back to Cambodia by talking with RCTC President Don Supalla, when I met Lori, an instructor on sabbatical and looking for something to do internationally. We talked and, with our President's approval, RCTC sent an exploratory group to Cambodia." But more than an exploratory group is needed for successful ISL. Like most 2-year institutions, RCTC lacks adequate funding and depends on faculty initiative for the requisite vision, organization, leadership, and logistics to set up ISL programs and plan for orderly and purposeful development and growth (Blum, 2006; Green, 2007; Hovland, 2009; McMurtrie, 2008; Raby & Valeau, 2007; Reams, 2003; D. J. Smith, 2007). Despite its inception by chance, RCTC followed the recommended practice of sending an initial representative team—faculty, administrators, and community members—to the host country to meet potential partners, discuss program goals, and investigate its feasibility for ISL (Eyler & Giles, 1999; Florman, Just, Naka, Peterson, & Seaba, 2009). Furthermore, an administrator's (a dean) physical presence as part of the contingent was an asset. An administrator's active support assured RCTC's president and cabinet of the commitment of the program's developers to its long-term success. This team-visit model is highly suggested to colleges initiating ISL programs (Eyler & Giles, 1999; Florman et al., 2009; Raby & Valeau, 2007).

"Best Practices"

Reference to "best practices," ostensibly useful for ISL programs, abound (Amerson, 2010; Annette, 2001; Hutchinson, 2005; Irie, Daniel, Cheplick, & Phillips, 2010; King, 2004; Kozeracki, 2000; Lough, 2009; Miller & Gonzalez, 2009; Raby & Valeau, 2007; Urraca et al., 2009; Ver Beek, 2002). Three practices, crucial to RCTC's program success, are examined: curriculum design and cultural immersion, student leadership and retention, and partnerships with Cambodian counterparts. Though fundamental to RCTC's success, best practices are easily misdirected if cultural factors are not monitored. ISL program leaders must take care to avoid choosing plans and measures that appear to be the smoothest path to realize a project goal yet result in patronage and charity rather than reciprocity and capacity building.

Best Practices: Course Curriculum and Cultural Immersion

According to Raby (2007), ISL curriculum must be "internationalized," that is, infused with "cross-cultural concepts, theories, and patterns of interrelationships . . . [accentuated by the] 'need to understand a variety of perspectives (geographic, ethnic, cultural, gender, etc.) by acknowledging similarities, but also in a way that respects and protects differences among multi-country diversities'" (p. 57). RCTC's curriculum choice, an intercultural communication course, is readily "internationalized." The course itself does not teach

"Cambodian culture" per se; rather, the course's purpose is to expose students to the "internationalized" curriculum of intercultural communication infused with "cross-cultural concepts . . . [and] underscored by a need to understand a variety of perspectives" (Raby, 1999, p. 1). Program students and participants, Cambodian and American, are put in a position where communication is demanded of them within a service context (e.g., hand-making and coloring English-Khmer flashcards, nonverbal communication while planting trees or collecting water samples together). This communication situation is fertile ground for mutual learning and reciprocity. Prior to the course, RCTC students acquaint themselves with the concepts and skills of intercultural communication and, through group meetings, reading packets, and online discussion and activities, learn the relevant theory, concepts, and skills to be practiced and observed once in Cambodia (e.g., interaction of language and social variables, evaluation of statements about a culture, cultural connotations of gestures, words, and phrases, etc.).

In Cambodia, students are given structured time for daily reflection on the meaning of cultural and/or service experiences in relation to their own personal and cultural values and experience. The curriculum includes non-service experiences such as touring the Tueol Sleng Genocide Museum, taking long van rides together, or even having a night at a karaoke club, which are often pedagogically powerful experiences that touch on personal values in a way that expand students' reflective and critical skills, especially when coupled with instructor mentorship (Durrant, Brown, Cluff, & Bevell, 2009; Furman, Coyne, & Negi, 2008; Vande Berg, Balkcum, Scheid, & Whalen, 2004). Mentored student reflection on their personal values in light of experience may elicit seeming paradoxes and uncomfortable situations that lead to deeper questioning, empathy, and understanding. Cambodian history and culture is unique in that it confronts students with both the depths and the sublime of which human nature is capable—providing student experience that potentially sparks student reflection critical for effective ISL and for personal transformation. Each year, the RCTC and CFO groups visit the Killing Fields, thus exposing students to the magnitude and character of the horrors human beings are capable of inflicting on one another (Hinton, 2005; Kamm, 1998). Students witness the crushing human poverty and the systematic inequity in Cambodian society. Daily, for example, when out in Phnom Penh or at a tourist site, students are accosted by hungry children, amputees, or mothers with infants and must make the quick decision of whether to give money. Later, students are asked to reflect on this experience: Is the giving of charity truly helpful? Why or why not?

Paradoxically, genocide and contemporary political and economic corruption in Cambodia present the sublime in humanity—students are able to sit and converse with Cambodia's first female labor leader and other activists who risk their lives daily striving for a better Cambodia. Students witness the hospitality and graciousness of the Cambodian villagers when visiting a project. The grandeur of Cambodian (Khmer) history is experienced in visiting the wondrous Angkor Wat temple and some of the lesser known, more remote temples. Time for guided reflection is given to process the experiential paradox that Cambodia poses (Cipolle, 2010; Kolb, 1984).

Reflection is crucial—though it is difficult to set aside adequate time with the demands and fast pace of student cultural immersion. Self-reflection with reference to personal experience and learning is a way in which we understand, connect to, and interpret the world in which we live. RCTC students examine the thoughts and feelings their experience elicits so they might develop the capacity to recognize better their own ingrained cultural biases and social conditioning, thereby moving beyond an "us and them" mentality, to identify more closely with the conditions of the Cambodian people (many of whom have become friends) and to see the systematic injustice present in Cambodian society. ISL thus allows students to learn in a way that is critical and potentially "transformational" (Cipolle, 2010; Freire, 1973; Kiely, 2004). Students may undergo a shift of consciousness in the way they view the world as they become aware of their own place in it, the ties that bind them with those of other cultures, and an understanding of the power structures of race, class, and gender that prevent social justice and personal happiness. Moreover, RCTC's experience has shown that transformation is not limited to the time frame of the ISL experience itself—an intercultural awareness and competence might burst forth as if planted from a seed after students return home.

Often, curriculum experiences are just as new to Cambodian NGO members as they are to RCTC students. As one CFO member wrote, "I have lived here my whole life; I never have been to the Garbage Dump. I feel ashamed I have never helped the children garbage-pickers before." Surprisingly, as well, many young Cambodians are unaware of the genocide. A tour guide at the Killing Fields seized an opportunity to teach the young, shifting from speaking in English to stress it in Khmer: "I was there, I saw this, and your generation does not believe your grandfathers. . . . I was there, I saw it." RCTC's program attempts to provide an experiential context in which a potentially transformative experience for both sets of students might occur.

RCTC's stay in Cambodia is short. A 2009 University of Minnesota study cited by Donnelly-Smith (2009) indicates that duration of stay is "insignificant" respecting the degree to which students—in this study, students engaged in study abroad only, not ISL—consider themselves to have become "globally engaged." RCTC's stay is short but intense, involving the immersion of faculty and students for 3 weeks in varied, exciting, and unfamiliar yet potentially uncomfortable settings (e.g., urban Phnom Penh's dump and orphanages, the NGO's school, venues of open prostitution, 2-day weddings, schools and villages with toilet and well service projects or other village work, an overnight stay on a small island in the Gulf of Thailand, etc.). RCTC students are immersed interculturally by working elbow to elbow with their Cambodian peers on goal-oriented ISL projects with host-villagers. Faculty, too, are affected by the immersion experience, for example, shared living space, multiple roles, faculty transformative learning, and so on (Warner & Esposito, 2009). This aspect of ISL merits future investigation.

Most RCTC students have never traveled far from home, much less immersed themselves in an international cultural immersion experience requiring learning through involvement with constant contact and interaction with their Cambodian counterparts, as well as villagers and schoolchildren (Kiely, 2004; Urraca et al., 2009). Immediate immersion in Cambodian culture requires students to quickly begin communicating interculturally in an unfamiliar environment. Most students adjust and adapt. However, the stress of intense cultural immersion causes a few students to distance themselves from others or from the goals of the ISL program, potentially posing a distraction from overall learning and service goals and, if not addressed, possibly interfering with the learning of others (Jones, 2002). One RCTC student refused to contribute the agreed-on $1.00–$5.00 donation for group meals when she did not like the food; neglected to put in the time and effort to get to know her CFO peers; and, despite being told repeatedly that the group would attend a traditional Cambodian wedding and should dress accordingly—a tasteful top with a khaki skirt covering her knees—instead appeared in short shorts. Fortunately, another student brought extra clothing. Though such experiences are rare, Jones (2002) remarked that some students at certain times "just don't get it," and despite care placed in curricular design and clear communication, some students may not be ready for a particular intercultural experience (p. 10).

Though theoretical concepts of intercultural communication are stressed at the first pretrip meetings and in Cambodia, instructors expose students experientially to aspects of authentic Cambodian culture. This means that, at times, the instructor's role, as coach and facilitator, is to understand when to get out of the way (Butin, 2006). Instructors must avoid the "banking model," where instructors possess the expertise and fill the students' heretofore empty bank account with their valuable knowledge, and avoid also the role of "academic patron" by not unduly dictating or narrowing the possibilities of course cultural curriculum (Freire, 2005). To illustrate, instructor academic expertise supplements, but does not substitute for, student experience as the basis for ISL learning; when being guided through the bone-laden paths of the Killing Fields by an actual genocide survivor, the instructor is not the real expert. Such an instance, however, is an opportunity for instructor mentorship, thus enhancing the learning experience (Durrant et al., 2009). Program instructors, particularly through deepening ongoing relationships with Cambodian NGO partners and, while in Cambodia, associating with village leaders, learn more about Cambodia each year and are better able to guide students to the opportunities Cambodia's rich culture offers, for example, visiting remote villages or connecting students with NGOs or other organizations and persons relevant to their individual course projects.

Given the trip's brevity, curriculum is applied in a before, during, and after approach. Before leaving for Cambodia, students are prepared using RCTC's online platform: Desire to Learn (D2L—similar to WebCT or Blackboard) to provide preparatory readings on intercultural communication theory and information and videos on Cambodian culture and history. D2L links to travel and cultural resources are also provided. Social networking (e.g., Facebook and Skype) connects RCTC students with their CFO peers before they leave for Cambodia, which, many students have remarked, eases the transition from American culture to Cambodian culture, and is a valuable medium to keep friendships flourishing after the experience.

Student course work consists of creating an individual service-learning project of their choice, submitting work online through five reading response essay quizzes, completing five online interactive discussion posts, keeping a journal during the trip, and recording reflections and analysis for a final paper or essay.

The student project is central. Before the trip, students begin brainstorming project ideas. Students are interviewed as to their major, career goals, and personal aspirations to clarify their reasons for signing up and what they hope to gain personally. The purpose of student projects is threefold: first, providing students theoretical structure from which to engage in and observe intercultural communication; second, incorporating local (i.e., near their home or school) service and mentorship before, during, and after the trip; and third, providing for academic reflection connected to their experience, thus creating a deeper awareness of self, increased awareness of the condition of others, an awareness of the social conditions and their relation to the poverty and suffering experienced, and perhaps an awareness that positive change is possible (Cipolle, 2010). Often, projects stem from a student's major. Examples include one law enforcement student who compared Cambodian and American law enforcement procedures; nursing students who prepared a hand-washing curriculum to teach in the United States at a preschool and adapted the lessons to teach children in Cambodia; a psychology student who designed a classroom activity for children that allowed her to observe how Cambodian grade school children would represent "family" in their drawings as compared to American children; a pre-med student who collected medical supplies from the Mayo Clinic, compared and contrasted Cambodian and American approaches to general medical care, and presented the findings to doctors at Mayo's Travel Clinic; and, most recently, students who engaged in social entrepreneurship by writing and obtaining a grant to purchase handicrafts from an NGO in Cambodia and are planning to open a store in the local Rochester area to sell these goods at a profit to, in turn, be returned to the NGO to bolster its sustainability. In a sense, the diversity of individual student projects reflects a dimension of the RCTC program that helps to shape an entirely unique experience each year. Though such projects may complicate trip planning and require additional individualized instruction, they deepen and enhance learning for both instructors and students.

Best Practices: Student Leadership and Retention

Former program students, or "returnees," the heart of the RCTC program, contribute much to the preparatory work for the trip and student ISL projects. Two to four returnees consistently travel to Cambodia each year, often arriving before the new RCTC ISL group, to volunteer directly with CFO, setting up projects in Cambodia. Two returnees, for example, spent one winter break traveling to the villages with CFO staff to collect data for assessing the toilet and well project and to test the water quality of wells. Another year, two returnees stayed in Cambodia to create an NGO and serve as interns teaching English at CFO's Phnom Penh school. Having roots in the Rochester community, many returnees are able to continue their service with the program by collecting donations of medical and school supplies, promoting the program locally, and presenting with faculty. Each year, new students are invited to join returnee groups' ongoing social and fund-raising events and are mentored to fund-raise themselves, if inclined to do so. Returnees mentor new students by introducing them to the program, providing them with opportunities to ask questions of RCTC's program, and offering, from a student's perspective, what to expect when doing ISL in Cambodia. Returnees, then, continue their service-learning—serving RCTC's program and new students and continuing to reflect on their experience—and now witness new students continuing the process.

ISL literature expresses concern that student learning develop beyond the parameters of one's own culture and toward a deeper understanding as a part of the global community, increased intercultural awareness and competence, personal growth and maturity, and continued participation in service (Borden, 2007; Eisenhardt & Ninassi, 2010; Eyler & Giles, 1999;

Florman et al., 2009; Kiely, 2004; Miller & Gonzalez, 2009; Sheil & Bahk, 2010; Sternberger, Ford, & Hale, 2005; Urraca et al., 2009). RCTC's role for returnees, in particular, is consistent with this concern. Returnees help prepare each year's cohort of students for their ISL and cultural immersion experience, serving as a peer resource while in Cambodia and maintaining and nurturing their intercultural competence once they return. Moreover, the enthusiasm of returnees is pivotal in recruiting students for RCTC's program.

RCTC's goal is to create a learning community among the various participants, addressing both individual and ongoing group projects in the process. Returnees play a crucial part in maintaining the learning community. Returnees, both the few who voluntarily return to Cambodia and those active in the Rochester, Minnesota, area, are allowed to help plan the group itinerary based on their previous experience as students and subsequent ongoing transformation. Indeed, gaps are intentionally left in the core schedule so that both new and returnee students can add programmatic suggestions before RCTC instructors, cofounder Kim Sin, and CFO president Thanak Ritchie plan the final itinerary. In contrast, prearranged "packaged travel/ study programs" are often costly and vary little from year to year; RCTC employs a collegial planning process, including student input, resulting in a greater variety of cultural experiences. Each year, returnee leaders make new requests, for example, touring the palace, seeing an animal sanctuary, talking with human trafficking survivors, and so on. While in Cambodia, CFO members and returnees sometimes lead small groups and split up in "different directions" for a couple of hours, thus giving students a healthy respite from the large group and a unique opportunity to bond and experience Cambodian culture outside of the "RCTC brochure" itinerary. Such programmatic flexibility allows for a collegial approach: Program experiences and, hence, learning itself are not dictated or "owned" by administration or faculty through dominance over itinerary—students are empowered by their input (Freire, 2005).

By design, after the ISL trip course students complete their projects through extended service locally, including speaking engagements at organizations and schools to present the results of their project and to educate local residents and schoolchildren about Cambodia. Besides local service, this course component helps students to stay involved in the group—perhaps becoming returnees. Social networking, in particular Facebook and Skype, allows the groups to share more than "hard-copy" photos. Past students interact daily online, be it with each other or with Cambodian friends. The American returnees and their Cambodian counterparts (many of whom are returnees in that they have been active in CFO for a few years) socialize regularly via social media (especially Facebook), and many believe that, though a community of learners, they have become a community of friends and family. Said returnee Alex, "Little did my fiancé know, or me for that matter, when I left for Cambodia that a year later, we would have twenty additional guests and my trip roommate would be a member of the wedding party." More research on the role of the returnee in RCTC's ISL program is being collected.

Best Practices: Partnerships With Cambodian Counterparts

The problem of patronage (i.e., those cultural forces outlined previously that steer RCTC's ISL program away from the delicate work of cultivating reciprocity and partnership and toward the vortex of charity) is the single biggest obstacle the program has faced in terms of establishing and maintaining partner relationships, providing student curriculum that comports with the actual ongoing service designed to meet the articulated needs of village-partners, and, ultimately, achieving sustainability—will the ongoing projects continue if there is change in CFO or if RCTC refrains from ISL in Cambodia for a couple of years? It is commonly mentioned in ISL literature that anyone can serve; this is indeed the case, but sadly, not everyone can serve well given the costs, complexities, and stakes of the ISL enterprise. Allan Keith-Lucas (1972) remarked, "To help another human being may sound like very simple process. Actually it is one of the hardest things that anyone can be called to do" (p. 119). This is important to ponder. After all, those who suffer most from ill-conceived and/or short-lived ISL are the desperately poor villagers.

Clearly, RCTC's strength has been its partnership with CFO, who has acted as a trusted mediator with project-villages, able to discern local needs and facilitate local cooperation. Frankly, CFO has made RCTC's short-term ISL viable. CFO has monitored our ongoing projects, such as wells and toilets and its ESL school, and continues to have new projects in the pipeline for our stay each year. However, despite CFO's integral place in the ISL partnership, at times RCTC still finds itself in a patron-like position that undermines the reciprocity necessary to a healthy partnership. For example, currently the CFO school in Phnom Penh is given money by some RCTC program members each month to pay its rent and pay its teachers. CFO is in an immediate financial crisis that is being met, at least for the short term, by monetary gifts—charity. Given current conditions, this culturally based solution is the path of least resistance. However, it plays into the cultural mind-set of CFO members viewing RCTC as a patron, subtlety gives RCTC patron-like power it should not wield, and raises questions as to whether CFO is being truly empowered by this arrangement. Moreover, outright charity cannot last. An important goal of RCTC ISL over the next few months is to work out an equitable and reciprocal arrangement with CFO that meets its pressing needs in a sustainable fashion.

To avoid the role of patron in a village-partner relationship, RCTC insists that village leaders and elders must possess a sense of their own important role in building and maintaining the project, thus creating capacity building and forging a reciprocal partnership. To this end, Nee and Healy (2003) emphasized that the community itself must determine and communicate its needs and be willing to take ownership of service projects by investing some of its own time and resources. Because of the power imbalance inherent in the patron-client system and its prevalence throughout Cambodian society and politics, many villages (or rather, village elders and patrons) are not necessarily willing to make this investment if it is not worth their while or if they anticipate a better "deal" from some other NGO "patron." CFO, when searching for potential village-partners, then, must have a good sense about the willingness of a village to take on a partner role. Ironically, many rural village leaders perceive CFO as reflective of the common Cambodian NGO reality, that is, hierarchical systems where much of the decision-making authority rests with the director. Thanak Ritchie, as CFO director, is conscious of this perception and tries to dispel it when meeting with village leaders. Still, it is difficult. Hierarchy, whether in the "organization or in the field" or in the village,

> is not conducive to participation or empowerment. It tends to diminish the sense of personal responsibility and self-discipline. . . . The power imbalance in the donor-patron relationship is an immediate and direct consequence of the donor having the funds and the right to decide whether or not this "partner" will continue to receive funding. (Nee & Healy, 2003, p. vii)

Both RCTC and CFO have found it difficult at times to set firm boundaries and to distance themselves from their perceived status as wealthy patrons. Indeed, it is easy for ISL programs to neglect to set firm boundaries. RCTC faculty found that the Cambodian cultural tendency of displaying a "willingness to please," that is, a ready agreeableness to all plans and proposals made so as to avoid conflict, is exhibited by host-villagers, and even CFO members, within the Cambodian patron-client context and feeds an ego-driven, unhealthy "helper high" on the part of the ISL leaders—especially students. Said one faculty member, "When discussing a project, it seemed as if dialog was taking place and a communal, reciprocal process was well under way, until, suddenly, it occurred to me that, in the end, it was my voice that was doing all of the expressing—all I heard from others was agreement." Perhaps in the Cambodian patron-client culture this interaction expressed a notion of leadership intertwined with the patron role, a "person who can speak on behalf of community members and has the ability to provide material and financial support to members when necessary," and what is paramount in Cambodian culture is trust between patron and clients, not transparency, accountability, participation, or the skills and competency of the leader (Nee & McCallum, 2009, p. 22; Ricigliano, 2009). Still, such roles impede capacity building and empowerment—the ultimate goals of ISL vis-à-vis village-partners.

Relationships between international service organizations (including ISL groups) and Cambodians may reflect misunderstandings resulting from cultural practices such as a culturally based excessive agreeableness and the patronage mind-set (Nee & McCallum, 2009; Seponski & Lewis, 2009). After building a number of toilets at host-villages, RCTC was told indirectly by members of one village, through CFO, that they lacked the means to empty the toilet's tanks once full—they could not simply call a truck to drive out to drain them. Also, to drain the tanks haphazardly in the area surrounding the village could be environmentally dangerous. RCTC's program, along with hard work from CFO, is currently resolving this issue with its host community partner. However, such an oversight was indicative of ignorance on RCTC's part and reluctance on the part of the village to communicate directly with CFO once the problem was realized, presumably because of a fear of disappointing RCTC as patrons. Through assessment via focus groups, a workshop to address this situation was organized and led by Dr. Meas Nee, an expert in capacity building. As a result, a business plan is being created that will transform village projects into "business opportunities" versus primarily RCTC-funded endeavors.

Another possibility RCTC's faculty, Kim Sin, and student leaders have discussed with CFO is composting toilets. Returnees mentioned its apparent popularity, especially near Angkor Wat, and the eco-friendliness of the idea (MaD [Making a Difference for Good in Siem Riep, Cambodia], 2010). RCTC and CFO had looked into the possibility of composting toilets earlier and were told by a number of vendors in Phnom Penh, including one particular Cambodian NGO, rightly or wrongly, that the villagers did not like them and would not use them. Yet, after mentioning that RCTC's program had heard this NGO did sanitation and that RCTC would pay for its composting toilets, suddenly this NGO's opinion changed, and it was willing to build composting toilets in rural villages. The quick change of position made program leaders suspicious. After many calls, RCTC and CFO leaders could not find a Cambodian business or an NGO to work with, so the CFO director volunteered his services, pledging he would find the plans and recruit members of CFO if RCTC ISL students could not participate. Three lessons might be drawn: First, once the sanitation NGO perceived RCTC as a "foreign" donor or patron, it was willing to accommodate us; as *foreigners* (the general Cambodian choice of term), RCTC is prima facie given more respect and status, presumably because as an American group it is assumed to possess more money than any Cambodian, or most other foreign, organizations. Second, CFO felt obligated to meet RCTC's "need" because discomfort on RCTC's part brought perceived disharmony to the relationship. And third, any village would accept any type of toilet we would offer as "donor" or patron. Often, in rural villages, RCTC students are the first foreigners the villagers have ever met, and group members are treated like royalty—causing embarrassment and discomfort among RCTC students. RCTC members are perceived as wealthy Americans; they are well fed, are usually White (light skin equates to status because it shows one does not work outside), and have paid much money to fly to Cambodia and drive in vans away from the excitement and lights of the city to rural villages. Typically, the poor are looked down on in Cambodian culture (O'Leary & Nee, 2001); therefore, the very act of attention given from the wealthy is anticipatory in nature. It leads villagers to believe that if something is given, more will follow.

RCTC continues to learn of the power of patronage in Khmer culture and to adapt to the role of outsiders. As outsiders, RCTC must trust and rely on CFO to choose project sites and subsequently monitor them—Cambodians planning projects for the benefit of Cambodians in Cambodia. Though this is seemingly obvious, as outsiders ISL developers must design projects with the appreciation that it benefits no one to try to fix that which is not in their place to fix. According to Ver Beek (2002), this lesson is lost on the "vast majority of service-learning experiences. . . . [Most ISL programs] neither understand nor address the true dilemmas of poverty and . . . provide little or no benefit to the poor. . . . Service based on a superficial understanding seldom empowers the poor or builds up their capacity" (pp. 55–56). RCTC, therefore, partners directly with CFO and indirectly with the villages. It was CFO who located ISL sites and assessed the needs of the villages—as voiced by the host-villagers. Next, CFO surveyed the new students' interests, consulted with returnees on fund-raising progress, and mapped out logistics with the U.S. and Cambodian program leaders and faculty. Additionally, CFO augmented and integrated into the group's schedule visits and days of service with affiliate NGOs. Finally, during the last trip, an assessment team composed of RCTC returnees and CFO students began to measure some of the projects' impacts on the villages by marking GPS locations, conducting well-water quality data tests, observing the condition of the toilets, and, when possible, interviewing village leaders regarding project satisfaction. From assessment, it became obvious it was beyond CFO to adequately monitor the success of those projects in some of the more remote northern provinces; therefore, CFO and RCTC elected to support another NGO with the same capacity-building mission focusing on sanitation and water projects. Thus, service from RCTC could be rendered during the tour of these provinces, but RCTC's participation could occur only under the direction of the third NGO's operation.

RCTC's assessment of its ISL impact necessitates keeping an ongoing relationship with site communities. When a project is built and a group does not stay involved, there is no assurance that the project's outcome in a village will be positive. In one case, 3 years ago, a rural village was hastily chosen out of convenience as an ISL project site for a toilet. The group had extra funds and knew the school did not have a bathroom, but it assumed that the village leadership wanted the project. Given the patron-client protocol, the villagers accepted the RCTC-CFO offer so as not to disappoint a potential patron, yet in reality village patrons (villagers with political connections, relative wealth, prestige, etc.) did not want the project—building this toilet, then, reflected foreign patron-based charity rather than partnership or village-initiated capacity building. Conversely, in another case, a CFO-chosen potential host-village openly talked over the project and, after internal discussions, agreed to the project's goal of building a bathroom, investing sweat equity, tools, and a small payment toward the project ($50.00). These arrangements gave the village and school a sense of ownership over the project as a full-fledged partner. To help sustain the partnership, RCTC asked a volunteer to work with the teachers at this school to create a sanitation education curriculum.

When RCTC returned a year later to visit each respective toilet project, students noticed that at the school where the toilet was given as charity, the doors to the facility were locked. When queried, the school's principal said, "We just locked it for the weekend early to protect it"; however, the noticeable cobwebs in and around the facility told another story. In contrast, the school that had deliberately invested in the project not only was using the toilets but also had added a hand-washing area, painted the interior, and adorned a school wall with hand-lettered Khmer directions on how to properly use the toilet. Faculty asked RCTC students to reflect and write about the differences between the two sites and its implications for how RCTC does ISL.

For RCTC, assessment proper has been largely confined to measuring student learning outcomes (e.g., personal reflection, critical thinking, cultural competence, etc.) and the effectiveness of the ISL program in terms of curriculum, leadership, logistics, NGO relationships, and returnee involvement. Absent, however, has been a formal, sustained assessment of project impact(s) on the host-villages. Proper assessment must ask, Is this project meaningful, and to whom? If ISL programs do not consider project goals and how they directly impact involved communities, as Crabtree (2008) observed, the following may occur:

> Local children become enamored with the foreign students and the material possessions they take for granted. Students and other visitors leave piles of used clothing and other "gifts" after project/trip completion. Members of neighboring communities wonder why no one has come to help them. Projects reinforce for communities that development requires external benefactors. (pp. 18–19)

Excuses for failing to conduct adequate assessment, at least for RCTC, are easily manufactured. Working at a 2-year teaching and learning institution, course instructors are distracted from thorough community outcome assessment by the magnitude of the task before them in light of other pressing responsibilities: teaching five classes per semester, scrambling to meet enrollment quotas, planning logistics of the trip, updating websites, promoting the program, and assuming—unreasonably—that their Cambodian partners have the time, resources, and ability to do assessment on the community level. Unfortunately, CFO, too, is understaffed and underfunded. As CFO president Thanak Ritchie remarked, "Much of my time is spent worrying of how we will fund and keep CFO alive—I know, though, we are making a difference in the provinces, and in our students' lives with the relationships." However, improvement of assessment on the part of RCTC is under way. During the most recent trip, Dr. Meas Nee provided expert feedback and conducted focus groups on collecting accurate assessment, and valuable data were collected. RCTC's task is now to sift through the data and use the findings for future guidance.

Conclusion: Assessment and Danger

Given RCTC's program growth, consistent assessment is necessary. RCTC will implement the Intercultural Developmental Inventory (IDI) assessment tool to determine if a link exists between ISL and student intercultural competence and also adapt it to assess the learning outcomes of CFO members from their experience with RCTC students. More important, as current relationships develop and new ones are formed with host-villages, a method of regularly assessing project impact and program presence needs to be designed and implemented. To this end, CFO support is essential. The remoteness of many of the villages precludes, at this time, regular personal visits by CFO personnel, and therefore third-party NGOs have been invited into the partnership to allow for assessment of remote villages. RCTC's first step, then, will be to consider creative ways of interviewing—via CFO—village schoolchildren, women, men, elders, and leaders individually, assuring them of the complete confidentiality of the interviews. It will be important to stress to them that project assessment requires honest feedback and that we will not sever ties with them for poor assessment results.

RCTC's program must be careful not to assess the danger out of its ISL experience. ISL is dangerous, asserted Butin (2005), "because it makes us confront the limits and possibilities of who we are and want to be as students and faculty in higher education." Quoting Pompa (2005) on ISL, Butin remarked, "I don't want my students to shake these encounters easily; in fact, I want my students to be shaken *by* them" (2005, p. 173). Once shaken, and then stirred, by the blatant corruption, economic and political inequality, and injustice in Cambodia, ISL students must question the dominant Western academic belief that there are many different cultures that must be regarded, as such, to be morally and ethically equal. This belief holds that the values, or ends, of one culture cannot be rationally shown to be better or worse than those of another because cultures are unique and irreducible to one another. No rational standard exists to judge between the two cultures or to evaluate one in light of the other. Moreover, this belief posits that any attempt to judge another culture violates the most fundamental principle of the science of cultures—that of tolerance and a universal respect for all cultures. Tolerance and respect for all cultures—multiculturalism—is the one value that transcends all cultures. Yet this paradigm, by its own principles, is unable to rationally demonstrate why tolerance is preferable to intolerance. It follows, therefore, that one cannot, on a principled basis, confront cultural norms and political and economic structures that are intolerant and oppressive. With the science of multiculturalism, unable to pronounce rationally on human matters of values, we are, as Weber (1949) put it, "specialists without spirit or vision, voluptuaries without heart." If ISL rests on such foundations, it becomes rather pedagogically limp—unable to be either critical or transformative—hoping to "promote students' grappling with socially consequential and politically volatile content knowledge—e.g., individual and institutional racism, and historical and contemporary structural inequities" (Jakubowski, 2003, p. 25). Instead, ISL pedagogy has nothing to say regarding the taking of land from the poor by the rich and politically connected in Cambodia or lacks any basis on which to evaluate the dark side of the patron-client relationship, which lies at the core of the corrupt authoritarian Hun Sen regime. ISL pedagogy thus becomes nothing but instructor opinion—indeed an instructor from a Western culture—and cannot be critically evaluated, and certainly the role of providing a change-agency toward democratic society is out of the question.

RCTC is moving toward a transformative and critical pedagogy surrounding gender concerns and human trafficking. In any case, RCTC's ISL presence and projects hope to demonstrate the need for positive change in Cambodia—if only beginning with "One Toilet at a Time"—and, ultimately, broaden the worldview and transform the cognitive, affective, and moral consciousness of all involved in the partnership nexus. This approach would, hopefully, provide positive ISL and mutuality, not charity, thereby shifting the consciousness of course students and, more important, RCTC's Cambodian counterparts and host-villages and in-service projects toward self-empowerment and capacity building. Cambodia will begin to truly change for the better only when entrenched systemic cultural, political, and economic injustice is recognized as such and called to account (Freire, 1998, 2005; Greenberg, 2008; Grusky, 2010; Jakubowski, 2003; King, 2004; Leonard, 2004; Mezirow, 1991; Monard-Weissman, 2003; Newman, 2008; O'Sullivan, 2003; Urraca et al., 2009).

Pedagogy for positive change is inconsistent with the cultural relativism associated with a narrow epistemology bound by the important, but not determinative, concepts of culture, class, race, and gender. RCTC takes seriously the pedagogy of positive change and the prospect that course students may grow as human beings from their ISL experiences. It holds that justice and the human good, though imperfectly understood and certainly imperfectly realized, exist independently of the confines of culture; there must be a standard, rooted in human nature and expressed in, say, the Universal Declaration of Human Rights, that allows for authentic critical and transformative pedagogy to occur. Hence, Western ISL programs and their values may work with (but not for) the powerless in Cambodian society toward establishing a process by which they may begin to better themselves and not depend on patron-leaders whose interests and allegiances lie more with increasing their own power and authority than with the concerns and real problems of the common people (Ricigliano, 2009). RCTC's pedagogy and program will not resign itself to the following long-held view and oft-heard phrase: "This is Cambodia. There is nothing I can do."

References

American Association of Community Colleges. (2010, August 1). *Community college trends and statistics.* Retrieved September 7, 2010, from http://www.aacc.nche.edu/AboutCC/Trends/Pages/default.aspx

American Association of Community Colleges & Association of Community College Trustees. (2006). *Building the global community: Joint statement on the role of community colleges in international education.* Retrieved September 3, 2010, from

http://www.aacc.nche.edu/Resources/aaccprograms/international/Documents/
aaccacct_jointstatement.pdf

Amerson, R. (2010). The impact of service-learning on cultural competence. *Nursing Education Perspectives, 31*(1), 18–22.

Annette, J. (2001). Global citizenship and learning in communities. *The Development Education Journal, 8*(1), 10–12.

Asma, S. (2005). *The gods drank whiskey: Stumbling toward enlightenment in the land of the tattered Buddha.* San Francisco, CA: HarperCollins.

Bell-Rose, S., & Desai, V. (2005). *Educating leaders for a global society.* New York, NY: Goldman Sachs Foundation.

Blum, D. E. (2006, October 27). Seeking to prepare global citizens, colleges push more students to study abroad. *Chronicle of Higher Education*, p. B10.

Boggs, G. R., & Irwin, J. (2007). What every community college leader needs to know: Building leadership for international education. *New Directions for Community Colleges, 138.* doi:10.1002/cc.278

Borden, A. W. (2007). The impact of service-learning on ethnocentrism in an intercultural communication course. *Journal of Experiential Education, 30*(2), 171–183.

Butin, D. W. (2005). Service-learning is dangerous. *National Teaching and Learning Forum, 14*(4). Retrieved December 1, 2010, from http://danbutin.org/ Service%20learning%20is%20dangerous.pdf

Butin, D. W. (2006). Disciplining service-learning: Institutionalization and the case for community studies. *International Journal of Teaching and Learning in Higher Education, 18*(1), 57–64.

Butin, D. W. (2010). *Service-learning in theory and practice: The future of community engagement in higher education.* New York, NY: St. Martin's Press.

Cipolle, S. B. (2010). *Service-learning and social justice.* New York, NY: Rowman and Littlefield.

"Community College Initiative." (n.d.). Retrieved August 5, 2010, from http:// www.whitehouse.gov/sites/default/files/uploads/White-House-Summit-on-Community-Colleges-Fact-Sheet-100510.pdf

Cone, D., & Payne, P. (2002). When campus and community collide: Campus community partnerships from a community perspective. *Journal of Public Affairs, 6*(1), 203–218.

Crabtree, R. D. (2008, Fall). Theoretical foundations for international service-learning. *Michigan Journal of Community Service Learning, 15*(1), 18–36.

Donnelly-Smith, L. (2009). Global learning through short-term study abroad. *Association of American Colleges and Universities, 11*(44), 12–15.

Durrant, M. B., Brown, R. B., Cluff, J. B., & Bevell, J. W. (2009). Mentored service learning and rigorous academics: Keys to successful international study abroad programs. *Journal for Civic Commitment, 8.* Retrieved from http://www.mesacc .edu/other/engagement/Journal/Issue8/Durrant.shtml

Eby, J. W. (1998). *Why service-learning is bad.* Retrieved August 27, 2010, from http://www.villanova.edu/artsci/assets/documents/college/servicelearning/ 4thhourreadings/WhyServiceLearningIsBad.pdf

Eisenhardt, A., & Ninassi, S. (2010). The application of international service learning principles. *The Journal of Academic Administration in Higher Education, 6*(2), 55–59.

Eyler, J., & Giles, D. E., Jr. (1999). *Where's the learning in service-learning?* San Francisco, CA: Jossey-Bass.

Fish, S. (1999). *The trouble with principle.* Cambridge, MA: Harvard University Press.

Florman, J. C., Just, C., Naka, T., Peterson, J., & Seaba, H. (2009). Bridging the distance: Service-learning in international perspective. *New Directions for Teaching and Learning, 118,* 71–84. doi:10.1002/tl.354

Foucault, M. (1973). *The order of things: An archeology of the human sciences.* New York, NY: Vintage Books.

Freire, P. (1973). *Education for critical consciousness.* New York, NY: Seabury.

Freire, P. (1998). *Pedagogy of freedom: Ethics, democracy, and civic courage.* New York, NY: Rowman and Littlefield.

Freire, P. (2005). *Pedagogy of the oppressed.* New York, NY: Continuum.

Furco, A. (2006). Is service-learning really better than community service? A study of high school service program outcomes. In A. Sliwka, M. Diedrich, & M. Hofer (Eds.), *Citizenship education: Theory-research-practice* (pp. 27–36). Waxmann Münster/New York, NY: München/Berlin.

Furman, R., Coyne, A., & Negi, N. J. (2008). An international experience for social work students: Self-reflection through poetry and journal writing exercises. *Journal of Teaching in Social Work, 28*(1–2), 71–86. doi:10.1080/08841230802178946

Green, M. F. (2007). Internationalizing community colleges: Barriers and strategies. *New Directions for Community Colleges, 138,* 15–24. doi:10.1002/cc277

Greenberg, D. J. (2008). Teaching global citizenship, social change, and economic development in a history course: A course model in Latin American travel/service learning. *The History Teacher, 41*(3), 283–304.

Grusky, S. (2010). *Service-learning: An exciting model for international development education.* Retrieved January 10, 2011, from http://www.worldhunger.org/articles/us/deved/grusky.htm

Hinton, A. L. (2005). *Why did they kill? Cambodia in the shadow of genocide.* Berkeley: University of California Press.

Hovland, K. (2009). Global learning: What is it? Who is responsible for it? *Association of American Colleges and Universities, 11*(44), 12–15.

Hutchison, P. (2005, March 3). *Service learning: Challenges and opportunities.* Retrieved September 5, 2011, from http://www.newfoundations.com/OrgTheory/Hutchinson721.html

Irie, E., Daniel, C., Cheplick, T., & Phillips, A. (2010). *The worth of what they do: The impact of short-term immersive Jewish service-learning on host communities; An exploratory study.* Retrieved September 16, 2011, from http://werepair.org/share/research/hss/repair_btw_twowtd_full_report.pdf

Jacoby, B., & associates. (1996). *Service-learning in higher education: Concepts and practices.* San Francisco, CA: Jossey-Bass.

Jakubowski, L. M. (2003). Beyond book learning: Cultivating the pedagogy of experience through field trips. *Journal of Experiential Education, 26*(1), 22–33.

Jay, G. (2008). Service learning, multiculturalism, and the pedagogies of differences. *Pedagogy: Critical Approaches to Teaching Literature, Language, Composition, and Culture, 8*(2), 255–281. doi:10.1215/15314200-2007-040

Jones, S. R. (2002). The underside of service learning. *About Campus, 7*(4), 10–15.

Kamm, H. (1998). *Cambodia: Report from a stricken land.* New York, NY: Arcade.

Keith-Lucas, A. (1972). *Giving and taking help.* Raleigh: University of North Carolina Press.

Kiely, R. (2004). A chameleon with a complex: Searching for transformation in international service-learning. *Michigan Journal of Community Service Learning, 10*(2), 5–20.

King, J. T. (2004). Service-learning as a site for critical pedagogy: A case of collaboration, caring, and defamiliarization across borders. *Journal of Experiential Education, 26*(3), 121–137.

Kolb, D. A. (1984). *Experiential learning: Experience as the source of learning and development.* Englewood Cliffs, NJ: Prentice Hall.

Kozeracki, C. A. (2000). Service-learning in the community college. *Community College Review, 27*(4), 54–71.

Kraft, R. J. (2002). International service-learning, University of Colorado, Boulder. In M. E. Kenny, K. Kiley-Babeck, & R. M. Lerner (Eds.), *Learning to serve: Promoting civil society through service-learning* (pp. 297–314). Norwells, MA: Kluwer Academic.

Ledgerwood, J. (2010, July 15). *Understanding Cambodia: Social hierarchy, patron client relationships and power.* Retrieved August 20, 2010, from http://www.seasite.niu.edu/khmer/ledgerwood/patrons.htm

Leonard, A. (2004, Summer). Service-learning as a transgressive pedagogy: A must for today's generation. *Crosscurrents, 61*–72.

Lough, B. J. (2009). Principles of effective practice in international social work field placements. *Journal of Social Work Education, 45*(3), 467–480.

MaD. (2010). *Water and sanitation project plan.* Retrieved February 5, 2011, from http://madcambodia.org/activities/rural-development/sanitation/126-mad-achievements

McMurtrie, B. (2008, October 17). Few study abroad from community colleges. *Chronicle of Higher Education,* p. A29.

Mezirow, J. (1991). *Transformative dimensions of adult learning.* San Francisco, CA: Jossey-Bass.

Miller, K. K., & Gonzalez, A. M. (2009). Service-learning in domestic and international settings. *College Student Journal, 43*(2), 527–536.

Milliron, M. D., & de los Santos, G. E. (2004). Making the most of community colleges on the road ahead. *Community College Journal of Research and Practice, 28,* 1105–1122.

Monard-Weissman, K. (2003). Fostering a sense of justice through international service-learning. *Academic Exchange Quarterly, 7*(2), 164–169.

Nee, M., & Healy, J. (2003). *Towards understanding: Cambodian villages beyond war.* North Sydney, Australia: Sisters of St. Joseph.

Nee, M., & McCallum, W. (2009). *Roads to development.* Retrieved June 10, 2010, from www.villagefocus.org/pdf/Road%20to%20Development_AFSC.pdf

Newman, J. (2008). Service-learning as an expression of ethics. *New Directions for Higher Education, 142,* 17–24. doi:10.1002/he.300

O'Leary, M., & Nee, M. (2001). *Learning for transformation: A study of the relationship between culture, values, experience and development practice in Cambodia.* Phnom Penh, Cambodia: Krom Akphiwat Phum/VBNK.

O'Sullivan, E. (2003). Bringing a perspective of transformative learning to globalized consumption. *International Journal of Consumer Studies, 27*(4), 326–330.

Ovesen, J., Trankell, I.-B., & Öjendal, J. (1996). *When every household is an island: Social organization and power structures in rural Cambodia.* Sweden: Uppsala.

Pompa, L. (2005). Service-learning as a crucible: Reflections on immersion, context, power, and transformation. In D. W. Butin (Ed.), *Service-learning in higher education: Critical issues and directions* (pp. 173–192). New York, NY: Palgrave.

Porter, M., & Monard, K. (2001). Ayni in the global village: Building relationships of reciprocity through international service-learning. *Michigan Journal of Community Service Learning, 8*(1), 5–17.

Raby, R. L. (1999). *Looking to the future: Report on international and global education in community colleges.* Sacramento: Chancellor's Office of the California Community Colleges.

Raby, R. L. (2007). Internationalizing the curriculum: On- and off-campus strategies. In E. J. Valeau & R. L. Raby (Eds.), *International reform efforts and challenges in community colleges: New directions for community colleges, Number 138* (pp. 57–67). San Francisco, CA: Jossey-Bass.

Raby, R. L. (2008, September). *Expanding education abroad at U.S. community colleges: Meeting America's global education challenge* (White Paper No. 3). Retrieved from http://www.iie.org/~/media/Files/Corporate/Membership/StudyAbroad_WhitePaper3.ashx

Raby, R. L., & Valeau, E. J. (2007). Community college international education: Looking back to forecast the future. *New Directions for Community Colleges, 138,* 5–14. doi:10.1002/cc276

Reams, P. (2003). Service learning in health care higher education: Risk or not to risk. *Education for Health, 16*(2), 145–154. doi:10.1080/1357628031000116835

Richards, L. (2005). *Engagement and global citizenship: Local roots and global reach.* Retrieved September 20, 2011, from http://www.compact.org/resources/future -of-campus-engagement/engagement-and-global-citizenship-local-roots-and -global-reach/4237/

Ricigliano, R. (2009). *Cambodia interagency conflict assessment.* Retrieved October 5, 2010, from http://www.global.wisc.edu/peace/readings/supplemental-ricigliano -cambodia.pdf

Rooney, M. (2002, November 22). Keeping the study in study abroad. *Chronicle of Higher Education,* pp. A63–A64.

Scott, J. C. (1972). Patron-client politics and political change in Southeast Asia. *American Political Science Review, 66*(1), 91–113.

Seponski, D., & Lewis, D. (2010). My grandmother and me: International service-learning in Cambodia with children infected and affected by HIV/AIDS. *Information for Action: A Journal for Service-Learning Research With Children and Youth, 3*(2). Retrieved July 14, 2010, from http://www.service-learningpartnership.org/site/DocServer/IFA-CambodianYouth.Vol3N02.pdf?docID=4204

Sheffield, E. C. (2005). Service in service-learning education: The need for philosophical understanding. *The High School Journal, 89*(1), 46–53.

Sheil, A., & Bahk, M. (2010). Exploring pedagogical outcomes of service learning in international public relations education. *International Journal of Innovation and Learning, 7*(3), 274–289.

Smith, D. J. (2007, October 10). How community colleges can work for world peace. *Chronicle of Higher Education*, p. 72.

Smith, M. L. (2008). *Two year faculty members using service-learning: Integration into practice.* Retrieved July 14, 2010, from https://getd.libs.uga.edu/pdfs/smith_marcy_l_l_200808_edd/smith_marcy_1_200808_edd.pdf

Stanton, T. (1990). Service-learning: Groping towards a definition. In J. C. Kendall (Ed.), *Combining service and learning: A resource book for community and public service* (Vol. 1, pp. 65–67). Raleigh, NC: National Society for Internships and Experiential Education.

Sternberger, L. G., Ford, K. A., & Hale, D. C. (2005). International service-learning: Integrating academics and active learning in the world. *Journal of Public Affairs, 8*, 75–96.

Tonkin, H. (2004). *Toward a research agenda for international service-learning: The international partnership for service-learning and leadership.* Paper presented at the Conference of the International Leadership Association, Washington, DC. Retrieved August 17, 2010, from http://uhaweb.hartford.edu/TONKIN/pdfs/TowardAResearch.pdf

Urraca, B., Ledoux, M., & Harris, J. T. (2009). Beyond the comfort zone: Lessons of intercultural service. *The Clearing House, 82*(6), 281–289.

Vande Berg, M., Balkcum, A., Scheid, M., & Whalen, B. (2004). A report at the halfway mark: The Georgetown Consortium project [Special issue]. *Frontiers: The Interdisciplinary Journal of Study Abroad, X*, 101–116.

Ver Beek, K. (2002). International service-learning: A call to caution. In G. Heffner & C. D. Beversluis (Eds.), *Commitment and connection: Service-learning and Christian higher education* (pp. 55–69). New York, NY: University Press of America.

Warner, B., & Esposito, J. (2009). What's not in the syllabus: Faculty transformation, role modeling, and role conflict in immersion service-learning courses. *International Journal of Teaching and Learning, 20*(3), 510–517.

Weber, M. (1949). *The methodology of the social sciences* (Trans. & Ed. E. Shils & H. A. Finch). New York, NY: Free Press.

Zieren, G. R., & Stoddard, P. H. (2004). The historical origin of service-learning in the nineteenth and twentieth centuries: The transplanted and indigenous traditions. In B. W. Speck & S. L. Hoppe (Eds.), *Service-learning: History, theory, and issues.* Westport, CT: Praeger.

Zlotkowski, E., Duffy, D. K., Franco, R., Gelmon, S. B., Norvell, K. H., Meeropol, J., & Jones, S. (2004). *The community's college: Indicators of engagement at two-year institutions.* Providence, RI: Campus Compact.

6

BUILDING STUDENT AND ORGANIZATIONAL CAPACITY

Assignments and Tools

Lori Gardinier
Northeastern University

This case study outlines and analyzes an assignment that was applied in several international service-learning (ISL) programs. This project applies a hybrid model incorporating "project-based" and "pure" service-learning in an International Human Services academic program operating in multiple locations, including Benin, Costa Rica, India, and Mexico. Although this model is a natural fit for students preparing for work in nonprofit professions, it could easily be modified to meet learning objectives in a variety of disciplines, including business, engineering, communications, health sciences, and others, as it requires students to implement a project that is grounded in their field of study. This assignment is the major component in a comprehensive integrated educational program that includes lectures, site visits to nongovernmental organizations (NGOs), direct service, structured group reflections, individual blogs, and a major research paper; students receive eight credit hours upon successful completion of this program. The primary goal of this assignment is to teach fundamental program assessment and implementation skills through service-learning while supporting nonprofit organizations.

Why International Service-Learning?

Institutions are increasingly interested in internationalizing campuses both in the United States and abroad. A survey conducted by the International Association of Universities (Knight, 2003) determined that 73% of respondents believe that internationalization of their campuses is "very much" a priority at their institution (p. 8). The Institute of International Education *Fast Facts* report (2008) indicated that about 40% of students studying abroad participate in semester-long programs, and 55% of U.S. students are opting for short-term programs (p. 2). Many of these emerging short-term programs are faculty led, and some are applying pedagogies used domestically, such as service-learning.

There is an absence of research focused on ISL; however, initial studies reveal high levels of student satisfaction with their experiences (see Gaines-Hanks & Grayman, 2009). Lewis and Niesenbaum (2005) found a range of benefits for students who participated in their short-term international program, including an increase in student willingness to take courses outside of their major, increased confidence to travel abroad in longer term programs, increased interest in interdisciplinary studies, and a more sophisticated perception of the costs and benefits of globalization. In addition to the high percentage of students participating in short-term programs, an American Council on Education (2008) report found that institutions are increasingly providing support for faculty who lead study abroad programs. Research has also shown that leading international programs has a positive impact on globalizing and enriching an instructor's domestic teaching (Sandgren, Elig, Hovde, Krejci, & Rice, 1999).

Service-learning is understood as an opportunity "to connect the personal and intellectual, to help students acquire knowledge that is useful in understanding the world, build critical thinking capacities, and perhaps lead to fundamental questions about learning and about society and to a commitment to improve both" (Eyler & Giles, 1999, p. 14). Grusky (2000) defined *ISL* as "an organized excursion taken by students (and often faculty or administrators) to different countries or different cultures where students and faculty live with local families and immerse themselves in a culture that is distinct from their own" (p. 859). Short-term international programs can provide unique challenges in service-learning facilitation, including creating an academic program design that is impactful, rigorous, and manageable for both faculty and students. As this is an emerging approach in international education, there is a dearth of literature guiding faculty interested in designing and implementing programs, and best practices are still being determined.

Short-term faculty-led service-learning programs differ from traditional study abroad models in several ways. The first is that students work with local organizations to service the community where they are staying, promoting depth in culture exchange that is different from what students can obtain by enrolling in a foreign university and interacting primarily with college-aged peers. The second is that students travel as part of a learning community and will often deepen their learning through facilitated reflection with peers who are having similar experiences. In addition, students are given an opportunity to develop a greater intellectual and professional connection with a faculty member, a factor that greatly influences students' overall satisfaction with their undergraduate experience.

Capacity Building as a Framework for Service-Learning

Capacity building is a term that has come into vogue in the NGO sector over the past couple of decades. It is meant to encompass a range of ways that organizations improve their effectiveness and/or efficiency. De Vita, Fleming, and Twombly (2001) defined *capacity building* as "the ability of nonprofit organizations to fulfill their missions in an effective manner" (p. 1). There is a range of ways that organizations may choose to undertake capacity building, including revamping operational activities to enhance their organizational capacity (increase staff training, make greater use of volunteers, do more public outreach, etc.), shifting or diversifying resources to more profitable activities or resources, or strengthening the organization through economic means (De Vita et al., 2001). One of the goals for this assignment is to use a capacity-building model to deepen the service-learning relationship with an organization. The use of a capacity-building approach is considered an important component of volunteerism. A United Nations Volunteers report (Pratt, 2002) explained,

> Capacity development is relevant to volunteering in two distinct but equally important senses. Firstly, volunteers undertake capacity development activities in many ways, and in so doing, engage with a range of individuals and organizations. Secondly, one particular dimension of capacity development is the fostering of greater and more effective volunteer activity. (p. 1)

Capacity-building activities often focus on elements of organizational infrastructure, leadership, and management. However, programmatic capacity building is also an important element for organizations trying to work more efficiently and effectively toward their mission. This approach is more appropriate within the scope of our academic structure, time constraints, and student ability level.

Students interning or serving in nonprofit organizations are quick to learn the economic realities and challenges encountered by management and staff. Students can provide organizations with new perspectives and energy, but as short-term outsiders they are not in touch with the complex decision-making mechanisms and structural realities both internal and external to the organization. One of the objectives of this assignment is to provide students with a framework for developing a more nuanced understanding of the mechanics of an organization and the forces that influence decision making during their short partnership.

Combining elements of both direct service models and problem-solving and project-based models is a good way to structure an ISL experience. In direct services students are exposed to the daily realities of the staff and clients and can have an opportunity for depth in their community engagement. Project-based service-learning approaches are appropriate for ISL because they are intended to be shorter term, have a specific goal and time frame, utilize the particular strengths of a group, and have the potential for a tangible benefit to the partner organization or community. A student in the India program explained in her blog,

> As the days went by it became less important to solve all of the problems in the rural villages in Hubli, and more important to accomplish our task. I began to understand how the work we were doing would fit into the larger picture of rural development. Learning about all of the work that BAIF was doing, and creating our service-learning project made me realize how progress is driven by community-centered approaches to problem solving.

This assignment gives students an opportunity to work closely with an organization and learn about program development while understanding that social change and impact can happen on a small scale.

Evolution of an Assignment

The profiles of students who generally participate in this program are undergraduates from a large research university who are preparing for work in the nonprofit field. Although many of the students are majoring in human services or have dual majors with international affairs, students from other disciplines, including business, psychology, communications, history, music industry, anthropology, health sciences, and others, have also participated. Students who participate in these programs are disproportionately female, a trend that is consistent with study abroad and the service field in general.

This project is the outgrowth of several iterations of a faculty-led program in central Mexico where students worked in a direct service-learning role with various nonprofit and social service organizations. In the first programs, small groups of students were placed with varied organizations, including orphanages, prisons, vocational training programs for homeless youth, residential programs for youth in the criminal justice system, English-language programs, and schools. Students would interact with clients, organize activities, or develop and implement education programs and reflect on how human service program design is influenced by culture, socioeconomic forces, and social policy.

The creation of the capacity-building assignment was intended to meet several learning objectives. One ojective was to add more academic rigor to the programs through the infusion of an organizational assessment and program-planning element, skills that are very relevant for practitioners in the field of human services. This would also provide students with exposure to fundamental language used in nonprofit settings and management tools. Another learning objective for this assignment was for students to conceptualize and implement a project as a group, a skill that is relevant in most fields. This assignment also allows for students to consider the relevance and applicability of some of the theoretical and philosophical tensions and debates dominating in development circles: What are the best models for aid and program planning? Who should be engaging in local change efforts? Do the West's efforts result in more harm than good? Are human rights universal?

The capacity-building assignment also allows students to get at a critical program development question: What makes for sustainable and impactful programming? As Light (2004) explained, "If capacity building is the answer, increasing organizational impact is the question" (p. 45). A student in the Benin program wrote the following in her blog:

> If sustainability only referred to the resources used by a project, its scope would narrow significantly. But by including a training program, sustainability expands to encompass human capacity, as it should. If Songhai simply grew fruits and vegetables, raised animals in an organic and energy efficient way, one that respected the land they used, and sold those products, it would be a sustainable practice, but only for the land on its compound. By training individuals in best practices, from Benin and elsewhere in the region, they are not only broadening the amount of land that is being cared for, but also improving food security in the country. DOHA, likewise, could simply take in girls who had nowhere else to go, providing them with food and shelter, but the organization goes beyond that, reaching out to the community to provide the girls with skills they need to care for themselves. Similarly, our capacity-building project did not just provide materials for the sewing program, but added another skill and potential product the girls could sell. What I've taken out of this week is a greater understanding of what sustainability can be, how it can be accomplished by individuals and organizations.

Engagement in this assignment requires students to critique how program interventions impact organizations and their constituents in the short term, midrange, and long term, through the application of the logic model (discussed later in this chapter). An overarching goal for this assignment is for students to develop an understanding of both the internal workings of an organization and the external forces that influence organizational behavior, including the larger culture in which they operate.

The original incarnation of this assignment was a singular project that students would complete as a class, determined through small group presentations, followed by a voting process. In the presentation students would present a logic model outlining a project that they determined to be worthy, one that would have impact and help the organization work toward its sustainable mission. Each program was provided a budget for implementation ranging from $300 to $1,000. The budget for this assignment varied because of other program-related costs such as travel expenses. The process for choosing a project varied greatly, due in part to the individual location, group dynamics and proposed projects, and the types of partnering organizations. In Mexico, students were able to see a range of organizations with varying degrees of financial and organizational stability, and the choice of the capacity-building partner was somewhat straightforward. For instance, students chose to put their resources into facilities improvements at an under-resourced orphanage, including improving safety conditions in the play area and putting running water into the girls' dormitory. This project was chosen over creating manuals for an English education program in a low-income community or a memory book for a better resourced orphanage. Students perceived this as a basic need, which took priority and was overwhelmingly supported by the group. In Benin, where each of the organizations had substantial need and were often only able to work fitfully because of inadequate funding, it was much harder for students to agree on which proposed project was the most "worthy." The reflection sessions would consist of very intense critiques of a project's possible longevity, sustainability, and impact.

Having a single project made the proposal process very high stakes, and students went to great lengths to articulate why their project was most compelling. This was lost a bit in the transition to multiple projects with funding generally ensured. The projects all had their own worth, but students had to consider which organizations were most likely to sustain their efforts and which had the potential to have the greatest impact for the organization and the community served. The ensuing debates, debriefings, and late-night discussions illuminated the difficulty that policymakers, funders, and organizational management have when determining how to distribute scarce resources, and forced students to consider what is meant by *impact* and have very intense discussions about whether addressing immediate human needs was more compelling than funding longer term organizational goals. After project selection, the group would develop a unified project, identify and assign subcommittees, and develop a memorandum of understanding with the selected community partner. The competition structure proved to be very meaningful to learning; however, it could have the potential to create disharmony within the group and taint the project and potentially damage the relationship with the community partner. For students to develop their presentations, they needed to interview management and staff within organizations and inform the partner as to whether the project was selected. This was a particularly difficult process in Benin, where the formal international volunteerism sector is extremely small, and there is a legacy of foreign financial involvement that in some cases influenced the relationship that students had with organizations. After three cycles of using this model, the assignment was restructured to encompass several small capacity-building projects, each with the potential for capital, occurring at the three-five sites. This would make it easier for students to understand the interworking of the organization while giving them an opportunity to collaborate closely with the leadership from their direct service-learning sites.

Steps, Strategies, and Techniques

Predeparture

This assignment requires a minimum of 4 weeks, but it can easily be expanded or built in as a component of a longer term program. Currently, it's a component of a multi-faculty-led semester program in southern India, and students are able to do some of the prep work for this assignment predeparture. Elements of this project include familiarizing students with the assessment tools that are to be used and facilitating discussion on the theoretical and philosophical frameworks for international volunteerism, partnerships, grant making, and aid. During this time students are also building their knowledge base about the economic, political, and social conditions of the location where the program will be based.

Predeparture students are provided with a description of each of the community partners where they will engage in service and are asked to pick their first, second, and third choices; they are then assigned accordingly. Student groups range in size from three to eight; larger group sizes can be as problematic, as can those that are too small, as decisions need to be made in a reasonable time frame. Ideally, students will have a service-learning orientation, including a definition of *service-learning* and an overview of how it complements the instructor's teaching philosophy, an overview of reflection as a learning tool and how it will be used in the program, instruction about appropriate conduct in an organization, and a facilitated discussion about students' expectations and what they hope to accomplish. A good deal of time is spent reviewing the goals of the assignment and an overview of some examples of capacity-building projects completed by previous groups. Another topic that is covered during the orientation period is the ethics of ISL. This is a great opportunity to discuss some of the real ethical dilemmas and scenarios that have arisen in past programs, and students are also required to complete several readings, including Ivan Illich's (1968) speech *To Hell With Good Intentions.* This is great way to engage students with the philosophical conflicts in international volunteerism. Ideally, faculty, students from previous programs, and the community partners upon arrival will lead orientations. Students should be presented with the overall mission of the organization, the role of volunteers, and an overview of their general service-learning responsibilities. Depending on the location, this can be more or less realistic. In Benin, where our partners were organizations that were more informal, this was a bit more challenging; in Costa Rica, our partner organizations operated in ways that are very similar to those in the United States, and in some cases had volunteer coordinators accustomed to hosting international students.

De Vita et al. (2001) explained that the existing literature does not provide an easy formula for building organizational capacity; however, one of the critical elements they identified was *determining the basic needs and assets of the community.* Students are often not on the ground long enough to conduct comprehensive community scans and/or surveys while meeting other program requirements. As with any international educational program, students will be made familiar with community indicators (literacy rates, mortality rates, poverty rate, access to health care, etc.). This is an important context for students who are seeking to understand the culture and the environment in which the organization is operating. This can be accomplished in the formal lecture sections of the program and reinforced in the reading. Data such as the United Nations Human Development Index can provide information on a national level, but students will have to depend on other sources to understand local conditions. This can also be reinforced through lectures by local government leaders and NGO staff and informally through conversations with local families and peers.

Week One

During the first week of the program, students develop an overall understanding of the organization's structure and mission. During this time service-learning groups will informally interview the staff of the community partner and collaboratively identify some of the perceived gaps in the organizations;

depending on their access to management, they may also start their conversation with the internal leadership. Gaps typically identified consist of capital improvements; material development, such as training manuals to improve trainings for volunteers; curriculum development for educational programs; or equipment for vocational programs. The objective is to find the intervention that best suits the needs of the organization in accordance with their organizational development and strategic plan.

Week Two

At the start of the second week, students are required to meet with the instructor for mini-conferences to discuss preliminary ideas, prepare their presentations, and develop their assessment and planning tools. The mini-conferences were a new strategy implemented in the most recent program and were very helpful to the overall success of the project. Considering the short-term nature of these programs, it is critical that students don't get too far in the process only to find that their proposal is unworkable or unwanted by the organization. A group of students proposed developing an "international volunteer manual" for an orphanage where they were doing their service, in response to their own experience as service-learning students. Although this seemed like a great way to build the quality of the organization's volunteer program, the students soon discovered that such a document already existed and was not being used, something that is very common in organizations. A student from the Costa Rica program explained in her blog,

> The first option my group discussed was to make a volunteer manual for our capacity-building project. The manual would cover everything from location descriptions, job summaries to commonly used phrases. With it, I feel as though we would be able to help out the organization in a productive manner from the start, and subsequently help the children. However to our disappointment, the following day, we were informed that ROBE-ALTO not only had a volunteer hand guide, but also key phrases and fun facts on their website. Since we want our project to be able to be incorporated into the program in a way that can be sustainable and present potential to foster the growth and development of the children they reach, we got back to work to decide on another project. We wanted to make sure that we did not come off as ignorant Americans like from the reading *To Hell With Good Intentions*.

Students are quick to learn that their ideas are not always in line with the actual needs of an organization. This experience is a great opportunity for us to discuss many of the insider-outsider debates that have emerged in development and community organizing circles. After a preliminary approval, students work in their groups with input from the organization to create three documents. The first document is a SWOT analysis (strengths, weaknesses, opportunities, threats) that highlights the external and internal influences of an organization and how resources can best be aligned with its current strategic plan. The SWOT is a tool that is used in corporate and nonprofit settings, and although the SWOT can be seen as an imperfect assessment tool, for purposes of developing a foundation for program assessment skills and analysis, it can provide a meaningful framework. This process allows students to articulate why the proposed project is aligned with where an organization is in its development. Conducting an assessment as an outside group, particularly one that is coming from another country, is an exercise that needs to be approached with deference and tact. Students have to collect their information from the view of the leadership within the organization and not based on the brief observations of the organization. During this experience students are required to consider the insider-outsider tensions that exist within development circles and reflect on how this experience has the potential to occur in the execution of their assignment. The second document students develop is a logic model that articulates how the proposed project fits into the existing organization and how it will have short-, mid-, and long-range impact. McCawley (n.d.) explained, "The application of the logic model as a planning tool allows precise communication about the purposes of a project, the components of a project, and the sequence of activities and accomplishments" (p. 1). This tool requires students to identify specific measureable outcomes that will be reached by virtue of the intervention that is being proposed. The third document students create is a grant application including a budget and a budget narrative for funds to implement their project; boilerplate models are available to reference including the Associated Grant Makers' common proposal, a form that can provide an idea of questions generally asked in proposals. Grant writing is a useful skill, not only because it's marketable in a range of fields but also because it forces students to provide a detailed rationale for their proposed project. All of these documents are for planning and evaluation purposes, and students understand that they are proposing these ideas and that they are subject to small modifications during implementation.

Week Three

During the start of the third week, students present their concepts using PowerPoint, showcasing and submitting the three documents. This week tends to be when students express the most stress and discomfort as the initial enthusiasm for being abroad may fade and the workload peaks. Students receive both academic and peer feedback, and because students are so familiar with the assignment, some of the most challenging comments come from peers. The peer feedback requires that students score the presentations on the degree to which they (a) provide an in-depth overview of the program's current strengths and challenges, (b) clearly identify an existing gap, (c) appear feasible within given time constraints and available resources, (d) maximize resources, (e) clearly identify that deliverables were proposed that are measurable, and (f) effectively apply the logic model and SWOT. Students also score the overall quality of the presentation. During the presentations students are expected to explain why this project has the capacity to maximize impact more than other projects that could be conducted at the same organization.

The faculty team, which can consist of the faculty leadership and community partners and teaching assistants, then makes determinations on how much to award each group, and students are notified by the middle of the third week so that they can prepare for implementation. Typically, one of the groups will need some more guidance on its project, and students will be required to attend an additional conference to refine their idea. Generally these problem areas fall into the area of sustainability or students overshooting their ability to implement the proposed project within the remaining time. Provided the project is feasible, students are then able to start their memorandum of understandings with the organization and develop a timeline for implementation.

The Final Week

The fourth or final week is dedicated to implementation, depending on the scale and scope of the proposed project some groups will implement over several days during their time serving on-site. Students tend to find this aspect of their project the most satisfying, as they can see their project go from idea to impact. The types of projects that students have selected have a wide range and are obviously influenced by the mission and needs of an organization. The students in the India program served at one of three sites. Eight students worked in schools implementing peace games–change-makers curricula. This program builds on the work being done locally in Boston by Peace Through Play (formerly Social Change Through Peace Games), a successful student-led program.[1] While in Hubli, students worked in several schools leading interactive exercises in the classroom to promote awareness and discussion about the qualities that make individuals peacemakers and change makers in their communities as a part of their direct service-learning. These placements were arranged with Akshara Foundation, a Bangalore-based Public Charitable Trust with the mission to ensure that every child is in school and learning. Students built on their direct service-learning relationship with Akshara to implement their capacity-building project. In collaboration with the leadership, they focused on the gap in the quality of materials for English as a second language (ESL) being used to prepare non-English speakers for entry into the primary schools. With this gap in mind, students worked in collaboration with several educators to create a comprehensive ESL curriculum, recorded a CD of children's songs in English, and bundled them with educational games and toys that reinforce the learning objectives identified in the curricula. The bundle was delivered to 10 preschools working to promote language readiness among some of the most underresourced children in the area.

Five students from this program were placed with RAPID, an organization that creates employment opportunities for women, particularly those who must provide livelihoods for themselves. RAPID has designed a project called Livelihood Creation for Young Widows and Deserted Women, which aims to provide underemployed and/or unemployed women with income-generating activities through employment and self-employment prospects. In their direct service-learning, students focused on job-creation activities through the promotion of RAPID's programming in local organizations, businesses, and hospitals. Students were able to secure commitments from approximately 15 employers with current openings to hire women from RAPID. For their capacity-building project, they were able to create a sewing and embroidery lab to prepare women for work as tailors, along with a sustained structure for peer-to-peer training. In addition, this group was able to put some capital behind a legal rights workshop with the aim of informing women about property rights, marriage, and domestic violence.

Another group worked with BAIF Institute for Rural Development, an organization that creates livelihood opportunities through community-managed integrated farming systems for 50 families living below the poverty line in two villages around Surashettykoppa in Kalghatgi Taluk. Students in this service-learning placement and capacity-building project focused on expanding BAIF's educational curricula to include health and nutrition materials. Students worked with leadership from BAIF and medical leaders to develop a pictorial flip-book highlighting strategies to reduce or prevent common health conditions through nutrition. All materials needed to be created in pictorial form, as most of the target population is not literate. Students created materials that illustrated the symptoms and nutritional strategies for illnesses such as anemia, scurvy, and fluorosis. An additional component of this capacity-building project was to develop model "kitchen gardens" to promote the growth of produce that can help families reach their nutritional needs. Although families that BAIF works with are farmers, they primarily focus on cash crops rather than subsistence farming. This capacity-building project has allowed for the creation of 10 model kitchen gardens that will be part of a comprehensive training program promoting access to nutrient-diverse foods.

A critical component of capacity building is monitoring and assessing progress on a periodic basis (De Vita et al., 2001). As many of these programs are run on an annual or semiannual basis, students have the opportunity to pick up where the last group left off, seeing how previous projects have been integrated, while accounting for program developments and changes. In addition, many of the students develop a rapport with the organization staff, and they continue to hear about program developments through e-mail.

Can Short-Term Capacity-Building Projects Have Impact?

The goal of this assignment is to deepen the academic outcomes for students and to impact the organization in a meaningful way. The addition of the capacity-building project has strengthened this program, increased the depth of learning for students, and encouraged students to consider organizational behavior in a cultural context. In addition to learning about their organization, students get the opportunity to learn more about the organizations of their peers. In the most recent program, students participated in small group capacity-building debriefing sessions with peers from other groups. This process highlighted the different types of obstacles that can be faced both internally as a group and with partner organizations. This process of mixed group reflection promoted a less myopic view of the assignment and their learning. This assignment can also help students see how they can be both students and teachers in this process of cultural exchange. One student from the Benin program explained,

> Even though we didn't know much about how things work in Benin, making soy cheese or even what ganulets were, I feel like our fresh set of eyes and knowledge from our college classes helped the women of Massavo/ Egbey Misogbey operate more efficiently so they can produce more and make more money. There is no way this project would have worked if we were just telling the women what to do or trying to find solutions without learning about Beninese culture and working with the women of the microenterprise.

As with domestic teaching, professors leading international programs are constantly retooling the structure of their assignments to more closely align with learning objectives. Structuring assignments in international experiential models presents unique challenges because the conditions are always changing, and operating as outsiders, faculty and students are not always fully in touch with shifts in organizational and local culture. A community partner that worked well one semester might not be viable the next because of any number of organizational developments, and that is not always apparent when students start their service. Faculty are charged with designing assignments that are manageable for all parties while challenging students and promoting learning, in addition to managing the demands of living abroad. The capacity-building assignment can provide the necessary structure to link many of the interrelated themes that arise in ISL programs, while striving to enhance organizational functioning. Outcomes and impact for partnering organizations have enjoyed varying degrees of success, which is consistent with capacity-building efforts in general. Light (2004, p. 46) explained,

> In theory, capacity building is designed to change some aspect of an organization's existing environment, internal structure, leadership, and management systems, which, in turn, should improve employee morale, expertise, productivity, efficiency, and so forth, which should increase organizational capacity to do its work, which should increase organizational performance. In practice, however, there is very little systematic evidence on whether and how capacity building works. It is impossible to know whether capacity building works, for example, without some standards of impact.

It's hard to isolate the impact that these student projects have had on organization, as they are often integrated into larger initiatives. In instances where students have implemented capital improvements, the impact is more obvious. There was an absence of running water in an orphanage, and the implementation of the capacity-building project that resulted in access to safe and consistent water has furthered the organization's mission of providing a habitable residence for children. When student projects fall into the realm of technical assistance or training, the impact is not always as obvious. However, many of our partners are able to conclude that the work we are doing helps bring them closer to their organizational goals:

> After obtaining a mini-grant from their university, the volunteers compiled and published a Volunteer Handbook that we now distribute to all of our in-country volunteers to support their work leading conversation groups for Costa Ricans. In a larger sense, our experience working with Northeastern University and Professor Gardinier also helped us move towards a volunteer model for our organization that not only involves volunteers in short-term activities, but also encourages them to create structures and materials that make a lasting impact. (Stanly-Obaando, personal communication, November 29, 2010)

What we have been able to determine through multiyear relationships with some of these organizations is that many of them are still working with the resources that the students have put in place.

Challenges and Cultural Considerations

The importance of preparing students predeparture cannot be overemphasized; however, there is only so much that students can conceptualize from a distance. Seeing firsthand the social challenges and economic conditions that organizations are working in can overwhelm students and take the focus off the learning. Some of the benefits of this assignment are that it is tangible, it requires students to focus on deliverables, and students are often able to see the impact that they can have on an organization in the short term rather than be overwhelmed by social conditions.

As with any program or research that has the potential to impact people's lives, faculty should facilitate discussion on the ethical elements that surround ISL. For this program students review several of the key standards discussed in the National Association of Social Worker (NASW) Code of Ethics. Students are often able to apply these ideas as they are conceptualizing their capacity-building project (see also Chapdelaine, Ruiz, Warchal, & Wells, 2005). In addition to setting expectations appropriately for students, community partners need to be informed of the goals and parameters of their project. It is unethical to suggest that the partnership will be anything more than what is prescribed within the academic program. In locations where ISL is not done frequently, it can be challenging to explain the limitations of the relationship, particularly when Western relationships have historically consisted primarily of the provision of aid.

Service-learning in general requires that both faculty and students assume a certain comfort level with ambiguity. The best laid plans can come off the rails for the student, the faculty, or the organization. It is important that students focus on the process rather than the product and that student expectations are managed and focused on what can be accomplished in a short period of time. This is particularly true in respect to international programs. Students seem to set the bar higher for impact when they are engaging in service-learning abroad. It is important to place an emphasis on the academic goals and remind students that they are a part of a change movement. Work being done in the capacity-building project is part of an integrated organization that strives toward a larger mission (educating girls, feeding children, improving housing conditions, etc.), and a student's contribution assists the organization in working toward these aims.

Students are often surprised by how much the "culture of volunteerism" differs in settings abroad. Research in this area looks at the role of volunteerism in relation to a country's development. Other studies look at the role of the family or church in societies and how it can influence the relevancy of the third sector and volunteerism. American students are often accustomed to working in organizations that have staff and infrastructure in place to support their domestic service-learning or volunteer experiences. This provides an opportunity to discuss with students the differing dependencies that societies and cultures have on external organizations. Students in these programs have also expressed discomfort with the close collaboration between churches and the nonprofit community, providing an opportunity to discuss a government's ability to provide for its citizenry and how critical a role these other institutions can play, including institutions of higher education.

One of the most satisfying successes of this program model has been the opportunity to promote collaboration between organizations that had been previously unengaged. For example, we were able to promote a partnership between an older day program that wanted to increase its English-language offerings through the use of volunteers with Multilingüe, a nonprofit committed to bringing together English-speaking residents of Costa Rica with Costa Ricans seeking to practice their conversational English. Both of these organizations were community partners with us but had not previously collaborated.

Considering Tension and Transformation

Insider-outsider tension has been a regular theme in community development and organizing in the United States. Lessons learned in that arena can be applied to ISL programs. Structuring the curricula and programming so that they emphasize the local community and leaders as the experts, and students as learners, is an important strategy for minimizing the potential for tension. This is a transferable skill relevant for students who intend to continue with community practice in the United States.

In this era of rapid globalization, institutions of higher education have an opportunity to create educational structures abroad that do more than expand a student's perspective. Applying a project-based service-learning structure can help to ensure that these experiences be transformative for students, local organizations, and, ideally, local communities. Through the application of comprehensive integrated educational programs, students can be learners, teachers, and collaborators, leaving a sustainable impact on the global community. In this program, students will often discuss their own tensions about participating in these programs, considering if it is reasonable to participate in service abroad or if they should focus solely on the communities where they live. This program encourages students to consider the possibility that it is not one *or* the other, that their international service experience can inform their understanding of domestic efforts, organizations, and social problems and promote a more holistic and global approach to social change that is grounded not only in ideology but also in practical skills that can have impact on organizations, communities, and individuals.

Endnote

1. Peace Through Play developed as a student group applying much of the Peace First curricula (formerly Peace Games), a national nonprofit organization.

References

Chapdelaine, A., Ruiz, A., Warchal, J., & Wells, C. (2005). *Service-learning code of ethics.* Bolton, MA: Anker.

De Vita, C. J., Fleming, C., & Twombly, E. C. (Eds.). (2001). *Building capacity in nonprofit organizations.* Washington, DC: The Urban Institute.

Eyler, J., & Giles, D. E. (1999). *Where's the learning in service-learning?* San Francisco, CA: Jossey-Bass.

Gaines-Hanks, N., & Grayman, N. (2009). International service-learning in South Africa and personal change: An exploratory content analysis. *NASPA Journal, 46*(1). Retrieved October 22, 2009, from http://publications.naspa.org/naspajournal/vol46/iss1/art5

Grusky, S. (2000). International service learning: A critical guide from an impassioned advocate. *American Behavioral Scientist, 43,* 858–867.

Illich, I. (1968, April). *To hell with good intentions.* Paper presented at the Conference on InterAmerican Student Projects, Cuernavaca, Mexico. Retrieved November 1, 2009, from http://www.swaraj.org/illich_hell.htm

Institute of International Education. (2008). *Fast facts.* Retrieved from http://www.iie.org/en/Research-and-Publications/Open-Doors/Data/Fast-Facts

Knight, J. (2003). *Internationalization of higher education. practices and priorities: 2003 IAU survey report.* International Association of Universities. Retrieved from http://www.pucminas.br/imagedb/documento/DOC_DSC_NOME_ARQU I20060214115459.pdf

Lewis, T., & Niesenbaum, R. A. (2005). The benefits of short-term study abroad. *The Chronicle Review, 51*(39), B20.

Light, P. C. (2004). *Sustaining nonprofit performance: The case for capacity building and the evidence to support it.* Washington, DC: Brookings Institute Press.

McCawley, P. F. (n.d.). *The logic model for program planning and evaluation.* Moscow, Russia: University of Idaho Extension Program.

Pratt, B. (2002). Volunteerism and capacity development. *Development Policy Journal, 2,* 95–117.

Sandgren, D., Elig, N., Hovde, P., Krejci, M., & Rice, M. (1999). How international experience affects teaching: Understanding the impact of faculty study abroad. *Journal of Studies in International Education, 3*(1), 33–56.

7

INSTITUTIONAL NETWORKS AND INTERNATIONAL SERVICE-LEARNING AT THE GRADUATE LEVEL

Stephanie Stokamer
Pacific University

Jennifer Hall
University of Technology, Jamaica

Thomas Winston Morgan
International Partnership for Service-learning and Leadership

This chapter will explore how best practices in service-learning partnerships apply to multilayered collaboration in an international and interdisciplinary service-learning master's degree program and examine the tensions that ultimately led to a program revision and partnership dissolution. The International Partnership for Service-learning and Leadership (IPSL) is an educational organization that has worked with multiple universities to offer a master's degree focused on international development and service. Each of these universities in turn partnered with multiple nongovernmental organizations (NGOs) to provide an extensive service-learning component to the curriculum. Using the service-learning scholarship on partnerships, contributing authors from the IPSL network will provide a case study of the IPSL master's program. The authors will consider which principles best apply to complex international service-learning partnerships, reflect on their experience with a partnership that changed course, and suggest modifications to ensure cultural competency and reciprocity in service-learning across borders.

Background

Although service-learning has blossomed as an area of scholarly publication in the past 15 years or so, very little of the resulting body of work has focused on the partnerships at the heart of service-learning. Not surprising, much of what has been published has focused on domestic service-learning, typically at the undergraduate level. For nearly 20 years, IPSL has offered a master's program with a study abroad component and service-learning in both domestic and international universities and their surrounding communities. The IPSL case can therefore provide a glimpse into complex, multilayered, international service-learning partnerships at the graduate level.

Furthermore, the longevity of the IPSL program has meant evolutions in personnel and partnerships that speak to the challenges of maintaining international service-learning programs over time. This chapter will highlight a 3-year period of transition in the IPSL program that involved both organizational and curricular changes and ultimately the dissolution of a partnership. By examining both the strengths of the IPSL approach and a particular partnership that was no longer viable, the true tensions of this work can be elucidated. This chapter will also explore how recent scholarship about service-learning partnerships has applied to the IPSL program and will discuss implications for practitioners of international service-learning.

The IPSL Master's Degree

The IPSL master's program is unique and comes with a long organizational history. IPSL was founded as an educational nonprofit in 1982—the first of its kind devoted to international academic service-learning. IPSL has consistently offered undergraduate international service-learning experiences and, beginning in 1996, a master's program as well. Originally based in New York, the organization relocated to Portland, Oregon, in 2008, and with the move came new staff and leadership, as well as a search for a new academic home for the master's program, all significant indicators of organizational transition. By 2009, an arrangement was made with Portland State University (PSU) to become the degree-granting institution for the master's program, and so began a time of change that offered exciting opportunities and partnership challenges.

The PSU master's program in international development and service in conjunction with IPSL reflected the need for graduates to understand a variety of perspectives and for leaders to navigate complex partnerships. Offered from 2009 to 2013 at PSU, the master's degree has always been interdisciplinary, drawing from the fields of global nonprofit management, educational leadership, and international sustainable development. The courses train leaders for professional careers with global nonprofits and educational and community development organizations with an international focus. At PSU the program was completed in 20 months and required 54 graduate credit hours.

Partnerships are central to the IPSL approach. The master's degree involves a multilayered collaboration within and among educational institutions and community-based organizations in multiple countries (see figure 7.1). In the PSU program, students spent the first year of study at PSU taking classes in the public administration (which houses nonprofit management), educational leadership and policy, and international studies departments. It was these key schools within the university that formed the basis of the partnership at PSU. During this time, students also served at local agencies and took a reflection seminar to solidify the learning from these experiences. In the summer, students attended the Summer Institute for Intercultural Communication in Portland, a program of the Intercultural Communication Institute.

After completing the Summer Institute, students departed for study abroad during the second fall term. They took classes at IPSL partner

Figure 7.1 International Partnership for Service-learning and Leadership partnership chart.

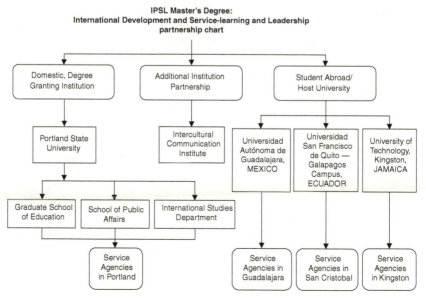

institutions—which at the time included the University of Technology (UTech) in Kingston, Jamaica; the Universidad Autónoma de Guadalajara in Guadalajara, Mexico; and the Galapagos Academic Institute for the Arts and Sciences at the Universidad San Francisco de Quito in the Galapagos Islands, Ecuador. These international partnerships have been in place for many years, serving as the host institutions for IPSL's undergraduate and graduate international service-learning programs. The IPSL-PSU-UTech partnership is examined in closer detail throughout this chapter's analysis.

While abroad, students lived with "homestay" families, served in local agencies, and prepared a proposal to address a problem of interest related to their service, applying in the field what they had learned at PSU. IPSL had developed relationships with nonprofit service agencies where the students did their service-learning work. Each of the partner institutions had a liaison with community organizations that helped place students in service-learning positions for the duration of their time in the host country. The reflection seminar continued and was cotaught by faculty at PSU and the IPSL partner abroad.

Student service in both Portland and the host community abroad offered a way to compare how agencies are operated, and this comparative work formed the basis of the culminating project of the master's student. Participants returned to the United States to complete their programs and earned their master's from PSU in their second winter quarter. In that final term students focused on their culminating project, a theory-to-practice analysis that brought together their course work, research, and service using a practical, problem-solving approach.

The partnerships that IPSL has forged over the years sustained the organization through the transition to Portland and provided the needed infrastructure to offer a totally unique master's degree that was truly international. Given the program's purpose to prepare students to work across organizational, disciplinary, cultural, and national borders, service and study abroad provided rich experiences for learning that complemented graduate-level course work. This strong foundation of experiential education sets IPSL apart from other programs. Even in the field of international studies, study abroad at the master's level is unusual and seldom as integral as it is at IPSL. Furthermore, service-learning placements generate ample experiences to analyze community problems, organizations, leadership, intercultural interactions, and the practice of service-learning itself. IPSL has been able to maximize the pedagogical value of experiential education through international service-learning (Crabtree, 2008; Lutterman-Aguilar & Gingerich, 2002) because of its extensive institutional partnership network. However, this kind of collaboration is not without challenges. The remainder of this chapter will therefore explore how the combination of effective partnerships and experiential learning provides a rich pedagogical palette for graduate-level learning and examine the specific challenges of a program in transition.

Service-Learning Partnerships

Partnerships in service-learning are grounded in egalitarian conceptions of service. Jacoby (2003, p. 7) used the Community-Campus Partnerships for Health definition of *partnership*, which is "a close mutual cooperation between parties having common interests, responsibilities, privileges, and power." Numerous authors have noted that relatively little published research has addressed service-learning partnerships (Dorado & Giles, 2004). However, the service-learning field has generated scholarship that helps practitioners to understand the nature of partnership work, stages of partnership development, and different partner perspectives in service-learning. The IPSL master's program provides an example of both the challenges of how partnership issues unfold in international service-learning and the application of best practices to continuously improve the program. An understanding of partnerships in service-learning is essential to the success of the IPSL program because of its widespread network. This section will review what the service-learning literature reveals about partnership work and examine how it applies to the international service-learning master's program at IPSL.

Though empirical data are relatively sparse, a few studies have examined service-learning partnerships. In 2006, Sandy and Holland reported results of their qualitative study of 99 experienced partnerships to examine how well community perspectives align with existing partnership models that have come out of higher education scholarship. In a similar vein, Stoecker and Tryon (2009) led qualitative community-based research gathering community partner perspectives on service-learning. Both of these studies reveal that community-based organizations value service-learning partnerships for a variety of reasons, such as direct impact on client outcomes, organizational capacity building, staff enrichment through working with students, and the development of the future nonprofit workforce. Nevertheless, participants in these studies also raised concerns about the influx of students at the start of a term (followed by their sudden disappearance at exam time); arbitrary requirements based on hours of service; unclear expectations related to supervision, training, and student learning objectives; and occasions of faculty assigning students service-learning projects with little to no prior planning with the organizations assumed to host them.

The concerns raised by Sandy and Holland (2006) and Stoecker and Tryon (2009) are particularly troubling given the importance of reciprocity in the theory of service-learning. Jacoby (2003) asserted, "As a program, a philosophy, and a pedagogy, service-learning must be grounded in a network, or web, of authentic, democratic, reciprocal partnerships" (p. 6). Reciprocity has long been a goal of service-learning (Kecskes, 2006; Sandy & Holland, 2006), but in practice it is a difficult ideal to achieve. In international programs this element is both additionally complicated and especially important.

International power dynamics, historical factors such as colonialism, logistical challenges, language differences, and varying cultural meanings of service all warrant special attention to the concept of reciprocity in international settings. Annette (2001) raised the need to consider the role of NGOs and local community organizations in equitable partnerships in international service-learning. Likewise, Lutterman-Aguilar and Gingerich (2002) suggested that because educators are not likely to perceive their purpose as "cultural invasion . . . they have a responsibility to work collaboratively with the local community to ensure that their relationships are built on mutuality and reciprocity and not on any kind of exploitation" (p. 70). In the IPSL program, partnerships with local educational institutions are one way of mitigating potential problems and ensuring authentic collaboration. At the same time, however, institution-to-institution partnerships add another layer of complexity to the international service-learning network.

Trust, Reciprocity, and Communication

The cofounder of IPSL and its former president Linda Chisholm (2003) offered three principles for international service-learning partnerships: "trust, mutuality of benefit, and open communication." IPSL has structured the master's program in such a way as to foster these principles. For example, most service-learning study abroad programs are those in which a professor travels abroad with a group of students, and they do work at an NGO, often one identified through that instructor's personal travels or connections (Annette, 2001). In contrast, IPSL partners with academic institutions abroad for the supervision of students, delivery of course material, and identification of community needs that can be in part addressed through student service. Although the divide between campus and community certainly exists in host countries as it does in the United States, IPSL's reliance on local partners to shape service-learning is a safeguard against the imposition of U.S. notions of "help" that can be detrimental to both service-learning projects and international relations.

IPSL service-learning placements are in agencies that have sprung up from the grass roots, where locals have identified a need and where the change effort is owned by them. In the organizations where IPSL students serve, the need is great for additional assistance of all kinds from the outside.

A single agency may need hands-on assistance from volunteers (direct service) or assistance in building capacity (indirect service) so that the agency can one day experience more stability in the delivery of its services. In actuality, because nearly all nonprofits experience resource scarcity, IPSL participants do a little bit of everything. And this is as it should be. Nothing says "I'm a partner in your community" better than a willingness on the part of a service-learning participant not only to do higher tasks but also occasionally to pick up a broom and sweep the floor so that the setting is clean and presentable. Such actions serve to change the view about Americans that are held by people in the communities in which IPSL has operated for many years. That is why many of the service agencies with which IPSL works have been partners for years.

Chisholm (2003) explained that trust means honesty, including fair assessment of what students will be able to accomplish or what skills they will have. Garcia, Nehrling, Martin, and SeBlonka (2009) of the Stoecker and Tryon research team reported that many of the organizational staff in their study prefer working with graduate students because of their maturity, commitment, and skill. Though IPSL runs undergraduate programs as well, master's students arrive at their service placements abroad with graduate-level course work under their belts. They therefore have a full range of services they can offer organizations, both direct and indirect. IPSL puts the community need first in arranging service-learning placements, trusting that students will gain valuable experience through effective reflection regardless of the task (as will be explored later in this chapter). This combination of high flexibility and high skill among graduate students means that IPSL partnerships can meet a variety of community needs. It is also important to note that IPSL is honest with students in this regard, even advising applicants during the admissions process that community need will determine the kind of service they are able to do and that as graduate students they will have a wide array of skills to offer, any of which could be more or less useful at any given time for an organization in which they serve.

In fact, communication is the key to trust and reciprocity. Numerous scholars have emphasized the importance of good communication for positive relationships and mutual understanding in service-learning partnerships (Chisholm, 2003; Jacoby, 2003; Sandy & Holland, 2006; Tryon, Hilgendorf, & Scott, 2009). Chisholm recommended communication that is both formal and informal, with opportunities to raise institutional and pedagogical concerns. At IPSL, such communication is necessary between faculty in different departments and institutions, between placement coordinators and service agencies, and between the program staff and students. Chisholm identified numerous factors to discuss in international partnerships that go beyond what might be necessary in domestic programs, such as housing, health care, costs, credit transfer, orientation, safety, and so on. Frequent and ongoing communication builds the human relationships of partnerships and opens the door to expressing and addressing concerns as they arise.

Of course, communication between parties in service-learning can be problematic. Sandy and Holland (2006) found that community partners use different language than institutions of higher education to describe their efforts, a by-product of different organizational cultures. Tryon et al. (2009) reported that community partners experience inconsistent communication with academic partners and struggle to find the time in their own schedules for adequate dialogue about student service-learning. Along with Chisholm (2003), Tryon et al. (2009) also noted that individual personalities and preferences enter into the partnership and that communication can be particularly difficult during times of transition because of staff turnover or other organizational changes.

Indeed, during the period immediately following IPSL's move from New York, communication proved to be a challenge. At IPSL, as well as at PSU and UTech, new staff were managing a program that either had just come to the institution (PSU) or had been inherited from previous players (IPSL and UTech). A new team of partners made decisions, perhaps without established expectations for what was communicated when and by whom, and each was influenced in different ways by factors such as risk management, geopolitical changes, shifts in institutional commitments, and the economic context. As a result, there were some unfortunate misunderstandings that affected the partnership, such as how severe security issues were and the ways in which program changes were determined and communicated.

Furthermore, communication in international partnerships is not without a unique set of challenges. Chisholm (2003) argued that international partnerships involve learning a new shared language related to practical program implementation, such as what "course" or "service" mean to each of the partners, as well as the roles of teacher and student. To that end, IPSL strives to communicate openly among partners and students about different meanings of service. Annette (2001) suggested that cultural anthropology can reveal cultural differences in meanings related to service-learning. Porter and Monard's (2001) article explored *ayni*, the Andean concept of reciprocal exchange relationships, provided an example of this approach. IPSL students are exposed to this and other ideas of service and reciprocity so that they are better prepared for culturally based differences in what it means to serve. Thus, given the range of ways in which students can serve in organizations, they are prepared to understand nuances of meaning due to culture, institution, sector, or nation.

Chisholm (2003) noted the negotiation necessary to maintain strong partnerships, especially in light of potentially differing values and cultures. In the multilayered collaboration of the IPSL program, varied interests come into play. Students, staff, faculty, institutions, and of course local community organizations all have different priorities. Finding the commonalities among them is essential to the long-term success of the program and represents one of its greatest challenges. For example, with academic partnerships, institutional size and structure created an unexpected hurdle in the partnership between IPSL and PSU. The union of a large public institution and a small community-based organization led to particular difficulties with decision making and finances because the relative importance each placed on the partnership was very different. In a small organization, the large institutional partner is likely to be seen as foundational to its survival. In contrast, the large institution—with myriad initiatives in place—may face challenges in bringing visibility to each of its community partnerships.

Another recent case illustrates how varied interests can operate on the ground in a program setting. The placement coordinator at an IPSL partner institution arranged a master's student service-learning at a government agency. Because this student had long-term career interests in nonprofit management, she preferred to work at an NGO. Unbeknownst to the coordinator, she canceled a meeting at the agency. This student, accustomed to American values of initiative and shared understanding of volunteerism, took it upon herself to seek a new placement—a task that turned out to be much more difficult than she anticipated, because NGOs in that host country are not often approached by American students looking for service-learning projects. Needless to say, her actions jeopardized the partnership between the local placement coordinator and the original agency. Moreover, her effort to arrange a placement at an NGO without introduction may have left a negative impression on the organizations she visited as she attempted to seek a better fit.

This vignette demonstrates several points. First, the role of the placement coordinator was critical. As a local resident, he understood immediately how the student's actions could be perceived and took strides to remedy the situation. With great diplomacy, he mended the relationship with the original agency so that its staff would still be amenable to future placements, and he visited the new organization to make sure its needs were being met with this student's service (and that it understood the goals of service-learning). His credibility as a local, his established connections, and his skill in negotiation prevented this tenuous situation from souring relationships all the way around. He was ultimately able to maintain trust with the community partners through honest communication and ensuring mutual benefit.

Second, this scenario also reveals both a gap and an opportunity in the student's learning. It appeared that this student did not understand the protocol for addressing concerns about a service placement. IPSL strives for good communication, but the nature of partnerships is a shifting kaleidoscope of factors beyond any one individual's or organization's control. Although the student acted in a way that would further her own learning and that in some situations would have been seen favorably—after all, she took initiative to solve a problem and meet her own learning needs—it was not appropriate in this particular cultural context.

Despite the fact that this case unfolded in a less than ideal manner (as can often happen in service-learning), such situations generate two important opportunities for growth. The first is the programmatic response. IPSL has since enhanced student orientation to better prepare students for this kind of situation. The challenges of international service-learning partnerships are landmarks on that ongoing path of program improvement. Jacoby (2003) noted that the Campus Compact benchmarks for Campus/Community Partnerships identify regular evaluation as a sign of advanced partnerships. Though IPSL has been at the forefront of international service-learning partnership work for nearly 30 years, no program is perfect, and an organizational (and individual) willingness to revisit mistakes and make changes accordingly is what has led to a strong master's program today.

The second opportunity that arises is for student learning. Chisholm (2003) suggested that given the unexpected developments that are inherent to international service-learning, intended learning objectives might not be met. Nevertheless, the experience can generate equally substantive and important learning. This authentic learning that makes use of experience is at the heart of IPSL. A part of the interview process involves preparing students for learning from experience and assessing their readiness for it. Students coming to the IPSL master's program thrive on this kind of experiential learning. The next section will address how the IPSL partnerships have become an additional source of learning through reflection.

Learning From Partnerships

Experiential Learning: The Foundation of IPSL

Service-learning involves the collaboration between the agencies and the communities they serve, the university and the agency, and the student and the instructor or facilitator and the relationship between them all (Berry & Chisholm, 1999). At IPSL, all of this exists amid the backdrop of a semester-long study abroad experience. For the students to experience the full impact of this international partnership network, they have to have a healthy appreciation for the unique learning that emerges from this pedagogy. As the foundation for the IPSL master's program, experiential learning creates an opportunity for students to meet program learning objectives and for the partners to continually improve the program.

Learning from experience is done by a series of actions and reflections on these actions. The value of reflection on experience as a way of enhancing learning has been posited from the early works of Dewey (1910). For Dewey (1938), reflection was more than talking or writing about what was done. He described it as a system based on doing and evaluating. Later, Kolb (1984) defined this *learning* as a process of doing and reflecting on one's experiences resulting in a modification of one's behavior. The idea is that as individuals continually reflect on an experience or task, they have more opportunities to modify and refine their responses and also understand the responses of others. These experiences help to produce learning and a change in practice for student and facilitator, which could lead to enhanced quality of both learning and teaching.

Lutterman-Aguilar and Gingerich (2002) discussed the extent to which study abroad is based on principles of experiential education. Drawing on the work of Dewey, Kolb, and Freire, they debunked the notion that study abroad is inherently educative, noting the range in program structures and degree of intentionality in using the experience in a way that can foster growth. As Parker and Dautoff (2007) observed, *service-learning* by definition is joined with reflection, so a study abroad program with a service-learning component has a built-in mechanism to facilitate students' learning about the international component of their experience along with the service component.

Service-learning embraces the idea that students learn to understand and show some mastery of the world around them through their service to others who truly need to be served and by reflecting on their experiences of engagement. Students cannot truly understand their roles as service providers and the assistance they provide to the community unless they continually reflect on what they do throughout the process (Dewey, 1938; Kolb, 1984). When service is linked to course work, it is "used as a 'text' that is interpreted, analyzed and related to the content of the course in a way that permits a formal evaluation of the academic learning" (Thomson, Smith-Tolken, Naidoo, & Bringle, 2008, p. 16). Reflection is essential to transform field experiences from simple volunteer activities to deeper learning. Without a significant reflective component, the connection between the intellectual work done in class and service-learning may not be made. If students' experiences and perspectives remained unexamined, students may simply reinforce and reify all their stereotypes or misconceptions and fail to meet the learning goals of the experience.

Educational institutions and more specifically educators, because of their pivotal role as facilitators of learning and giving service, must keep curricula relevant. It should be transformative and capable of translating theory into practice for the benefit of the student, the community, and the institution. The IPSL program reflects such integration. It is designed to provide students, through theory, practice, and engagement in service in a culture not their own, with the experience necessary for understanding the operation of NGOs. This service-learning also helps them to utilize their skills to provide assistance in the satisfaction of a human need, which would otherwise remain unmet. The experience gained in the agency placement enhances students' knowledge of the larger society, fosters linkages with their academic work, and develops an appreciation for the role of their homestay. Most relevant to this chapter, however, is that international service-learning facilitates student understanding of the partnerships that are central not only to their master's program experience but also to the international NGO management careers for which IPSL is preparing them. The reflection seminar is the primary way in which the IPSL program helps students to draw these linkages.

The IPSL Reflection Seminar

Throughout their program, IPSL students participate in a reflection seminar designed to maximize their learning from service placements. For Eaton and O'Brien (2004), reflection is a tool that deliberately incorporates creative and critical thinking by students so they can understand and evaluate what they did, what they learned, how it affected them personally, and how their services affected society on a broader scale. In addition, they noted that it is more than telling a personal story and is distinctly different from displaying the acquisition of the objective, factual content of a course that might be assessed through tests or observations made in community-based settings and reported in a field journal. Good reflective work, they argued, prompts students not only to document what they have learned but also to think about how they have learned it.

The seminar format utilizes both written and dialogical reflection that provide the student, the faculty, and potentially the institution with rich data about how and why particular instructional strategies succeed or fail and can lead to more effective teaching and learning. Patton (1990) stated that qualitative inquiry cultivates the most useful of all human capacities—the capacity to learn from others. In this spirit, reflection in the IPSL master's program is source of data for both student and educator analysis.

Furco and Billig (2002) asserted that students will not be successful at meeting their learning objectives unless facilitators guide them to make the desired connections between the service performed and the course content. Engaging learners in activities that encourage them to document and assess their own learning is essential because it gives both the learner and the educator insights into how well the learner is learning and how well the learning experiences are contributing to the student's process and progress toward the learning goals (Eaton & O'Brien, 2004). It is for this reason that the seminar meets weekly and issues for discussion are identified by both the instructor and the students.

For the IPSL students studying abroad, their experiences are in the context of a new culture. Their academic discourse, homestay, and service-learning placement form an interplay that allows them to assess and reassess themselves on their journey in the host country. In a cross-cultural environment, many misunderstandings may occur based on past and present perceptions, assumptions, prejudices, and biases. These are sometimes influenced by families, friends, the media, or the students themselves. Interestingly, students may not remember the objectives of a course, an assignment, or a visit to a cultural site, but various perspectives may surface in a reflective exercise. Being able to recognize, interpret, and react correctly to these perspectives, however, is important to help students achieve understanding. Challenging students' assumptions through reflection eventually encourages the development of the students' cognitive ability. For some, the misperceptions change quickly, whereas for others this may take a longer time as they try to understand the host culture.

In international service-learning, the facilitator must, however, be proactive in assessing students' progress in reflecting. This is done by reading their journals and noting how they draw conclusions about issues or problems that may be controversial. This review helps in understanding how students' perspectives may have changed as they go deeper into understanding how the culture works. Having students share aspects of their journals with the entire class helps to reinforce, affirm, or reject opinions; clarify views; or offer suggestions. On completion of the reflection seminar, study abroad students should therefore be able to separate assumptions based on their own background from those of the host culture. They should also experience what Chisholm (1998) referred to as "critical incidents"—those moments in which a particular issue or cultural puzzle is encapsulated. IPSL educators have read journals, listened to students, and observed them reach such moments. It is pleasurable for some and shocking or painful for others when those moments of truth present themselves. Although service-learning literature often points to interactions with "the other" as the source of such critical incidents (Dunlap, Scroggin, Green, & Davi, 2007; Jay, 2008), in the IPSL program the network of partnerships that enable the service experience is a source of learning too.

IPSL master's students are training to be professionals in global nonprofit management, educational leadership, and international sustainable development, all areas in which skillful partnerships will be vital to the organizations for which they work. Students' understanding of the depth of communication necessary for success, the concepts of reciprocity and institutional power, and the cultural and organizational history will be an asset in their future work. Reflection can help students identify the aspects of their experience that are impacted by partnership issues, such as a miscommunication or expectation based on previous students' work. As these experiences surface in reflection, facilitators can turn the partnership itself into an additional text.

Furthermore, Schön (1987) asserted that one is able to refine one's artistry or craft in a specific discipline. In a 1996 review of reflective practice, he wrote that reflection involved deliberate consideration of one's experiences as knowledge is applied to practice while professionals in the field coach the process. This personal reflection, complemented by observations by other professionals, increases learning. In this respect, international service-learning at the graduate level entails meeting a community need, professional socialization in partnership work, and development of a reflective practice. While the IPSL program was in transition with UTech and PSU, students were not immune to partnership challenges and in some cases were caught in the middle of miscommunications. Though not easy to facilitate, the reflection seminar in this case became an essential tool for processing their experience, at once creating space for the validation of feelings such as frustration and contextualizing that experience in light of organizational change and the challenging reality of collaborative processes.

Finally, reflection is not only a pedagogical tool but also a partnership tool. Clayton and Ash (2005) argued that reflection extends beyond understanding to move toward informed and effective action. Students' reflective writing is one way of capturing the potpourri of experiences—school, home, and service—and can be an important diagnostic tool for the faculty member. Pedagogically, reflective writing offers an insight into gaps in student learning. The process of reviewing student papers and facilitating discussions is a type of formative assessment that allows for modification to instruction—changes in teaching strategies and to content—and program revision.

In partnerships reflection can reveal how students experience the collaboration. Those miscommunications or unspoken expectations that shape students' experiences and emerge in reflection can alert the facilitator to a problem that can perhaps be addressed to improve the situation. Although maintaining student confidentiality is necessary, at the graduate level, transparent, diplomatic, and culturally appropriate action to remedy a concern models effective problem solving in partnership work.

Moreover, unlike traditional disciplines where underlying principles and theories are grounded in established norms and mores and in particular years of research, service-learning as an academic discipline is still in its infancy. It is amorphous and culturally peculiar (Hodelin, 2006). The learning process is dynamic, and the opportunities for serving and learning are constantly changing. It is often through reflection that faculty members know to take action to improve both curriculum and partnership to enhance the service-learning experience.

To that end, through observation of students' experiences and reflective practice, the partners in the collaboration between IPSL, PSU, and UTech all learned from the challenges that we faced. As primary players in the partnership between IPSL, PSU, and UTech, we can attest to the difficult period of change that we went through together. Over time we realized that despite our good intentions, our institutions were no longer well suited to each other in this endeavor. That our interests no longer aligned felt in some ways untidy, as the tensions of international service-learning are bound to manifest themselves through students' experiences or our own dissatisfaction with the experience of collaboration.

And yet, we did the best job we could to steward the partnership through many changes. In the process, we learned that partnerships are living organisms that change over time and react to many external influences. We learned that partnerships rely on honesty, integrity, and open communication. And we learned that effective partnerships require work well beyond good intentions. A constant nurturing is necessary in order to air the varied interests of all stakeholders such that everyone involved in international service-learning—students, faculty, academic institutions, and NGOs—can together read and reflect on the partnership itself as the text of change. In so doing, we create another means for the potential transformation of international service-learning to occur.

Indeed, though the partnership between IPSL, PSU, and UTech has now dissolved, the opportunities for student transformation go on through a revised program. IPSL, which has now become a limited liability corporation, developed a new partnership with Concordia University–Portland to redesign the graduate program in a way that integrated various ideas generated from student and partner reflections during the many years of program operation. In particular, IPSL has built on the experiential learning piece that resonates with a wider audience, particularly AmeriCorps alumni and other students who have a history and love of service. In addition, IPSL has expanded the means for students to experience firsthand what international development looks like in both developed and emerging economies by placing students in communities abroad for two semesters as opposed to just one.

PSU has continued an internationalization effort, whereas UTech (Faculty of Education and Liberal Studies) has not engaged in another exchange program since the last cohort of IPSL students left its campus in 2010.

Conclusion

IPSL has been building partnerships since its founding over 30 years ago. Many of the academic institutions and community organizations that IPSL works with today have been partners for decades. It would be disingenuous to suggest that the IPSL master's program has had flawless partnerships or programming, yet the design of this complex, multilayered, international service-learning partnership has facilitated continual program improvement, genuine student learning, and authentic assistance to communities in need—precisely the kind of transformation that international service-learning seeks to engender. Organizational and human relationships in the IPSL network have been nurtured over time by the principles of trust, reciprocity, and communication articulated by Chisholm (2003) and others. Graduate-level preparation increases the range of needs that students can meet through service, and their learning is deepened through structured reflection that can lead to both cognitive and professional development. Partnership work is intentionally examined for both student learning and program evaluation.

Jacoby (2003) cited the Center for the Advancement of Collaborative Strategies in Health's conceptualization of "partnership synergy." She explained that in partnership synergy, "the partners work together to create something new and valuable, a whole that is greater than the sum of its parts. Partnership synergy enables a partnership to think and act in ways that surpass the capacities of the individual participants" (pp. 7–8). The IPSL master's program is a whole greater than the sum of its parts. Partnership challenges are par for the course in international service-learning. Ultimately, however, the challenges provide an opportunity for student learning and our own.

References

Annette, J. (2001). Service learning in an international context. *Frontiers: The Interdisciplinary Journal of Study Abroad, 8,* 83–93. Retrieved from http://www.frontiersjournal.com/

Berry, H., & Chishom, L. (1999). *Service-learning in higher education around the world: An initial look.* New York, NY: International Partnership for Service Learning.

Chisholm, L. (1998). *Charting a hero's journey.* New York, NY: International Partnership for Service Learning.

Chisholm, L. (2003). Partnerships for international service-learning. In B. Jacoby & associates (Eds.), *Building partnerships for service-learning* (pp. 259–288). San Francisco, CA: Jossey-Bass.

Clayton, P., & Ash, S. (2005). Reflection as a key component in faculty development. *On the Horizon, 13*(3), 161–169.

Crabtree, R. (2008). Theoretical foundations for international service-learning. *Michigan Journal of Community Service Learning, 15*(1), 18–36. Retrieved from http://quod.lib.umich.edu/m/mjcsl/

Dewey, J. (1910). *How we think*. Boston, MA: Heath and Company.

Dewey, J. (1938). *Experience and education*. New York, NY: Collier Books.

Dorado, S., & Giles, D. (2004). Service-learning partnerships: Paths of engagement. *Michigan Journal of Community Service Learning, 11*(1), 25–37. Retrieved from http://quod.lib.umich.edu/m/mjcsl/

Dunlap, M., Scroggin, J., Green, P., & Davi, A. (2007). White students' experience of privilege and socioeconomic disparities: Toward a theoretical model. *Michigan Journal of Community Service Learning, 13*(2), 19–30. Retrieved from http://quod.lib.umich.edu/m/mjcsl/

Eaton, M. (2002). *Searching for the "New University": Changing faculty roles* (Project on the Future of Higher Education Working Paper). Retrieved from http://www.pfhe.org

Eaton, M., & O'Brien, K. (2004). *Creating a vital campus in a climate of restricted resources: Role of student self-reflection and self-assessment*. Retrieved from http://www.cielearn.org/wp-content/theme/creating_a_vital_campus_climate

Furco, A., & Billig, S. H. (2002). *Service-learning: The essence of the pedagogy*. Greenwich, CT: Information Age Publishing.

Garcia, C., Nehrling, S., Martin, A., & SeBlonka, K. (2009). Finding the best fit: How organizations select service learners. In R. Stoecker & E. Tryon (Eds.), *The unheard voices: Community organizations and service-learning* (pp. 38–56). Philadelphia, PA: Temple University Press.

Hodelin, G. (2006, January). *Report on integration of voluntary service (community service and service learning) into academic curriculum at the* University of Technology, Jamaica. Submitted to the Academic Policy Committee, University of Technology, Jamaica August 9, 2006.

Jacoby, B. (2003). Fundamentals of service-learning partnerships. In B. Jacoby & associates (Eds.), *Building partnerships for service-learning* (pp. 1–19). San Francisco, CA: Jossey-Bass.

Jay, G. (2008). Service-learning, multiculturalism, and the pedagogies of difference. *Pedagogy, 8*(2), 255–281.

Kecskes, K. (2006). Behind the rhetoric: Applying a cultural theory lens to campus-community partnerships. *Michigan Journal of Community Service-Learning, 12*(2), 5–14. Retrieved from http://quod.lib.umich.edu/m/mjcsl/

Kolb, D. A. (1984). *Experimental learning: Experience as the source of learning and development*. Englewood Cliffs, NJ: Prentice Hall.

Lutterman-Aguilar, A., & Gingerich, O. (2002). Experiential pedagogy for study abroad: Educating for global citizenship. *Frontiers: The Interdisciplinary Journal of Study Abroad, 8*, 41–82. Retrieved from http://www.frontiersjournal.com/

Parker, B., & Dautoff, D. (2007). Service-learning and study abroad: Synergistic learning opportunities. *Michigan Journal of Community Service Learning, 13*(2), 40–53. Retrieved from http://quod.lib.umich.edu/m/mjcsl/

Patton, M. (1990). *Qualitative evaluation and research methods.* Newbury Park, CA: Sage.

Porter, M., & Monard, K. (2001). Ayni in the global village: Building relationships of reciprocity through international service-learning. *Michigan Journal of Community Service-Learning, 8*(1), 5–17. Retrieved from http://quod.lib.umich.edu/m/mjcsl/

Sandy, M., & Holland, B. (2006). Different worlds and common ground: Community partner perspectives on campus-community partnerships. *Michigan Journal of Community Service Learning, 13*(1), 30–43. Retrieved from http://quod.lib.umich.edu/m/mjcsl/

Schön, D. A. (1987). *Educating the reflective practitioner.* San Francisco, CA: Jossey-Boss.

Schön, D. A. (1996). *Educating the reflective practitioner: Toward a new design for teaching and learning in the professions.* San Francisco, CA: Jossey-Bass.

Stoecker, R., & Tryon, E. (2009). *The unheard voices: Community organizations and service-learning.* Philadelphia, PA: Temple University Press.

Thomson, A. M., Smith-Tolken, A., Naidoo, T., & Bringle, R. (2008, July). *Service learning and civic engagement: A cross cultural perspective.* Paper presented at the International Society for Third Sector Research Eighth International Conference, Barcelona, Spain. Retrieved from http://www.istr.org/conferences/barcelona/WPVolume/Thomson.Smith-Tolken.Naidoo.Bringle.pdf

Tryon, E., Hilgendorf, A., & Scott, I. (2009). The heart of partnership: Communication and relationships. In R. Stoecker & E. Tryon (Eds.), *The unheard voices: Community organizations and service-learning* (pp. 96–115). Philadelphia, PA: Temple University Press.

8

WHEN SERVICE-LEARNING MEETS STUDY ABROAD

Locating International Service-Learning Institutionally and Abroad

Amye Day Ong and Patrick M. Green
Loyola University Chicago

As higher education institutions develop more international service-learning (ISL) opportunities for students, the origin may be a faculty-led trip, a third-party provider, an institutionally commissioned experience encouraged by administration, or a study abroad office initiative. Highly developed ISL programs exist across institutions in various places throughout the world. For example, Santa Clara University has developed the Casa de la Solidaridad program in El Salvador, in which students work in the field several days of the week and attend classes the other days. Loyola University Chicago has developed service-learning opportunities at the John Felice Rome Center in Rome, Italy, where students work with refugees during the week while studying human rights in class. Marquette University has developed a service-learning program in South Africa as well. Regardless of global location, colleges and universities have moved quickly in the past decade to participate in the race for ISL programs. Yet, what are the desired learning outcomes for such programs and the desired goal for the global communities in which the students and institutions work? The response to this key question in ISL lies more in where ISL is located at an institution rather than where it takes place globally.

In the limited literature on ISL programs, it is clear that the evolution of ISL lies at the intersection of international education, study abroad, service-learning, and global citizenship (Brewer & Cunningham, 2009; Bringle & Hatcher, 2011; Lewin, 2009; Tonkin, 2011). Given the many iterations of

ISL, however, it is less clear how ISL is situated within individual courses and academic programs, educational organizations, and higher education institutions. Plater (2011) noted the emphases that colleges and universities place on preparing students for global citizenship in an interdependent world. This is juxtaposed with how higher education institutions are required by the job market to graduate individuals who demonstrate global experiences and knowledge (Plater, 2011). The tension between educating through a global experience and intentionally facilitating experiences that educate about global citizenship is at the heart of the locality of ISL. In this regard, service-learning and study abroad provide the most direct intersection to create ISL experiences.

The fields of study abroad and service-learning currently are both experiencing growing participation and institutional prominence across U.S. institutions of higher education (Jacoby, 2009). Lewin (2009) described the increase in study abroad as a revolution, because more students are traveling abroad to a larger variety of global locations. Service-learning has become more institutionalized in higher education institutions, with an increase in faculty instructing service-learning courses and the institutionalization of service-learning offices (Campus Compact, 2009; Strong, Green, Meyer, & Post, 2009). Both areas have experienced dramatic growth in the past two decades (Bringle & Hatcher, 2011; Lewin, 2009).

With this success comes the impetus in both fields to diversify and enrich the experiential learning opportunities offered. For study abroad, this includes incorporating individualized service-learning options into more programs or creating service-learning-themed study abroad programs. For service-learning, growth has given rise to extending the borders of service beyond local communities to more commonly include international sites. In practice, the implementation of these programs may take many shapes, as there are more than 20 types of variability of ISL courses (Jones & Steinberg, 2011). Support structures in the form of study abroad offices and service-learning centers often serve a peripheral role, depending on whether the ISL is faculty led or institutionally sanctioned.

Such variability leads to the concern that ISL programs often do not address the study abroad or service-learning fields, as program planners haphazardly seek collaboration from higher education professionals who are experts in the field. ISL program development may be too narrowly focused on the tension of the question "Are we internationalizing service-learning or incorporating service-learning into study abroad?" Programs designed to merely internationalize service-learning or incorporate service-learning into study abroad limit the transformative potential for both students and local communities by giving one field prominence over the other. The experiential learning component that both study abroad and service-learning share, according to Pusch and Merrill

(2008), creates twice the opportunities for transformative learning (Mezirow, 1997), but these rewards cannot be reaped if this intersection is ignored.

Through the use of two case studies at Loyola University Chicago, including assessment and program evaluation data, we explore the intersection between study abroad and service-learning. Loyola University Chicago is a Catholic research institution located in the large midwestern urban center of Chicago. Loyola University Chicago's ISL programs in Vietnam during the summer of 2009 and in Peru during the summer of 2010 demonstrate both successful and disjointed attempts at collaboration between service-learning and study abroad. Through both indirect and direct assessment measures, program evaluation research demonstrates how the collaboration of service-learning and study abroad offices created ISL programs that impact transformative learning for students. Because these two case studies reveal ISL programs that are institutionally driven, commissioned by administration, the tension between programmatic design, marketing, and recruitment efforts is highlighted. The two programs also bring to light how the merging of study abroad and service-learning best practices raises new conflicts for practitioners and academicians seeking to promote and advance ISL on their campuses.

Case Study: Missed Opportunities in Vietnam

In the summer of 2008, the administration of Loyola University Chicago commissioned the professional staff to increase global initiatives and to begin planning self-designed ISL programs to be carried out in the summer of 2009. The two selected program locations, Peru and Vietnam, were locations where the university had developing connections in-country. In Peru, Loyola was developing a partnership with the Universidad Antonio Ruiz de Montoya (UARM), a young Jesuit university located in Lima. In Vietnam, Loyola was on the brink of receiving official permission from the Vietnamese government to establish the first U.S. university representative office. These in-country connections allowed Loyola to act on its larger commitment to service-learning, as exemplified by the creation of Loyola's Center for Experiential Learning in 2007, and move it into the international arena. The institutional context was ripe to foster ISL.

However, the first attempt at these two ISL programs was rife with miscalculations in planning, which ultimately led to opportunities for learning and growth. New dimensions of program development are required for consideration in ISL, such as student recruitment, marketing, and developing a growth plan for staged implementation. Although the initial planning for both programs began in the summer of 2008 and student recruitment for the programs was launched in October 2008, many major programmatic components, such as developing service placements and connecting academic courses, were still being finalized as late as March 2009, the time of the application deadline.

Issues in program development began with student recruitment and marketing. Although target numbers were set at a realistic number of 10 (the minimum number of participants required for these programs in order for them to be financially self-supporting), enrollment was slow. The incomplete and inconsistent recruitment message for both programs resulted in very low enrollment at the time of the application deadline, with 3 students having applied for Peru and 4 for Vietnam. The Peru program was canceled, and the in-country partner UARM was notified. For Vietnam, however, the decision was made to redouble recruitment efforts and extend the application deadline in hopes of obtaining a few more applicants. The final enrollment numbers reached a total of 7 students.

Issues for the Vietnam 2009 program did not end with recruitment. During the program participating students communicated with the on-site staff and Chicago-based staff regarding complaints related to the poor scheduling of program components (i.e., class time, meals, social activities, excursions, and required events), location of the housing well outside the Ho Chi Minh City (HCMC) center, lack of access to transportation, and poor communication between on-site staff and students. Attempts were made to address concerns during the program, but some issues, especially those related to the housing location and lack of transportation, could not be rectified mid-program. On the postprogram evaluations, all students did score the overall program experience as average. When asked on the postprogram evaluation about the most challenging or unpleasant aspect of the experience, students reiterated their earlier complaints:

> Living outside the city, not having a plan (or not knowing the plan) for most the trip.

> Miscommunication! Micromanagement! No autonomy! We did not have much time to explore HCMC because of the distance from our guesthouse. . . . Not enough immersion!

> The frustration of miscommunication or no communication at all. Schedule was off sometimes making it hard to plan to do anything.

> The residence location completely changed what I expected my experience to be and was a huge disappointment.

Although the Vietnam pilot program fell short regarding student satisfaction, it also failed to provide an environment where authentic service-learning could occur because of the program structure. With the first 4 weeks of the 6-week program devoted to class time, activities, and events, the actual service work was entirely relegated to the final 2 weeks. Although students did have a final reflection paper for the class due after their service placement had ended, there were no regular class meetings taking place concurrently with the service work. The reflection component was limited to only the final paper. The program structure, in essence, deprived students of both the opportunity for facilitated and professor-directed reflection and the time to process such experiences or do more substantive service at their sites, all of which are essential components of service-learning.

The weakness of the Vietnam 2009 program, however, led to more program development for the first iteration of the Peru program in the summer of 2010. Planning for 2010 in Peru was postponed until the conclusion of the Vietnam 2009 program assessment and program evaluation. The complaints of the Vietnam 2009 students regarding structure, housing, and immersion informed the redesign of the Peru program. The failures of the Vietnam pilot program led to an opportunity for close cooperation between study abroad and service-learning staff.

Case Study: Collaboration and Transformation in Peru

The collaborative approach for service-learning and study abroad generated a different program model than the one attempted the prior year. The central component of the planning process for Peru 2010 was the development of a contract between UARM and Loyola University Chicago that included detailed descriptions of every major program component, as well as addenda for the program budget and the two final course syllabi. Loyola's Center for Experiential Learning, which was more deeply involved in the redesign of the Peru program, reviewed each draft of the service-learning course syllabus prior to endorsing the final version that was included in the program contract. In the early fall of 2009, the exhaustive planning and discussions between Loyola and UARM, as well as between Loyola's Office for International Programs and its Center for Experiential Learning, allowed the program to be marketed beginning in November 2009 with comprehensive program details. Students responded well, and in March 2010, the program had received 17 applications. In the end, 12 students confirmed their participation in the program.

Indirect and direct assessments of the Peru program demonstrated that the extensive collaborative program development resulted in a stronger ISL program. Direct assessments included on-site program observations, classroom visits, interviews with the faculty from Peru, and interviews with the students in the program. Indirect assessments included a postprogram survey sent electronically, with questions focused on student satisfaction and student perception of achieving the learning outcomes of the program. Interviewing the students revealed overall positive responses from the participants and identified some distinct program gaps. Using a five-point Likert scale, survey questions indicated that students rated the program as *above average*. Students scored the overall Peru program experience as *good* to *excellent*, with 4.18 and 5.0, respectively. The qualitative student responses on the Peru 2010 postprogram evaluation also had a markedly different tenor than those from the students in Vietnam 2009:

> Overall, my experience living in Peru, my discussions with my peers, the service work, and the class along with it broadened my global understanding of poverty, development, and both our opportunities and limits to be agents of inclusion.

> Often hard and frustrating but also incredible and life-changing.

> I will never forget the relationships I built at my service placement. . . . I learned so much through this experience and am walking away with more than I could ever give.

> My placement made me sure that I want to become a doctor. It also helped me realize that when I have more medical skills I want to use them for more than monetary gains, I want to give back to the community in which I live and work.

> Overwhelming and inspiring at the same time. All the work only made me grow as a person.

The qualitative responses from the open-ended survey questions reveal the transformative educational experience students had in Peru 2010 and also make clear that the service work and reflection were central elements of the program, unlike in Vietnam. The extensive program development that occurred through collaboration from study abroad and service-learning professionals was integrated in the student responses.

Of course, there are always program components that can be improved, and the assessments revealed gaps in the program. The students gladly highlighted those aspects of the program they felt were challenging or needed to be altered in the future:

> It felt like we had very little free time to experience Lima, especially with the amount of service we did and the amount of homework we had.

> The language was very challenging, but in the end I was able to communicate and have improved my Spanish greatly.

> In general, not having as much independence and ability to choose things for myself: schedule, food, etc.

> The workload was really stressful for me. . . . You are always exhausted after service days because they are long and in a different language and then there is your host family that you have to talk to [and] you're trying to experience Lima all at the same time. If the workload had been a little less I think it would decrease the stress of the experience a lot.

Figure 8.1 Comparison of student survey responses, Part I.

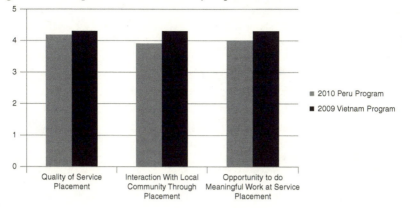

In many ways the tight structure of the Peru program, which was likely reinforced by the detailed planning, led to the principal complaint by students of too little free time.

Figure 8.1 and figure 8.2 demonstrate that the student participants in both Vietnam and Peru rated their experiences *above average* quite similarly, except for overall quality of the program. The Peru service-learning program received a distinctly higher score on average from students, and the students' qualitative responses on the open-ended questions of the survey validate this as well. These data are also supported by the interviews with students and the direct observations in the site visit.

Figure 8.2 Comparison of student survey responses, Part II.

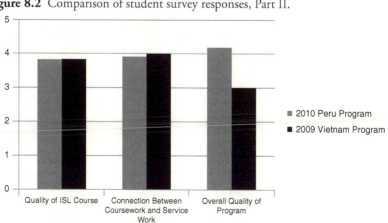

The Burden of Student Recruitment: Tension Between Learning and Financing

By taking service-learning opportunities abroad, ISL program leaders become subject to the many restrictions that have long affected study abroad programs, including the need for a quorum of students in order to make the program financially self-supporting. In addition to balancing a program budget, a minimum number of students may also be required in order to carry out in-country service projects outlined by the community partners. No matter the principal motivation, meeting student recruitment goals is a necessity for any ISL program. In light of the reality of student recruitment, there are competing interests with regard to the students' academic and financial priorities and the program's pedagogical goals. The tension between institutional educational objectives and individual student priorities is significant.

In the field of study abroad, the student is often treated as the consumer, carefully choosing the most attractive study abroad program from myriad options. Loyola offers well over 100 programs in 55 countries, and this variety affords students the opportunity to be very selective when comparing the academic and financial aspects of potential programs. Academically, students seek study abroad programs whose courses fulfill one or more requirements for a student's degree. Consequently, an ISL program that offers students only general elective credit will be a much less attractive option than an ISL program whose course fulfills a core, major, or minor requirement and is academically appealing to a wide range of students. For example, when the 2009 Peru program was designed, students could initially only earn political science credit through the service-learning course and Spanish credit for the second course. This dramatically narrowed the pool of potential students. Through strategic collaborations with academic departments, the academic course offerings were reorganized to more broadly attract students of all majors. For example, the Spanish course was dropped as a requirement and replaced with a not-for-credit Spanish-language tutorial during the first week of the program. This allowed Loyola to recruit students from beginning-level Spanish students to those who were native speakers.

Just as students seek a clear understanding of how an ISL program will contribute to their academic progress, they are drawn toward programs with a clearly demonstrated financial value. This does not necessarily mean that the cheapest program garners the most applications. Instead, students want to know, in the current economic climate more than ever, that funding their participation in the program will be money well spent. Loyola ISL programs are divided into tuition and program fees, with the tuition encompassing in-class instruction and academic excursions and the program fee including housing, meals, in-country transportation related to the program, social activities or nonacademic excursions, and program on-site support. The tuition rate for ISL programs and other study abroad programs is near identical to on-campus tuition, because students have already demonstrated the ability to pay that amount, and the quality of instruction is on par or superior to that offered in traditional classes. Although the costs of actual in-country instruction and academic excursions are likely to be less than the tuition the home university charges, any revenue generated by the university through the program tuition helps compensate for the time and effort invested by the university in the program's development and maintenance. The program fee, however, is priced to merely break even, because its additional cost to the student, as well as airfare and other personal costs, can be a great burden to some students and diminish the accessibility of ISL to the home university's entire student population.

In addition to offering students a comparable tuition charge and at-cost program fee, ISL programs can recruit students and demonstrate financial value by weighing academic credit and program length. On average, students seek to earn academic credit that correlates directly with or exceeds the number of weeks they will be in-country. That is to say, students will consider a 3-week program in which they earn three credits or more but will be less likely to apply for a 6-week program in which they earn only three credits. For summer ISL programs, this is especially important, because students have the option to work full-time, take classes full-time, or do both part-time during the summer. If a program lasts for 6 weeks but offers students the opportunity to earn only three credit hours, as was the case for the Vietnam 2009 summer program, students are essentially attending class part-time but forfeiting the opportunity to also work part-time. The correlation between cost, credit, and program length was underscored during the Peru 2010 program site visit when students unanimously voiced exhaustion over the intense nature of the program and great amount of homework assigned. They also simultaneously indicated, when questioned, that they would not have attended the 6-week program if they were earning only three credits.

As study abroad professionals can attest, ISL program leaders are wise to take heed of student academic and financial preferences when designing a program if recruitment is to be successful. However, the need to cater to students as consumers is in conflict with the ISL goal to have students, institutions, and local and global communities in solidarity. The tension is palpable, as developing attractive ISL programs can redirect the focus away from developing authentic service-learning international partnerships. The consumer-provider relationship occurs not only between students and U.S. universities but also between the U.S. university and its in-country partners.

This mentality can easily be counterproductive to the spirit of collaboration that ISL aims to foster. From a student recruitment standpoint, some of the latent consumer catering can be offset by careful selection of language that fosters reciprocity in program recruitment materials. ISL programs advertised as providing students the opportunity to "work alongside," as opposed to "help," local communities will take the first step in setting the stage for establishing a mutually beneficial relationship between the in-country partners, institutions, and students.

Balancing the Ideals of Global Impact With the Realities of Institutional Responsibility

Many domestic service-learning programs already operate in accordance with the best practices set by the field. However, the more recent and quickly developing expansion of service-learning internationally adds new imperatives with regard to program transit safety and student orientation already familiar to professionals in study abroad. U.S. universities providing ISL programs have an obligation to consider these issues carefully, as institutional liability extends beyond the borders of our country. Though institutional responsibility regarding student safety abroad may limit ISL program design, study abroad theory regarding student immersion will often aid in fostering the transformative learning environment ISL program leaders seek.

Providing both a mandatory predeparture orientation in the months prior to a program start and an on-site orientation in the initial days of a program is standard practice in the field of study abroad. The predeparture orientation is often the only time program participants and program leader(s) meet prior to the program start and can set the tone for the entire experience, including how students should expect to relate to their partners at the service sites. This U.S.-based orientation is an opportunity to discuss preparations regarding health (e.g., vaccines, prescriptions needed over the course of the program, international health insurance, etc.), visas, final paperwork (e.g., university risk and release policy), and what to pack. It is also an ideal time to review with all participating students what the expectations should be regarding the arrival procedure, behavior in-country, service sites, program schedule, necessary safety precautions, and proper method for reporting concerns or issues.

For the Peru 2010 program, representatives from both the Office for International Programs and the Center for Experiential Learning were able to meet with all students and, therefore, had the opportunity to address issues related to both study abroad and service-learning. On-site orientation ideally is the first event on the program calendar immediately following airport arrival and can last anywhere from 1 day to 1 week. The function of the on-site orientation is to reiterate program expectations that were first discussed at the predeparture orientation—especially those regarding health, safety, and emergency procedures—and to introduce the students to their new host country and culture. In the case of the Peru 2010 program, the on-site orientation week was also a time when students participated in a language tutorial to refresh their Spanish conversational skills in preparation for their service placements. Students received an excellent orientation by UARM to Lima and its safety considerations, but all of the service placements were in the outskirts of Lima in the high-poverty neighborhood of Pamplona Alta, which had its own specific safety concerns. For that reason, in 2011, the program added a specific on-site orientation component that more formally introduced students to the community organization partners and their neighborhood.

Transportation for domestic service-learning is often not a dominant concern, as students are usually able to drive themselves to their service site or use public transit as they so choose. However, ISL programs are responsible for directly arranging or advising students as to the preferred method of transit to their service site abroad. Given the high poverty, and occasionally high crime, areas in which students are working and the likelihood that a student may stick out in the local community, it is essential that ISL program leaders work with in-country partners to understand and mitigate the risks associated with student service. Occasionally, sacrifices regarding immersion or solidarity with the community must be made in order for an institution to do its due diligence in ensuring student safety. For example, in the Peru 2010 program students were transported via privately arranged taxis from their homestays in central Lima to their service sites in Pamplona Alta. UARM advised Loyola that this was necessary, as public transit via this route that would take well over an hour each way had greatly increased risks, in comparison to the public transit routes students could take from their homestays to UARM for class. Clearly a student arriving to the service site via privately arranged taxis sets them apart from the local community, who are almost exclusively commuting by foot or by public transit microbuses. Yet in the debate between student safety and community solidarity, the well-being of students must be paramount.

Although safety concerns with regard to transportation may limit a student's ability to identify with the local community, using the traditional study abroad housing option of host families can compensate by providing increased immersion experiences. The relationships a student develops by living in a local homestay can provide just as many opportunities for personal connection and learning as the student's service site. In addition to increasing overall program immersion, housing students with a host family or local roommate is also likely to give students the opportunity to discuss societal issues and injustices they are confronting at their service site with locals who are sure to have their own perspective as well.

In the Vietnam 2009 program, students were told at a predeparture meeting that local roommates could be arranged, and a number of students selected this option. However, logistical issues ultimately eliminated the option, and all seven of the students were either paired with each other or put in a single room. The lack of local roommates and limited interaction with Vietnamese students made the isolation of participating students more acute, as they were already displeased with their housing location well outside HCMC. The missed opportunity for immersion housing in Vietnam, however, ultimately provided organizers the impetus to use the homestay housing option when planning the Peru 2010 program.

In the Peru 2010 program, the host family experiences were a significant part of the program structure, and the evaluations revealed that the students consistently reported this as a highlight of their overall experience. Students wrote passionately about the importance of living with a host family:

> They were really amazing; I mean my host mother especially took me out and was always making sure I had everything. We talked a lot and had a great time together. The best part was that her sister is also in the program and was hosting another student so I felt like I got an extended host family too.

> They were very sweet and always looked after us. We would always have a family lunch on Sundays and spent really quality time with them during dinner. They were truly sincere and generous.

> [My host parents] are very welcoming people who want you to be actively involved in their culture. . . . They took us around during the weekend when they were not obligated to. They were a wonderful family and a perfect fit for me.

In the postprogram evaluations, the homestay placements were scored by students as 4.45 and 5.0. The host family immersion experience contributed to building the students' cultural competency, language acquisition, and interpersonal skills, as students built strong relationships with in-country homestays.

The Final Frontier: Fostering Collaboration With In-country Partners

Collaboration between service-learning and study abroad offices is a challenge, and although each seeks to provide students with a transformative learning experience, professionals come to the table with conflicting practical priorities. Although the study abroad professional is likely to focus on student safety, orientation, housing, and student recruitment, the service-learning professional is more apt to devote time and attention to the location of the service placement, type of work performed, intersection of service with course work, and desired learning outcomes for students. When these professionals are discussing these competing, but ultimately complementary, priorities, it can be easy for the concerns of the in-country partners and local community to be lost in the shuffle. Although the in-country partners were substantial planning partners for both the Vietnam and Peru programs at Loyola University Chicago, future experiences in these settings seek to include the in-country partners more intentionally. For any ISL program to be successful long term and live up to the ideals of reciprocity, the in-country partners and local community must be brought to the same table that service-learning and study abroad now share.

References

Brewer, E., & Cunningham, K. (2009). Capturing study abroad's transformative potential. In E. Brewer & K. Cunningham (Eds.), *Integrating study abroad into the curriculum: Theory and practice across the disciplines* (pp. 1–19). Sterling, VA: Stylus.

Bringle, R. G., & Hatcher, J. A. (2011). International service learning. In R. G. Bringle, J. A. Hatcher, & S. G. Jones (Eds.), *International service learning: Conceptual frameworks and research* (pp. 3–28). Sterling, VA: Stylus.

Campus Compact. (2009). *Campus compact annual membership survey* [electronic version]. Retrieved April 6, 2011, from www.compact.org/about/statistics

Jacoby, B. (2009). Facing the unsettled questions about service-learning. In J. Strait & M. Lima (Eds.), *The future of service-learning: New solutions for sustaining and improving practice* (pp. 90–105). Sterling, VA: Stylus.

Jones, S. G., & Steinberg, K. S. (2011). An analysis of international service-learning programs. In R. G. Bringle, J. A. Hatcher, & S. G. Jones (Eds.), *International service learning: Conceptual frameworks and research* (pp. 89–112). Sterling, VA: Stylus.

Lewin, R. (2009). The quest for global citizenship through study abroad. In R. Lewin (Ed.), *The handbook of practice and research in study abroad: Higher education and the quest for global citizenship* (pp. xiii–xxii). New York, NY: Routledge.

Mezirow, J. (1997). Transformative learning: Theory to practice. *New Directions for Adult and Continuing Education, 74*, 5–12.

Plater, W. (2011). The context for international service learning. In R. G. Bringle, J. A. Hatcher, & S. G. Jones (Eds.), *International service learning: Conceptual frameworks and research* (pp. 29–56). Sterling, VA: Stylus.

Pusch, M. D., & Merrill, M. (2008). Reflection, reciprocity, responsibility, and committed relativism: Intercultural development through international service-learning. In V. Savicki (Ed.), *Developing intercultural competence and transformation: Theory, research, and application in international education* (pp. 297–321). Sterling, VA: Stylus.

Strong, E. C., Green, P. M., Meyer, M., & Post, M. A. (2009). Future directions in campus-community partnerships. In J. R. Strait & M. Lima (Eds.), *The future of service-learning: New solutions for sustaining and improving practice* (pp. 9–32). Sterling, VA: Stylus.

Tonkin, H. (2011). A research agenda for international service learning. In R. G. Bringle, J. A. Hatcher, & S. G. Jones (Eds.), *International service learning: Conceptual frameworks and research* (pp. 191–224). Sterling, VA: Stylus.

9

MULTIDISCIPLINARY LEARNING

Interdisciplinary Teaching and Community Service-Learning in Jamaica

A. Rafik Mohamed
Clayton State University

John Loggins and Carlton D. Floyd
University of San Diego

June 2013 marked the eighth consecutive summer of the University of San Diego's (USD) Jamaica study abroad program.[1] Since its inception, this 3-week immersion program has been overseen by two primary professors and a university staff member whose full-time commitment is to community service-learning. The philosophical foundations of the program are rooted in the belief that the independent island nations making up the Caribbean are central to a comprehensive understanding of modern global societies, the difficulties faced by the majority of postcolonial nations in the developing world, and the privileges associated with citizenship in postindustrial "first world" societies.

Through an interdisciplinary curriculum and a required community interaction component involving formal partnership with local community agencies and opportunities for informal student exchanges with local community members, our Jamaica program is structured to achieve four academic goals. First, we seek to provide students with an overview of Caribbean society and culture from the beginning of the transatlantic slave trade to the present. Second, we ask students to consider how European colonization shaped Jamaican society and culture for the bad and, to a lesser extent, the good. Third, through meaningful interaction with Jamaican community members, students experience the day-to-day lives of people who live and work in a region with an identity that is inextricably tied to its colonial past and a contemporary dependence on American and European tourism and trade. Fourth, we seek to have students gain an understanding of the mechanisms through which a cultural identity of resistance and immodest independence can be forged in spite of ideological and economic systems that continue to promote dichotomous and unequal master-servant societies (Giovannetti, 2006; Lewis, 1983).

In moving toward these four primary academic goals, once again through both service-learning and multidisciplinary in-class curriculum, the program also seeks to have students develop an appreciation for the intrinsic value of Caribbean literature, music, and culture; understand how the world's most powerful nations have shaped the economies and cultures of less powerful nations in ways that often detract from the self-determination and global competency of these less developed nations; and use Jamaican culture as a lens through which they can critically evaluate their racial, ethnic, gendered, national, and socioeconomic selves. Ultimately, it is the objective of this 3-week program to have student-participants return to the United States with greater cultural competency and critical thinking abilities than when they left for Jamaica.

Choosing the Appropriate Location in Jamaica

Jamaicans often refer to their country as the "land of contradictions," and it was our aim to locate this study abroad program in a site that reflected some of the more stark economic and identity-based challenges confronting Jamaican people on a daily basis. Indeed, long before Christopher Columbus claimed the island for the Spanish crown in 1494, Jamaica had all of the trappings of what would ultimately become the cornerstone of Caribbean plantation societies: Its climate is warm and tropical, its soil is fertile and ideal for year-round agricultural production, it has navigable channels that could accommodate the era's tall ships, and the island had an indigenous population incapable of fending off colonial encroachment. Most of these same characteristics, coupled with warm clear-blue waters and sandy beaches, are precisely what made Jamaica an appealing tourist destination both during and after slave times.

In a contemporary sense, the specific contradictions we sought to highlight through our program were those revolving around the paradoxes of living in "paradise," particularly as they relate to relationships between the Jamaican people and the tourism industry that has become the island's postcolonial hallmark. Initially, we considered basing the program in Kingston, Jamaica's capital city, and utilizing dormitory and classroom facilities at the

University of the West Indies. However, this consideration proved untenable and ultimately inconsistent with our ultimate educational goal of students learning about Jamaica's postcolonial existence and the struggle for dignity faced by the bulk of Jamaicans who find themselves dependent on the Caribbean tourist economy and foreign remittances for their livelihood.[2] We therefore concluded that locating the program nearer to, but not directly in, one of Jamaica's north coast tourist hubs would make for a better academic fit. Although development and considerations for tourists can be found across much of the island, the majority of resorts are located along the island's north-central coast on the 70-mile ocean-front stretch between Montego Bay and Ocho Rios and, to a lesser but more concentrated extent, in Negril on Jamaica's west end. Although the entire island is a truly tropical paradise, we reasoned that it would be a powerful learning tool to have students experience on a daily basis the juxtaposition of north coast resort opulence with the dire poverty that exists directly outside the resort gates— literally across the street on what Jamaicans call "the gully side." And, finally, through this combination of competing existences, we wanted our students to contemplate how life for real Jamaicans differs from the "no problem" and "irie" Jamaican stereotypes promoted by the Jamaican travel industry in the United States and Europe.

Ironically, the very water and the white sand beaches that have, throughout Jamaica's history, attracted outside interest are increasingly becoming off-limits to everyday Jamaicans. Because of the proliferation of coastal resort development and a desire by investment firms and the Jamaican Tourism Board to construct a tourist-friendly sanitized Jamaican experience for visitors to the island, many Jamaican locals are welcomed at the resorts only as employees and otherwise have the access to their country's nicer beaches blocked by prohibitive tariffs. For example, to access one beach near our program's home base in Duncans, Jamaica, locals must pay a day rate of US$50, roughly the weekly wage of the average worker in the area. Beyond direct water access, from Lucea (a small town approximately midway between the north coast city Montego Bay and the west end city Negril) to Ocho Rios, foreign mega-resort development continues to obscure sight lines and has made it increasingly difficult for Jamaicans to even see the waters that draw in tourists. As one of our community partners, Melvin Thompson, commented during a drive between Montego Bay and our program's base town, "This used to be a beautiful drive. Now all you see are hotels."

Indeed, over the past 8 years that we have been administering the Jamaica study abroad program, no fewer than three massive hotel complexes and one colossal beachfront condominium have been constructed and opened for business along this already hotel-laden 100-kilometer stretch. As one columnist for Jamaica's most significant newspaper, *The Gleaner*, adulated, "Jamaica has the potential to be a world superpower in tourism."[3] Although certainly a noble aspiration and beacon of progress for a country that does not have many other licit avenues to compete in the global marketplace, the often overlooked issue and certainly the question of greatest importance to everyday Jamaicans is, at what cost does this progress come? In contemplating this question and the others stemming from this paradise paradox, we have our students read Jamaica Kincaid's (1988) *A Small Place* during their flight to Jamaica. As Kincaid wrote of her similarly situated homeland, Antigua, "It is as if, then, the beauty—the beauty of the sea, the land, the air, the trees, the market, the people, the sounds they make—were a prison, and as if everything and everybody inside it were locked in" (1988, p. 79).

To maximize student learning along these themes of contradiction, we ultimately chose to locate the program primarily in Duncans, a small town of approximately 2,500 located about 25 miles east of the north coast's major port city, Montego Bay. Duncans was appealing and has proved to be an ideal program location for several reasons. As we noted earlier, whenever traveling abroad with a large group of people clearly identifiable by racial and other markers as outsiders, safety is a paramount concern. Duncans is only 15 minutes driving from at least one substantial resort located in the somewhat larger town of Falmouth and within a half hour to either the east (toward Ocho Rios) or the west (toward Montego Bay) of literally dozens of resorts of all sizes. However, the town, which is not marked on most tourist maps of Jamaica, is still secluded and far enough away from the typically beaten tourist path to minimize student encounters with "hustlers," other people who may prey on the naïveté of people unfamiliar with Jamaican folkways and even other tourists. Furthermore, from an immersive educational standpoint, many of the people who reside in Duncans are employed by resorts or are in some other tangential way dependent on tourist dollars for their livelihood (e.g., bus, route taxi, van drivers, etc.). Accordingly, our residing near Duncans allows our students to experience firsthand the daily lives of people they would otherwise encounter only in the more formally choreographed tourist-meets-resort-employee fashion. And of course, the opposite is true as well: Our Jamaican counterparts are able to see nontourist (in the traditional sense) foreigners who can also challenge their perceptions of the other.

Because Duncans is in the "country,"[4] students develop a better sense of the communities that resort workers and other everyday Jamaicans return to after a day of posing as "the happy servant."[5] This is a relatively unique experience for American visitors to Jamaica because employee protocol deliberately constructs a cultural distance between those who work at the resorts and those who visit the island as guests of the resorts. When tourists travel any distance from the resorts, they are often escorted by resort personnel and take part in highly structured tours designed to perpetuate the image of the happy native and beautiful countryside while downplaying poverty and other fundamental features of day-to-day Jamaican life. As a student commented after completing our summer 2009 program, "I was, or at least tried to be, completely immersed. I felt like I saw a side of Jamaica I couldn't see without this program."

The relatively small size and slower pace of Duncans also allows students to develop meaningful bonds with local people, relationships that many of our students have maintained after returning to the United States. Indeed, this interconnectedness and sense of kinship is a deliberate part of our program. Building strong relationships between our students and the local Jamaican community has always been a goal central to our program's learning outcomes, and service is the primary tool we use to achieve this goal. It is in fact the only way we can attempt to break the "one-up" cycle. Whether it is the dichotomy of master-slave, tourist-servant, or service provider-service recipient, we try to avoid fostering a dynamic that creates or reinforces hierarchy and instead adopt a more "critical service-learning" approach that strives to make students aware of the social justice issues present in their international experience (Mitchell, 2008; Rice & Pollack, 2000; Rosenberger, 2000). We are also aware that acknowledging cultural difference in conjunction with an intrinsic sense of human equality is central to effective community-based service-learning. As Tania D. Mitchell wrote, "The challenge is to create relationships that neither ignore the realities of social inequality in our society nor attempt to artificially homogenize all people in the service-learning experience" (Mitchell, 2008, pp. 58–59). This justice-oriented service-learning model puts our students and our Jamaican partners on a trajectory toward self-awareness and solidarity. And, as Radest (1993) suggested, building solidarity is central to the development of authenticity and an earnest commitment to social justice (Mitchell, 2008).

Regarding specific service-learning options available in our program, Jamaica summer students have the choice of participating in community service-learning activities at one or more of the three primary sites with which we have formal community partnerships. Each of these sites is intentionally structured around children, who are far less intimidating to students and serve as ideal gateway to the broader community. The first partner site, and in fact the first community partnership we were able to establish in Duncans in 2006, is the Duncans all-age school. The all-age schools in Jamaica are roughly equivalent to elementary and middle schools in the United States. Our students serve as teacher's aides, assist in the special education wing, teach computer skills to Jamaican children, and help set up and staff an annual children's fair. The second partner site is the Place of Safety located in nearby Granville. Jamaica has several of these residential facilities designated for minor delinquent and "thrown away" girls located around the island. Ostensibly, our students tutor the girls and otherwise help them with their schoolwork and other life-skills-oriented activities. However, our students spend most of their time at the Place of Safety more simply interacting with the girls and sharing life stories. Our third, and most recent, partnership site is the Trelawny Community Resource Center. Here, our students engage in activities with preschool students and also provide assistance to adults who participate in a number of career development workshops.

Beyond these more formal partnerships, student service-learning activities also take place in more casual or informal settings. These informal encounters are an integral and very intentional part of the program. Program faculty are constantly modeling these encounters to encourage students to follow suit and to help strengthen the relationships within the community. Adjacent to the students' neighborhood housing in Jamaica is Jacob Taylor Beach, a working fisherman's beach where local fishermen, artisans, and small shop owners congregate from the predawn hours until well into the night. Our students customarily visit with locals at Jacob Taylor to discuss topics that range from the daily struggle for dignity experienced by many Jamaicans, to local and global politics, to perceived misogyny in Caribbean music and culture. Students also routinely mingle and chat with locals in the Duncans town square, attend Sunday church services with some of the women they have met in the community, or play football (soccer) with Jamaicans at a community field we helped clear in 2008. In all, these structured and unstructured community experiences have proven invaluable assets in achieving our student learning outcomes. These unfettered opportunities provide our students a way to engage Jamaicans on their own terms, based on their own interests, and offer an additional layer of connectedness that is valued by both our students and the Jamaicans they meet. As one student from the summer 2010 program commented when asked what the program highlights were, "Being able to work in the community and being able to meet such awesome people in Jamaica."

Curriculum Development and Program Organization

From the outset, we intended this to be a multidisciplinary program with a synergistic community service-learning component (Howard, 1998). It is certainly possible to explore an aspect of Jamaican society through a more

MULTIDISCIPLINARY LEARNING

singularly oriented curricular focus. However, our hope was to structure a diverse array of community-based and cultural experiences around the relatively brief time students spend in Jamaica so that the student participants could return to the United States with a more comprehensive understanding of Caribbean life and develop a real sense of feeling connected to Jamaica. Therefore, we determined the broader lens offered by this multidisciplinary approach to be the most appropriate and most effective method we could use to help students find something about Jamaica that would resonate with them. Whether it be the real and powerful explanation of the slave trade that challenges their sense of justice, or a beautifully written Jamaican poem that sparks their imagination, or the opportunity to have a conversation with a "thrown away" youth at Place of Safety, our students have multiple opportunities to connect themselves authentically to the community.

Ultimately, on the basis of the interdisciplinary strengths that the core program faculty brought to the table and the intended student learning objectives, we offered two upper-division course options rooted in four primary academic subject areas. The first course offered is titled "The Black Atlantic" and can be taken for credit in sociology, ethnic studies, or international relations. The course explores the development of Black identity in the Caribbean, particularly how and why it has taken shape in ways similar to and different from Black identity in the United States. In doing so, the course places specific emphasis on the themes of colonization, slavery, culture, and resistance in the African diasporas. Our second course, "Post Colonial Studies: Black Caribbean Literature," allows students to earn academic credit toward either English or ethnic studies. Through the lens of Caribbean writers, with specific effort to incorporate the essays, plays, short stories, and poetry of Jamaican authors, students are exposed to themes of African cultural heritage, the Middle Passage, the postslavery colonial experience, and the postcolonial English-speaking Caribbean experience. Beyond this more traditional academic curriculum, as we have already noted, a required community service-learning component is built into our program.

Driving the structural and curricular development of this program were three shared pedagogical understandings. First, as reflected in USD's mission and pedagogical research on interdisciplinary teaching abroad, college educators and administrators have increasingly realized the need to prepare students for citizenship in a global society (Lessor, Reeves, & Andrade, 1997). Our view of the global citizen is not simply someone who has been exposed to cultures and international perspectives different from their own. Rather, we see global citizens as people who, through structured contemplation in conjunction with immersion in cultures different from their own, develop a critical understanding of how they are symbiotically related to other people in the world, even if they never come into direct contact with the vast majority of these people. It was our belief that this citizenship should not be limited to those international perspectives typically brought into the relational discussion that characteristically revolves around first world societies, particularly because these first world societies are directly and indirectly responsible for many of the economic, social, and political challenges faced by the developing nations left out of these conversations.

Second, our program augments the dominant study abroad paradigm and provides an opportunity for our students to explore subaltern studies from the historical and firsthand perspectives of those who, in a global context, appear to hold comparatively subordinate positions. This departure from a focus on cultures and places traditionally deemed worthy of study abroad has not come without overt and implied challenges to its academic merits. Even after 8 successful years with the program, we continue to endure questions from colleagues, students, parents of students, and administrators regarding the academic legitimacy of study in the Caribbean, questions most would not dare ask about studies abroad on the continent.

Third, but by no means the least significant influence on the development of our program, was and continues to be USD's identity as an independent Catholic institution "committed to advancing academic excellence, expanding liberal and professional knowledge, creating a diverse and inclusive community, and preparing leaders dedicated to ethical conduct and compassionate service." Since the start of our program, the university also established an international center focused on creating a campus environment that builds theoretical and practical skills necessary for effective interaction in contemporary global society. Accordingly, university faculty members are openly encouraged to design international research and study abroad experiences that promote cross-cultural understanding and global citizenship. The result of this positive institutional attitude toward internationalization is seen in the fact that nearly 80% of all undergraduate students participate in some form of study abroad experience during their career at USD, placing the university second in the nation in doctorate-degree-granting institutions sending students abroad.

Daily Life: Class Structure and Community Service-Learning

With the exception of most weekend days and weekdays on which we have planned day trips to sites of cultural and historical significance, formal classes are conducted every day for approximately 3 to 4 hours, beginning in the late morning. In the earlier morning preclass hours, students are given the opportunity to participate in one of several community service-learning options by working with preschool students at a basic school or primary school students at a local all-age school with which we have established community partnerships. Our classes are conducted in seminar style so that each student is accountable for the course readings and has an opportunity to reflect critically on the readings and share thoughts on how these readings tie into their community experiences. Although students may receive academic credit for only one of the two courses offered through our program, in an effort to maximize what we see as the benefits of interdisciplinary learning in an abroad setting, we elected to "team teach" the courses. Therefore, all of the approximately 20 to 25 student participants are exposed to and responsible for the multidisciplinary content, and all program faculty attend each class and serve as discussants. Also, as part of our regular course curriculum, we incorporate both planned and spontaneous reflection opportunities so that students can engage in structured dialogue about their experiences with the local Jamaican community and we as program faculty can guide the conversations to ensure these experiences are captured in the context of course reading materials. Through these reflections and daily conversations, we find that our students not only begin to make connections between their Jamaican experience and the readings but also begin to connect their readings and experiences to themselves. As instructors we attempt to listen carefully to what is resonating with each student and, on the basis of these interactions, provide students opportunities to explore those sentiments in connection with the community. It also seems to be the case that when our students venture out into the community as curious to learn about themselves as they are about the community, Jamaicans begin to open up and more actively and authentically engage our students. The one-up dynamic dissipates, and everyone becomes engaged in the learning and teaching process.

In making this choice for collaborative instruction, each year we attempt to identify course materials that complement each other and reflect, from different academic perspectives, the major historical and cultural shifts experienced in Jamaica from the beginnings of the transatlantic slave trade to the present. For example, while we have students read Robert Harms's (2002) vividly grim account of an 18th-century slave ship and Obiagele Lake's (1998) more sociohistorical work documenting slavery and capitalism in Jamaica, we simultaneously ask students to consider Claude McKay's slave-themed poem titled "In Bondage" and Vera Bell's "Ancestor on the Auction Block." Similarly, while having students contemplate the relationships between reggae music and Jamaica's colonial past, we read Paul Gilroy's and Stephen A. King's more political-anthropological accounts of the roots of reggae music in conjunction with other assigned works like Victor Stafford Reid's "The Cultural Revolution in Jamaica After 1938" and Linton Kwesi Johnson's poem "Reggae fi Dada." In planning a classroom-based curriculum that could be used as a tool for students to interpret their community experiences, we felt this balancing of more analytical academic pieces with thought-provoking and emotive literary pieces would make the learning process more immediately relevant for students already distracted by their status as "strangers in a strange land." We also felt strongly that this choice would allow students drawn toward different pedagogies and students whose strengths lie in different modes of academic analysis to have equal ownership in our discussions of Jamaican culture, history, and politics. We have consistently revised the curriculum and expanded the kinds of service-learning and immersion experiences available to our students over the program's 8 years, and student response suggests that our approach has been an effective one. We routinely receive formal student evaluation feedback saying things like, "I feel that the reading really related to what I saw and experienced in the communities and I loved the community service part of the class. I will take so much from this trip."

As a prelude to the summer experience, specifically as it relates to what students may expect to experience in the community and through the service-learning component of the program, we offer a spring semester one-credit-hour orientation course designed to acclimate students to Jamaican culture prior to their arrival on the island. The intention behind this course is to minimize "culture shock" and help students adjust as quickly as possible to a cultural environment that is foreign to most of them. Accordingly, the principal instructor for this mini-course, our community service-learning director, covers subjects like the basis of Jamaican Patois; Jamaican norms, religions, and cultural practices; Rastafarianism; and the centrality of reggae music and Bob Marley to Jamaican identity. The instructor also invites Jamaican guest speakers residing in the San Diego area to make presentations geared toward interacting and engaging with the people students may encounter while visiting Jamaica. Over the years, this precourse seems to have functioned well as a precursor of the program's required service-learning component, as students are primed to build meaningful relationships. Indeed, our goal has been to prioritize building meaningful relationships, albeit brief, over some of the more traditional service-oriented projects organized around meeting identified community needs. We certainly are not calling into question the merits of these more traditional approaches to service, and we in fact provide several opportunities for students to participate in hands-on projects. However, as we tell students during our predeparture meetings, if they are willing to open themselves up to the community experience, they are certain to learn more from everyday conversations and interactions with Jamaican people than we could possibly teach them in the classroom. We think this approach of stressing cultural immersion and face-to-face interaction over other modes of service has been an effective one, as we typically receive student responses like this offered after our summer 2009 program: "I learned more outside the classroom than in it!"

It certainly has taken time to develop and cultivate the requisite relationships and community trust necessary to achieve our goals, but over the years we have been able to offer our students largely unimpeded access to Duncans and the surrounding areas. Because we view our relationship with our friends and community partners in Duncans as one characterized by reciprocity and mutual respect, we likewise offer Duncans community members regular access to program activities and interaction with students, and we host several community-themed events during our time in Jamaica. We have subsequently managed to codify authentic interactions that make for deeper, more meaningful, and in many cases lasting relationships between our students and people in Jamaica. When reflected on in formal and informal settings, these very personal, genuine experiences enable participants to expand their capacity to challenge their perceptions and realities. They also enable the program faculty to work with what is emerging within the students, make adjustments to existing opportunities, and set up additional opportunities to continue challenging and steering students in the direction of interconnectedness and solidarity.

Challenges and Reflections

We certainly faced a series of challenges in both the developmental and implementation stages of our study abroad program in Jamaica. Even though USD has a robust rate of student participation in studies abroad, when we proposed the program, ours was the only study abroad experience at USD with a devoted, formally embedded, community service-learning component.[6] Moreover, in building our program we realized that the literature was sparse on study abroad programs that successfully incorporated service-learning. We knew what worked in conventional or local service-learning situations but not what worked in nontraditional, international settings.

An additional challenge that we found remarkable in scope was the extent to which studying in Jamaica has been considered bereft of academic merit—merely a vacation thinly veiled as an academic program. Beyond this more trivial challenge, we have certainly experienced some difficulties associated with building meaningful relationships over the course of a short-term international service-learning program. And, as Jennie Smith-Paríolá and Abíódún Gòkè-Paríolá (2006) noted of their service-learning program also based in Jamaica, a basic concern with any short-term international service-learning program is that it could end up reinforcing and intensifying, rather than challenging, ethnocentric views students pack with them when traveling abroad. We think this is a particularly acute challenge for programs that bring students to the Caribbean. Mythologies, like that of the carefree "yah mon" Jamaican, are routinely reinforced by the cultural distortions packaged in tourism marketing, as well the firsthand experiences of students and their associates who have traveled to the Caribbean but have never experienced "the gully side" or, more simply, the everyday lives of people on the other side of the tourist coin.

Another challenge faced by all service-learning programs, whether domestic or international, is student reluctance to shift out of the "passive learner" role that typifies most classroom-based instruction. For students to take more ownership of their educational experiences, it is important that they shift into a more "active learner" role in which they intellectually grow through meaningful discussion and interaction. This challenge is particularly acute when students are immersed in an international environment where class, race, language, and cultural differences may cause them to feel intimidated and withdraw. We certainly experienced some of this in our Jamaica program and try, early on in each summer session, to break down these barriers by offering children-based service-learning outposts and incorporating Jamaican friends of our program into early-stage activities.

A final challenge that we think worthy of note revolves specifically around our efforts to explore the tensions of learning about Jamaica's postcolonial existence and struggle for dignity through meaningful interactions with Jamaicans. We encourage our students to actively consider through respectful and evocative conversation with Jamaican people what it would be like to live a postcolonial existence in which life choices were fairly limited to careers or jobs in the service sector, specifically that economic sector that caters to predominantly White American and European tourists. However, this ambition poses several challenges. On the one hand, we do not wish our students to "talk down" to the local Jamaicans or present airs of superiority. Furthermore, getting people whose lives are inextricably tied to tourism dollars to speak candidly about their existence to people who, at the end of the day and in spite of their student status, are still tourists can be difficult. And, finally, because our ambition is for our students to develop constructive critiques of postcolonial socioeconomic arrangements, we did not want them to withdraw into resentment or despair.

Conclusion

Smith-Paríolá and Gòkè-Paríolá (2006) made the following statement concerning service-learning, with which we strongly agree:

> A key characteristic of service learning, then, is that it challenges instructors and students to link intellectual engagement with civic engagement and theory to practice. We would argue that, particularly in the context of the United States, closing the gap between academic study and action, between ideas and real world problems, has never been more important. (p. 72)

Despite many of the challenges that come with international service-learning programs, there remains the tremendous potential for transformative experiences that stimulate student development and create deep, meaningful connections with community members abroad. Through our experiences in Jamaica over the past 8 years, we conclude that academic instruction abroad that does not involve a service-learning component can often widen the distance between students and the communities from which they could actively learn so much. By offering students largely unimpeded access to the Duncans community and likewise offering the Duncans community access to program students and staff, we have worked with some success to codify authentic interactions that make for deeper, more meaningful relationships. When reflected on, these very personal, genuine experiences enable student participants to expand their capacity to challenge their perceptions and reconsider their realities.

Ultimately, although we encountered several obstacles both at home and abroad, our case has largely been a success story. At the end of each year's program, student participants complete instructor and program surveys. To date, we have collected over 160 of these evaluations documenting the impact that the Duncans community and Jamaican multidisciplinary international service-learning experience had on our student participants, and they have been largely outstanding. Students uniformly make comments like "This class was an amazing experience" and "This course challenged me emotionally. It also opened my eyes to issues that need to be looked at on a more macro-level. My perspectives have been challenged and changed." Beyond this admittedly gratifying feedback, and perhaps more important, the lasting friendships and partnerships that we and our students have formed with the people of Duncans are a testament to the potential for multidisciplinary international service-learning programs to enhance greatly and transform the way students, faculty, and staff see the world.

Endnotes

1. While still housed primarily at the University of San Diego, this program is also run in partnership with Clayton State University.

2. Current estimates place remittances—nominal money that flows from friends and relatives in industrialized countries back to Jamaica—at nearly 15% of Jamaica's gross domestic product.

3. Mark Titus, "More Trained Labour Force Needed," *The Jamaica Gleaner*, June 3, 2007.

4. Jamaicans typically refer to Kingston as a town and accept Montego Bay as a city, but they refer to most of the smaller communities like Duncans as the country.

5. This is an allusion to the "myth of the happy slave" discussed throughout a good bit of the contemporary literature on colonial plantation life.

6. USD has a well-established and nationally recognized center for community service-learning, and the center staff has for years overseen international service trips. And at least one other study abroad program on campus had opportunities for students to spend time after class once per week with local community members. However, a service-learning component had never been formally embedded in a USD program abroad.

References

Gilroy, P. (1993). *The Black Atlantic: Modernity and double consciousness*. Cambridge, MA: Harvard University Press.

Giovannetti, J. L. (2006). Grounds of race: Slavery, racism and the plantation in the Caribbean. *Latin American and Caribbean Ethnic Studies, 1*(1), 5–36.

Harms, R. (2002). *The diligent: A voyage through the worlds of the slave trade*. New York, NY: Basic Books.

Howard, J. (1998). Academic service learning: A counternormative pedagogy. *New Directions for Teaching and Learning, 73*, 21–29.

Kincaid, J. (1988). *A small place*. New York, NY: Farrar, Straus and Giroux.

King, S. A. (2007). *Reggae, Rastafari, and the rhetoric of social control*. Jackson: University of Mississippi Press.

Lake, O. (1998). *Rastafari women: Subordination in the midst of liberation theology*. Durham, NC: Carolina Academic Press.

Lessor, R., Reeves, M., & Andrade, E. (1997). Interdisciplinary team teaching on sustainable development in Costa Rica. *Teaching Sociology, 25*, 134–149.

Lewis, G. K. (1983). *Main currents in Caribbean thought: The historical evolution of Caribbean society in its ideological aspects, 1492–1900*. Baltimore, MD: Johns Hopkins University Press.

Mitchell, T. D. (2008, Spring). Traditional vs. critical service-learning: Engaging the literature to differentiate two models. *Michigan Journal of Community Service Learning*, 50–65.

Radest, H. B. (1993). *Community service: Encounter with strangers*. Portsmouth, NH: Praeger.

Rice, K., & Pollack, S. (2000). Developing a critical pedagogy of service learning: Preparing self-reflective, culturally aware, and responsive community participants. In C. R. O'Grady (Ed.), *Integrating service learning and multicultural education in colleges and universities* (pp. 115–134). Mahwah, NJ: Lawrence Erlbaum.

Rosenberger, C. (2000). Beyond empathy: Developing critical consciousness through service learning. In C. R. O'Grady (Ed.), *Integrating service learning and multicultural education in colleges and universities* (pp. 23–43). Mahwah, NJ: Lawrence Erlbaum.

Smith-Paríolá, J., & Gòkè-Paríolá, A. (2006). Expanding the parameters of service learning: A case study. *Journal of Studies in International Education, 10*(1), 71–86.

Titus, M. (2007, June 3). More trained labour force needed. *The Jamaica Gleaner*. Retrieved January 17, 2014, from http://jamaica-gleaner.com/gleaner/20070603/business/business3.html

10

TRANSFORMING PRACTICE

International Service-Learning as Preparation for Entering Health Care

Joy Doll, Keli Mu, Lou Jensen, and Julie Hoffman
Creighton University

Caroline Goulet
University of the Incarnate Word

Today's health care professionals face challenges in understanding the complex nature of patient care in this diverse world (Carter-Pokras & Baquet, 2002). Providers must not only be prepared to diagnose and treat within their respective scopes of practice while addressing restriction in participation but also possess the skills to appreciate the impact of clients' and patients' culture and health beliefs on the enablement process. It is not enough for providers to simply understand how a disease or disorder affects a patient biologically; providers must recognize how it influences engagement in activities of daily living and quality of life (Kumagai & Lypson, 2009). Furthermore, factors such as health disparities, low English proficiency, and sociocultural beliefs complicate the knowledge and understanding providers need in order to successfully identify and treat the needs of patients (Bass-Haugen, 2009; Brach & Fraserirector, 2000).

One approach for preparing health professions students to practice in this complex and diverse environment is to engage in learning philosophies that promote critical consciousness. Critical consciousness "involves a reflective awareness of the differences in power and privilege and the inequities that are embedded in social relationships" (Kumagai & Lypson, 2009, p. 783) and facilitates critical thinking based on the concepts put forward by Paulo Freire (1970). An individual who engages in critically conscious thoughts engages in critical self-reflection, moving beyond focus on self to exploring others and injustices that impact others. Critical consciousness is more than simply a thought process; it includes action based on a broad understanding of health and injustice (Kumagai & Lypson, 2009).

Service-learning can act as a pedagogy to help health professions students develop critical consciousness. In authentic service-learning contexts, students must face the complexities of society and make decisions of how to interact with individuals and respond to presented needs (Flecky & Gitlow, 2010). Students are then asked to reflect on these experiences, pulling forth what they have learned about both themselves and others. Service-learning outcomes demonstrate that service-learning increases student self-efficacy, improves awareness of social issues, and facilitates students' awareness of their own values (Astin, Vogelgesang, Ikeda, & Yee, 2000; Mayne & Glascoff, 2002). For health professions students, community service-learning has been demonstrated to impact professional growth and formation, enhance critical thinking skills, and help students develop social responsibility as professionals (Callister & Hobbins-Garbett, 2000). Through an intensive immersion, international service-learning (ISL) provides an opportunity for health professions students to explore a different culture and health care system (Vogel, 2009) and to develop the critical consciousness of caring health professionals. If well designed, ISL can produce and develop professionals who can not only contribute to the health of individual patients but also role model professional behaviors for other providers both internationally and locally (Bentley & Ellison, 2007; Clark, 2000). Furthermore, ISL provides faculty a venue for exploring pedagogy through the Scholarship of Engagement and the Scholarship of Teaching and Learning by developing best practices and exploring student transformation (Boyer, 1990). Fundamentally, international partnerships allow academic institutions to collaborate with international partners to meet the needs in developing countries and to collaborate to define how those needs can continue to be met in a sustainable and community-centered manner (Ansari, Phillips, & Zwi, 2002; Buys & Burnsall, 2007). ISL is best expressed and learned about through experience; however, ISL holds unique challenges requiring strategic thought and consideration needed for each ISL program (Wittmann-Price, Anselmi, & Espinal, 2010). Careful planning and strong institutionalization is needed to ensure a positive impact on both community partners and students (Steiner, Carlough, Dent, Pena, & Morgan, 2010).

Case Example: Institute for Latin American Concern

The Institute for Latin American Concern (ILAC) at Creighton University supports ISL experiences in the Dominican Republic based on the philosophies of Jesuit education. The mission of ILAC is to support "collaborative health care and educational organization that exists to promote the integral well-being and spiritual growth of all its participants" (S. Laird, personal communication, October 2008). The ILAC program offers participants support that includes trained ILAC staff to aid in logistical coordination, food services, and a lodging site for experiences in the Dominican Republic. Furthermore, ILAC helps faculty in identifying community needs and the development and maintenance of service-learning programs that meet the needs of the people. The goal of the program is to provide an immersion experience in the culture and country of the Dominican Republic and offer an opportunity for students to apply their acquired clinical knowledge and skills, along with meeting the ongoing needs of the Dominican people. ILAC offers programs for students across multiple health disciplines including dentistry, medicine, nursing, occupational therapy (OT), pharmacy, and physical therapy (PT).

Student experiences with ILAC last from 3 to 6 weeks depending on the program. Prior to the international immersion, students participate in faculty-developed and faculty-facilitated preparation sessions. These preparation activities vary slightly based on discipline, but the focus includes exploration into the Dominican culture and health beliefs of the people, concepts of global health care practice, and preparation for growth both personally and professionally through the development of reflection skills. A significant focus of the service-learning experience is to examine the role of a health care provider in an underserved global health setting and begin to grasp the role a provider can play in an underserved community. During the experience, students engage in cultural exploration of the Dominican culture, implementation of evaluation and intervention, and patient education. All health-related activities have been identified as important community needs by the Dominican community, the ILAC staff, and the faculty. Outside of clinical learning, reflection and discussion are the main methods used to promote student growth during the experience. Both are facilitated and led by experienced faculty members to help students extract both personal and professional development and promote critical consciousness.

Clinical experiences vary for each discipline based on community needs identified by *cooperadoras* and *promotoras* (i.e., lay health providers trained by ILAC). Some programs are rurally based, providing medical and dental care for rural communities that have no providers and little access to health care. Others are based in Santiago, the city where ILAC is housed, and provide a variety of services for Dominicans with a wide range of physical and cognitive disabilities. For example, in the OT program, an ongoing partnership has been developed with a community-based rehabilitation program. Through this partnership, the OT students and faculty provide in-home therapy assessments and educate lay health providers (i.e., *promotoras*) to provide ongoing care for a variety of children with disabilities. These lay health providers are often mothers of children with disabilities themselves and have a true desire to help both their own and other children in their community. During the experiences, the OT students collaborate with Dominican families and caregivers in the home environment. Furthermore, the students develop recommendations for family members and caregivers based on the in-home assessment to enhance health care and garner skills in international clinical settings. Through clinical interactions, students explore and gain an awareness of the everyday activities and health beliefs of the Dominican people while providing basic care to parents and women who otherwise would not receive it. Students are required to communicate with families in Spanish and, through these interactions, explore the complexities of an underserved international setting and the challenges of a cross-cultural interaction as a provider.

Health professions students receive a variety of credit hours for the ISL experience with ILAC based on their time spent in the country. The inherent success of the program lies in the ongoing partnership with local communities and community organizations that identify health needs that faculty and students can address. A service-learning model ensures the existence of a partnership where both the Dominicans and the students collaborate to meet health needs of the people, developing a critical consciousness in students that carries back to their personal and professional lives in the United States.

Faculty and administrative commitment is critical to the program's success. Administrators support the ILAC program by supporting faculty to immerse themselves with students in the country and also by assisting in financing faculty travel. Faculty are committed to the program sustainability by facilitating the program year after year and training newer faculty to ensure program success relies not on one person but on a collaborative effort. Leaders in the department of each discipline assess faculty interest. On the basis of interest and ability to participate, faculty develop a plan for faculty participation in ISL and collaborate with the lead faculty to prepare students to engage in the experience. Through this process, mentorship and collaboration occurs and ensures the program maintains sustainability. Emphasis is on the ownership of the programming by the entire faculty and not simply an activity assigned to one faculty member. Last, the mission of the institution clearly complements the program and lays the groundwork for the explicit curriculum of the development of clinical skills and the implicit curriculum of developing professionals who exemplify characteristics and behaviors beyond service provision to provision of "care" that not only meets need but also addresses the human spirit.

Case Example: China Honors Immersion Program

The China Honors Immersion Program (CHIP) was launched in 2008 at Creighton University in collaboration with the Third Medical Hospital of Hebei Province to help promote cultural understanding and exchange, cultivate cultural sensitivity and competency, foster international leadership, and increase international collaborations in health education and research. CHIP was developed as a cross-cultural, interprofessional, and collaborative program involving faculty and students from Creighton's School of Pharmacy and Health Professions' OT and PT programs, School of Nursing's nurse practitioner (NP) program, and medical doctors and rehabilitation specialists from a university medical center in China. The underlying premise was that such international collaborative efforts could mutually benefit the professional education and provision of health care services, especially rehabilitation, in both the United States and China. This goal is of particular importance as China's rehabilitation system and services are developing (Zongjie, Hong, Zhongxin, & Hui, 2007). CHIP also exemplifies Creighton University's mission in action: "Service to others . . . and appreciation of ethnic and cultural diversity."

CHIP originated out of the ongoing active involvement between university-affiliated hospitals and medical universities in China initiated and developed by a Creighton OT faculty member who garnered administrative support. CHIP consists of a two-credit-hour interprofessional elective course offered to OT, PT, and NP students at Creighton University. Through interprofessional service-learning in hospital settings in China, this course intends to increase participants' cultural awareness and competency, facilitate clinical reasoning, and foster leadership development for societal and global health concerns, along with educate the people of China.

Because of the resources of the partners in China, a limited number of students can participate in CHIP. This interprofessional education course is competitive in nature, requiring students to apply or be recommended by faculty. Students must be in good academic standing, submit a reflective essay expressing their desire to participate, and complete an interview. A member from each academic discipline participates in the ISL experience to China to provide clinical expertise and guidance to the students. Faculty have been identified and developed through a train-the-trainer model to ensure faculty are prepared for the ISL experience and foster a sustainable program.

The train-the-trainer model is an important aspect of the sustainability of the programming. Furthermore, sustainability is a critical component of ISL, and the preparation of faculty cannot be overlooked in the development and implementation of sustainable ISL programs (Pechak & Thompson, 2009; Steiner et al., 2010). The model for CHIP works through the rotation of faculty participants as leaders of the program. Each year, two faculty members participate in leading the program, with one main leader mentoring the other faculty member. To garner faculty support and interest, the leaders in each department poll faculty members to determine who desires to participate in the ISL experience in China. On the basis of this survey, faculty are assigned and must commit to the program for 2 years. In a faculty member's first year of participation in CHIP, he or she assists in communicating with partners in China and preparing the students. The second year, that faculty member takes the lead and mentors the secondary faculty member for leadership the following year. Thus far this model has been a success, and with the commitment of multiple disciplines, it ensures that one department does not always take the lead, avoiding faculty burnout.

Students engage in the interprofessional education course that includes preparation followed by an immersion in China. Students and faculty participate in a series of five seminars focused on awareness of cultural competency, understanding of the Chinese culture, and preparatory activities for the clinical learning experience consisting of developing patient-care presentations for rehabilitation personnel at facilities in China. During a mid-semester break, students and faculty engage in the 10-day ISL experience in China. During the ISL, students work in interprofessional small groups (e.g., two to four OT, PT, and NP students) under the supervision of the faculty to provide direct rehabilitation services to patients in the hosting hospitals in order to meet patient needs and educate Chinese providers. Students interview patients and families to determine patients' participation restrictions, evaluate functional abilities, and develop long-term and short-term rehabilitation goals and objectives.

Through the provision of hands-on direct patient care, students teach and demonstrate therapeutic theories and specific rehabilitation techniques, as well as the use of adaptive equipment to maximize the function and participation of the patient. With the assistance of interpreters, students also instruct and coach patients and families in home programs to maximize patients' independence and strengthen preventative care such as managing skin issues and maintaining appropriate positioning in beds and wheelchairs. In addition, students and faculty engage in various educational sessions for rehabilitation personnel in the local and regional areas. These sessions include group presentations, small workshops, and modeling of the value of interprofessional, holistic patient care. These educational offerings are designed to improve the Chinese rehabilitation personnel's awareness and understanding of OT, PT, and nursing service delivery in the United States and deepen and broaden their knowledge and skills in rehabilitation and advocate for evidence-based rehabilitation.

Throughout the experience, students are exposed to the Chinese culture through sharing in the day-to-day life of their Chinese colleagues, including visiting homes, sharing meals, and participating in social and professional activities. It is of critical importance to emphasize that the Chinese partners desire to learn more about the American health care system and that the education and interventions are based on feedback from the health professional partners in China and not the desire of Creighton University. The purpose and goal of the program is not to encourage the partner to adopt American health care practices but, instead, to be aware of the benefits of rehabilitation as offered in the United States. Rehabilitation professions such as OT and PT are not widely used or understood in China, making them of interest to the partner.

Ambassadors of the host hospital strive to ensure the CHIP faculty and students are well cared for during their time in China and that they gain exposure to many aspects of the Chinese culture. The daily schedule is full of structured time at the hospital, visits to local cultural and historical landmarks, and traditional Chinese meals that last several hours and allow collegial exchange of customs and discussions. Because of the desires of the host country and the culture, a scarcity of free time in which to engage in structured reflection during the immersion exists. However, while participating in the daily activities of the immersion experience, students are always encouraged to engage in reflection by posing questions and through prompting from the faculty, much as a clinical instructor would do with a student. Because of these important factors, the bulk of formal and structured reflection also comes once the CHIP participants return to the United States in the context of the interprofessional course.

Upon returning from China, students are required to take part in a debriefing session in which reflection and synthesis of the experience is encouraged. They also gain experience in a leadership role by sharing their ISL experience through a presentation to faculty, staff, and students at the school. The intent of these activities is to benefit other students of the school through such peer-to-peer education and facilitate students to develop a critical consciousness by reflecting on the larger meaning of the ISL experience. Other discrete strategies such as short journal entries could also be implemented in the future to promote students' reflection.

Development and Maintenance of International Partnerships

Community partnerships have been demonstrated as a successful approach to addressing health concerns (Becker, Israel, & Allen, 2005; Roussos & Fawcett, 2000). A critical piece for any service-learning experience is the community partner. Essentially, service-learning cannot be a successful pedagogy without partnerships in place that connect students to community members and in which students help meet needs an organization cannot address alone, as exampled with both ILAC and CHIP. Obviously, the challenges to community health cannot be addressed without collaboration, and health care practitioners need to engage in collaboration to be successful in addressing community need and ensuring the need being addressed is that identified by the community and not the provider (Becker et al., 2005; Fazio, 2008). Research has shown that academic-community partnerships can aid in improving student education, addressing health disparities, and increasing health care access for communities (Commission on Community-Engaged Scholarship in the Health Professions, 2005). These types of partnerships are common models for implementing service-learning, both locally and internationally. Despite the benefits, collaborating and developing community partnerships can be time-consuming and challenging, further complicated in international settings where cultural differences and language barriers may be factors (Becker et al., 2005). Research has shown that developing and maintaining partnerships takes time, commitment, and open communication to develop the mutual trust required for true exchange in a partnership (Burhansstipanov, Dignan, Wound, Tenney, & Vigil, 2000; Kagawa-Singer, 1997; LaMarca, Wiese, Pete, & Carbone, 1996; Poole & Van Hook, 1997). Faculty and administration must be committed to allow time for the partnership to develop to ensure all entities benefit from ISL. Examples of both of these important factors in ISL occur with both ILAC and CHIP in which both programs are faculty and administratively supported with strong commitments to sustainability.

A complication of ISL is the integration of multiple cultures. Faculty must be knowledgeable and capable of cross-cultural brokering in order to develop and maintain international partnerships. For example, in CHIP, the faculty member who started the program originates from China and was critical in developing the program. In some cases, distrust among community partnerships can be due to cultural differences among partners, rather than misintention (Bringle & Hatcher, 2002). Learning the culture and dealing with the challenges of cross-cultural relationships presents a challenge for an outsider. In most ISL experiences, the program leader may come from a different cultural background than the partner and the community being served. This is certainly the case for ILAC in which no faculty who participate in the program come from a Dominican background, requiring each faculty member involved to learn about the culture and country prior to participation. A lack of cultural awareness and cultural sensitivity can cause challenges due to potential differences in communication and health beliefs among cultural groups (Bringle & Hatcher, 2002). Furthermore, faculty members have to be aware of their cultural biases and not let these infiltrate the partnership or the service-learning program. Faculty must not only learn the culture and health beliefs of the country in which the service-learning occurs but also be aware of the health care infrastructure and how providers are viewed. All of this information is critical to ensure service-learning is successful not only for the students but also for the international partner.

One approach to developing a reliable and sustainable service-learning partnership is to recruit faculty committed to learning about the culture, health beliefs, and health care infrastructure of any country where ISL is done. These faculty members will become role models for others in terms of cultural sensitivity and health beliefs. For the sake of building and developing sustainable partnerships, faculty members must understand the importance of continuity and be willing to commit for more than a onetime experience. To have more than one faculty member involved every year helps develop the continuity and sustainability of the programming. In both ILAC and CHIP, the commitment of multiple faculty has been critical to not only the ongoing sustainability of the programs but also the success and growth of the programs.

Another approach is to allow a faculty member to immerse him or herself in the country prior to taking or being responsible for students. This immersion may occur with another group or through a fellowship such as Fulbright. Faculty members who have had time and experience with the culture are better prepared to both lead and teach a group of students. For example, the OT ILAC program coordinator participated in two trips with the PT group to gain cultural knowledge and experience prior to developing an OT program in the Dominican Republic. Through these trips, the faculty member was able to grasp community needs, cultural beliefs, and trip logistics and begin to develop a relationship with a community partner. The dean of the school provided the financing for these trips, ensuring the professional development required for the OT faculty member to be successful in developing, implementing, and maintaining the ISL experience. To address the language barrier, the faculty member took it upon herself to learn basic Spanish and currently provides community service with a local community partner that requires her to communicate in Spanish to maintain her skills.

Maintenance of partnerships is key to ensure ongoing sustainability of ISL (Adams, Miller-Korth, & Brown, 2004). Faculty members must commit to getting feedback from international partners about the service-learning experience to continue to improve the experiences and meet community needs. Furthermore, faculty members must engage in ongoing communication with

community partners to continue to develop the relationship when not residing in the country. In the examples of ILAC and CHIP, this occurs through
ongoing communication seeking feedback through dialogue and electronic
communication. ILAC sponsors yearly visits by partners to Creighton for
meetings and collaboration. To support CHIP, Creighton has hosted three
physicians from China in the United States for a semester to learn about
health care in the States and demonstrate the reciprocity of the partnership.
Administrators need to allot faculty time to revise ISL experiences as needed
to ensure their ongoing success.

Health Professions Student Preparation for ISL

Students may be excited about international experiences but are in need of
preparation prior to such an experience. Student preparation is critical to
ensure that students can be successful in ISL experiences where culture shock
and language barriers can pose significant challenges to student learning
(Haq et al., 2000). Both ILAC and CHIP have preparation programs that
provide students with opportunities to be thoughtful in their preparation
for the culture and the needs of patients. On the basis of the experience
and expertise of the faculty members involved in ISL, preparation reduces
the impact of culture shock and orients students toward critical consciousness both during the experience and beyond. Students tend to be anxious
about logistical factors of the experience, like where sleeping occurs and what
will be eaten. Although meals can be rich cultural experiences, they can also
quickly be a barrier if a student is not prepared and unsure of what to do at
mealtime. Student preparation and faculty support can reduce some of these
challenges.

Faculty should be careful not to build false expectations for students but
to provide them with objective information about logistics and an introduction to basic cultural beliefs like greetings, proxemics, and proper eating
procedures for meals (Imperato, 2004). These preparation experiences also
demonstrate to students how to explore and gain their own cultural knowledge in preparation for future practice with diverse individuals, both locally
and abroad. All of this is discussed in the preparation curriculums for both
CHIP and ILAC. For example, the concept of White privilege often arises in
the Dominican Republic, so students spend time reading about and exploring the concept of White privilege, and faculty leaders provide examples of
how White privilege influences the relationships during the ILAC experience.
Another important aspect is that the preparation curriculum is developed
around faculty experiences and emerged out of the observation of issues and

students facing challenges dealing with the concept of White privilege during the experience. Preparation experiences also provide students an opportunity to begin to gain skills in critical consciousness by reflecting on cultural differences and their expectations for health care provision (Chiang & Carlson, 2003). Students are highly influenced by the belief that the American health care system is the "best" and can often let that bias infiltrate care when faced with different practices in vastly different cultural contexts. Faculty need to prepare students both before and during the experience to reflect on these biases and resolve professionally how they will act when health care delivery services differ from theirs (Imperato, 2004). In both CHIP and ILAC, this preparation is done through the use of cases and faculty sharing their experiences and challenges with cultural differences.

Reflective Practices for ISL

Reflection remains a critical component to the application and processing of knowledge in service-learning pedagogy. Reflection has long been studied since being introduced by Dewey (1933) and further studied by experts like Kolb (1984). Reflection is a valuable teaching tool, helping students "develop the capacity for critical thought if they are challenged both by surprising experiences and by reflective teachers who help them explore these experiences and question their fundamental assumptions about their world" (Eyler, 2002, p. 521). Reflection, as mentioned, is important to developing critical consciousness.

Research in service-learning has demonstrated that service-learning experiences with high levels of reflection promote students' abilities to problem solve complex issues, a skill needed by health care providers (Eyler, 2002). But reflection is not automatic and needs to be constructed for students in a way that challenges them to engage in critical thought processes (Eyler, 2002). Eyler (2002) argued that for reflection to be effective in impacting cognitive development in students, it has to be rich and occur at multiple levels. Students should reflect individually, in small groups, and with community partners on a continuum from prior to the service, during service experiences, and after the service experience.

The implementation of the ISL programs of CHIP and ILAC have revealed the following best practices for reflection based on experience and support from the literature:

1. Daily group reflection is a critical component to the learning experience. However, an experienced faculty member can read the group to

determine whether more frequent reflection is needed. As students progress individually at different rates and learn different concepts from the experience, some students may require one-on-one reflection with a faculty member to explore and delve into issues. Participants are also encouraged to reflect informally with one another. After the experience, students are asked to engage in an online reflection about 2 weeks to 1 month after their experience to continue to explore the meaning of the experience.

2. Guiding questions need to be provided to help students form a starting point, but reflection should be open to what the students feel is important to discuss. In the course syllabus for both ILAC and CHIP, reflection questions are provided to students to give them a guide and framework for effective reflection. On the basis of the mission of the institution, the Ignatian values are used as a framework for reflecting and promoting reflective practice.

3. The faculty member should monitor the reflection, allowing students to express themselves in a constructive manner, and guide the group toward constructive reflective practices. Reflection sessions should not be a time to complain but, instead, be an opportunity for students to explore uncomfortable feelings and thoughts. Students are also encouraged to engage in individual, private reflection to continue to hone this professional skill. Spontaneous reflection is important as well and may be needed when a group has experienced something atypical or unpredicted. In both ILAC and CHIP, faculty recognize the need to be available to students for reflection before, during, and after the ISL experience.

Administrative Support for ISL

For ISL to be viable and sustainable, administrative support is crucial (Bringle & Hatcher, 2000). Faculty members with a desire to develop and implement ISL courses need assistance in the development and maintenance of partnerships. Institutionalization of ISL ensures that the programs are ongoing and can continue educating students and meeting international needs (Bringle & Hatcher, 2000). The development of electives brings in revenue; however, the institution needs financial support to fund faculty travel and stay during ISL experiences.

In both CHIP and ILAC, administrative support for ISL is in congruence with the mission of Creighton University where both programs are housed. As a Catholic, Jesuit, and comprehensive university, Creighton exists for students and learning. Creighton is committed to service to others and appreciation of ethnic and cultural diversity. The strong administrative support also comes from a clear vision for and understanding of the inherent benefits of ISL to both student and faculty development, along with the formation of critical consciousness in the health care providers of tomorrow. Furthermore, accreditation standards across the health professions require educators to address cultural awareness, which can be honed during ISL. Accreditation standards facilitate a need to offer such experiences to health professions students and for administrators to support such efforts.

It should be highlighted that implementation of ISL programming is not without hesitation, roadblocks, and challenges for both administrators and faculty (Hartley, Harkavy, & Benson, 2005). In addition to the top-down administrative support, bottom-up individual commitment is also crucial for the success of such programs, as is demonstrated with both CHIP and ILAC. Strong personal interest, desire, commitment, and dedication from faculty and staff are also key ingredients for the realization and success of ISL. Faculty collaboration and the commitment of a department to a program are critical to its sustainability and have ensured the success of ILAC and CHIP.

Conclusion

ISL can provide a profound pedagogy for educating health professions students in preparation for current health care practice. Developing critically conscious health care providers both ensures quality care for individual patients and promotes tomorrow's professionals to advocate for social injustices commonly associated with the health care system (Kumagai & Lypson, 2009). Both ILAC and CHIP demonstrate the importance of faculty and administrative commitment to international partnerships to develop and implement ISL programs meaningful to patients served and to maximize student learning. Although ISL may appear challenging, if well planned and developed, it can offer learning experiences to health professions students that are transformative. CHIP and ILAC both demonstrate the importance of faculty recruitment and training for maintenance of strong ISL experiences. For successful and sustainable ISL, as demonstrated through both CHIP and ILAC, student preparation is critical to success of the program to ensure students have a positive learning experience and are accurately able to serve community partners during the experience. Collaboration with community partners ensures that ISL remains community centered, focusing on the needs of communities rather than the academic institution. Despite its complexities, ISL can be done well, with strong intention, and can transform the lives of faculty, students, and community partners.

References

Adams, A., Miller-Korth, N., & Brown, D. (2004). Learning to work together: Developing academic and community research partnerships. *Wisconsin Medical Journal, 103*(2), 15–19.

Ansari, W. E., Phillips, C. J., & Zwi, A. B. (2002). Narrowing the gap between academic professional wisdom and community lay knowledge: Perceptions from partnerships. *Public Health, 16*(3), 151–159.

Astin, A. W., Vogelgesang, L. J., Ikeda, E. K., & Yee, J. A. (2000). *How service-learning affects students*. Los Angeles, CA: Higher Education Research Institute.

Bass-Haugen, J. D. (2009). Health disparities: Examination of evidence relevant for occupational therapy. *American Journal of Occupational Therapy, 63*, 24–34.

Becker, A. B., Israel, B. A., & Allen, A. J. (2005). Strategies and techniques for effective group process in CBPR partnerships. In B. A. Israel, E. Eng, A. J. Schulz, & E. A. Parker (Eds.), *Methods in community-based participatory research for health* (pp. 52–72). San Francisco, CA: Jossey-Bass.

Bentley, R., & Ellison, K. (2007). Increasing cultural competence in nursing through international service-learning experiences. *Nurse Educator, 32*(5), 207–211.

Boyer, E. (1990). *Scholarship reconsidered*. Princeton, NJ: Carnegie Foundation for the Advancement of Teaching.

Brach, C., & Fraserirector, I. (2000). Can cultural competency reduce racial and ethnic health disparities? A review and a conceptual model. *Medical Care Research and Review, 57*, 181–217.

Bringle, R. G., & Hatcher, J. A. (2000). Institutionalization of service-learning in higher education. *Journal of Higher Education, 71*(3), 273–290.

Bringle, R. G., & Hatcher, J. A. (2002). Campus-community partnerships: The terms of engagement. *Journal of Social Issues, 58*(3), 503–516.

Burhansstipanov, L., Dignan, M. B., Wound, D. B., Tenney, M., & Vigil, G. (2000). Native American recruitment into breast cancer screening: The NAWWA project. *Cancer Education, 15*, 28–32.

Buys, N., & Burnsall, S. (2007). Establishing university-community partnerships: Processes and benefits. *Journal of Higher Education Policy and Management, 29*(1), 73–86.

Callister, L. C., & Hobbins-Garbett, D. (2000). "Enter to learn, go forth to serve": Service learning in nursing education. *Journal of Professional Nursing, 16*(3), 177–183.

Carter-Pokras, O., & Baquet, C. (2002). What is a "health disparity"? *Public Health Reports, 117*, 424–434.

Chiang, M., & Carlson, G. (2003). Occupational therapy in multicultural contexts: Issues and strategies. *British Journal of Occupational Therapy, 66*(12), 559–567.

Clark, G. (2000). Messages from Josefa: Service learning in Mexico. *Language and Learning Across the Disciplines, 4*(3), 76–80.

Commission on Community-Engaged Scholarship in the Health Professions. (2005). *Linking scholarship and communities: Report of the Commission on Community-Engaged Scholarship in the Health Professions*. Seattle, WA: Community-Campus Partnerships for Health.

Dewey, J. (1933). *How we think: A restatement of the relation of reflective thinking to the educative process.* Boston, MA: D.C. Heath.

Eyler, J. (2002). Reflection: Linking service and learning; Linking students and communities. *Journal of Social Issues, 58*(3), 517–534.

Fazio, L. (2008). *Developing occupation-centered programs for the community* (2nd ed.). Upper Saddle River, NJ: Prentice Hall.

Flecky, K., & Gitlow, L. (2010). *Service-learning in occupational therapy: Philosophy and practice.* Boston, MA: Jones & Bartlett.

Freire, P. (1970). *Pedagogy of the oppressed.* New York, NY: Continuum.

Haq, C., Rothenberg, D., Gjerde, C., Bobula, J., Wilson, C., Bickley, L., Cardelle, A., & Joseph, A. (2000). New world views: Preparing physicians in training for global health work. *Family Medicine, 32*(8), 566–572.

Hartley, M., Harkavy, I., & Benson, L. (2005). Putting down roots in the groves of the academe: The challenges of institutionalizing service-learning. In D. Butin (Ed.), *Service-learning in higher education* (pp. 205–222). New York, NY: Palgrave Macmillan.

Imperato, P. J. (2004). A third world international health elective for U.S. medical students: The 25-year experience of the state university of New York, Downstate Medical Center. *Journal of Community Health, 29*(5), 337–373.

Kagawa-Singer, M. (1997). Addressing issues for early detection and screening in ethnic populations. *Oncology Nursing Forum, 24*(10), 1705–1711.

Kolb, D. A. (1984). *Experiential learning: Experience as the source of learning and development.* Englewood Cliffs, NJ: Prentice Hall.

Kumagai, A. K., & Lypson, M. L. (2009). Beyond cultural competence: Critical consciousness, social justice, and multicultural education. *Academic Medicine, 84*(6), 782–787.

LaMarca, K., Wiese, K. R., Pete, J. E., & Carbone, P. P. (1996). A progress report of cancer centers and tribal communities: Building a partnership based on trust. *Cancer, 78*(Suppl. 7), 1633–1637.

Mayne, L., & Glascoff, M. (2002). Service learning: Preparing a healthcare workforce for the next century. *Nurse Educator, 27*(4), 191–194.

Pechak, C. M., & Thompson, M. (2009). A conceptual model of optimal international service-learning and its application to global health initiatives in rehabilitation. *Physical Therapy, 89*(11), 192–204.

Poole, D., & Van Hook, M. (1997). Retooling for community health partnerships in primary care and prevention. *Health and Social Work, 22*(1), 2–4.

Roussos, S. T., & Fawcett, S. B. (2000). A review of collaborative partnerships as a strategy for improving community health. *Annual Reviews of Public Health, 21*, 369–402.

Steiner, B. D., Carlough, M., Dent, G., Pena, R., & Morgan, D. R. (2010). International crises and global health electives: Lessons for faculty and institutions. *Academic Medicine, 85*(10), 1560–1563.

Vogel, A. (2009). *Advancing service-learning in health professions education: Maximizing sustainability, quality and co-leadership.* Retrieved from https://depts.washington.edu/ccph/pdf_files/Amanda%20Vogel%20Doctoral%20Dissertation.pdf

Wittmann-Price, R. A., Anselmi, K. K., & Espinal, F. (2010). Creating opportunities for successful international student service-learning experiences. *Holistic Nursing Practice, 24*(2), 89–98.

Zongjie, Y., Hong, D., Zhongxin, X., & Hui, X. (2007). A research study into the requirements of disabled residents for rehabilitation services in Beijing. *Rehabilitation in Practice, 29*, 825–833.

11

INTERNATIONAL SERVICE-LEARNING IN FAITH-BASED CONTEXTS

Paul Kollman and Rachel Tomas Morgan
University of Notre Dame

L ong before the recent proliferation of international service-learning (ISL) courses across a range of U.S. universities, a number of universities and colleges had made international experience a prominent part of their desired undergraduate curricula. For many, the international experience was part of a desire to instill a vocation to serve in their students, a desire often rooted in their institutions' founding religious traditions.[1] The Center for Global Education at Augsburg College in Minnesota, the Human Needs and Global Resources (HNGR) program at Wheaton College in Illinois, and the Study-Service Term at Goshen College in Indiana are excellent examples of early ISL pioneers, and each reflects the faith-inspired values of its Christian tradition: respectively, Lutheran, nondenominational Evangelical, and Anabaptist-Mennonite.[2]

In this chapter we will explore a number of critical questions that arise in connection to ISL when it is pursued at religiously affiliated (or faith-based)[3] universities, a topic largely overlooked in service-learning literature.[4] We will do so by focusing on the International Summer Service Learning Program (ISSLP) at the University of Notre Dame,[5] a program whose approach is informed by and rooted in the faith-based mission of its Catholic sponsoring institution. Drawing on experiences with the course, in particular recent assessment data on outcomes of the course that showed significant changes in the worldviews of student participants, we will make a twofold argument. First, ISL in faith-based contexts has important potential to help students connect their deepest convictions—often rooted in their religious self-understanding—to their broader education. It thus behooves religiously affiliated universities to utilize their distinctive religious foundations as they integrate ISL into their broader educational goals. Second, the field of ISL can also benefit from faith-based universities' ISL efforts in two interrelated ways. First, ISL at faith-based universities, like service-learning in general, offers models for how universities as institutions can become productive members of the variety of communities they engage—locally and globally. Second, by helping to responsibly integrate religious identity in learning, it assists in attempts to help U.S. university students bring various facets of their education into a coherent and integrated process in pursuit of preparation for responsible global citizenship.[6]

To advance these two arguments—one addressed to religiously affiliated universities in particular, the other to the ISL field as a whole—we will first describe the ISSLP and then discuss results from a recent assessment undertaken to determine its outcomes among students. We then use such results to consider tensions that inevitably arise because of the course's theological orientation and, by implication, the university's Catholic character in light of broader conversations in the U.S. academy about the place of moral and civic education in universities more generally. Without denying these tensions, we will conclude this chapter by making suggestions for ISL based in other religiously affiliated universities and also consider what such universities' efforts in ISL might contribute to the broader field.

Notre Dame's International Summer Service Learning Program

Since its inception in 1983, the Center for Social Concerns at the University of Notre Dame has closely aligned itself with the university's mission, which includes as a stated goal the following:

> To cultivate in its students not only an appreciation for the great achievements of human beings, but also a disciplined sensibility to the poverty, injustice, and oppression that burden the lives of so many. The aim is to create a sense of human solidarity and concern for the common good that will bear fruit as learning becomes service to justice.[7]

The center has sought to fulfill the university's mission through community-based learning, research, and service.[8] Beginning in 1998, the center has also granted opportunities for students to pursue the ideals of Notre Dame's mission within a global context through the ISSLP, which places students in service-learning settings with nongovernmental and faith-based organizations around the world.

When the ISSLP was being developed in the mid-1990s, the term *international service-learning* was virtually nonexistent in service-learning literature.[9]

Promising practices in service-learning were then evolving with more clarity, but they mostly focused on the domestic U.S. context.[10] In designing the ISSLP, the program's founding director researched programs that combined community service and alternative models for study abroad then under way.[11] Since then the course has evolved in a variety of ways, though the fundamental structure has remained constant.

The ISSLP operates as a two-part "bookend" course, so that its formal class time occurs in two courses that meet within the semesters before and after the 8-week overseas summer service-learning field component. Both courses are housed in Notre Dame's Department of Theology. The first is a one-credit, spring-semester course, the "Global Issues Seminar," that prepares students for the summer abroad experience. Adopting an interdisciplinary approach, most of the spring seminar's weekly 2-hour sessions are led by faculty from various units and departments in the university or prominent experts in a particular field who are invited as guest lecturers to introduce students to pertinent global issues.[12] Class topics include globalization, human rights, global health, immigration and migration, the UN Millennium Development Goals, global poverty, international development, and security. The overarching framework of the seminar, in line with that of the Center for Social Concerns as a whole, is the Catholic social tradition and social analysis inspired by that tradition, which together provide a critical lens through which students are invited to interpret an array of global issues.[13]

One significant element of the spring course is a reflective weekend gathering that becomes an occasion for powerful community building and discernment. The students leave campus for a few days together in order to prepare their minds, hearts, and spirits for the summer. Along with the theological and spiritual aspects discussed next, a significant part of the weekend focuses on sensitivity to new cultural realities. A cross-cultural simulation activity is followed by a discussion with a social anthropologist, which then leads into a series of panel sessions featuring past ISSLP students. Former participants describe practical issues living abroad, share their struggles with intercultural communication, and discuss the phenomenon of reverse culture shock and other reentry issues. They also share what they learned and how they continue to live out their ISSLP experience.

The summer field component itself and reentry requirements in the fall semester compose the second theology course, titled "Confronting International Social Issues." During their service-learning abroad, students continue their academic reading and writing. Upon return to campus, they complete evaluation forms and assessment surveys, select journal excerpts for submission and evaluation, and prepare an integrative paper or project.[14] They also participate in a reentry weekend and several class sessions focusing on continued integration of their summer experience with the academic readings. Each student has an individual debriefing session with a member of the ISSLP staff aimed at further distilling the learning that has occurred, drawing out the challenges the students faced, and exploring the questions that surfaced for them. Returnees finally give a public presentation on their ISSLP, often in their residence hall.

At the heart of the ISSLP is of course the 8-week service-learning experience abroad. The course has grown steadily in interest over the years, recently selecting 50 students from several hundred applicants and placing them in pairs in 16 countries in Latin America, Africa, and Asia. Students are selected and matched by their interests, prior community service or service-learning experiences, skills, and academic disciplines with the organization's mission, scope of work, and other selection criteria. The ISSLP prioritizes partnerships in developing countries in accordance with a key principle of Catholic social teaching:[15] a preferential option for the poor. Such partnerships allow students to serve and learn in a variety of contexts, including health care, education, orphan care, microenterprise, capacity building, advocacy, and increasingly through project- and community-based research initiatives. Although varied in scope, all the service-learning placements are carefully selected to fulfill the course objective of providing for students a multidimensional understanding of poverty through the critical and analytical lens of Catholic social teaching.

The International Summer Service-Learning Program Assessment and Research Findings[16]

The ISSLP was developed specifically to challenge students who already had domestic service-learning experiences. The program articulates three learning goals,[17] hoping students will gain the following: (a) an understanding of the multidimensionality of poverty in the developing world by analyzing root causes and identifying strategies for social development and poverty alleviation; (b) an awareness of global social issues in light of Catholic social teaching, specifically through the themes of solidarity and the preferential option for the poor; and (c) increased cross-cultural competency.

Since the inception of the program, evaluations have been collected from students and site partners that have informed and improved the ISSLP course design in line with these goals. Yet evaluations are only a fraction of the assessment process, a rather rough tool to gather feedback for improvement on aspects of course design and instruction. Broader assessment asks, What have our students learned, how well have they learned it, and how successful have we been at what we are trying to accomplish?[18] Results from assessment are then used to improve strategies for learning and to provide evidence of impact.

Anecdotal evidence and evaluations have been used to reshape and adapt the ISSLP from the beginning. Recently, however, the Center for Social Concerns has devoted significant resources to study more formally the outcomes of its courses and programs on student learning across a variety of measures. In 2008–2009, it conducted an assessment of its service-learning and community-based-learning courses, which range in duration from 48-hour and 1-week seminars to the 8-week domestic and international summer service-learning programs.[19] All such courses are credit bearing and include academic readings, written assignments, and classes before and after the field component. Among the results were findings that showed that students in the summer service-learning programs, both domestic and international, showed significant changes in five variables or outcomes measured, all related to justice and inequality: openness to diversity, an empowerment view of helping, belief in a just world, social dominance orientation, and a self-generating view of helping.[20]

Two of these, *belief in a just world* (BJW) and *social dominance orientation* (SDO), merit special attention. Both are widely employed in psychological research, and they are considered personality variables that gauge deeply felt worldviews and assumptions. BJW identifies the extent to which one believes that the world, as it is, is a just place, that is, that people deserve their lot in life: In general, good things happen to good people, and bad things happen to bad people (Dalbert, Montada, & Schmitt, 1987). It is linked to the just world hypothesis that states, "Individuals have a need to believe that they live in a world where people generally get what they deserve" (Lerner & Miller, 1978, p. 1030). One's degree of that need can be measured in terms of BJW.

SDO conveys one's acceptance of, and even preference for, inequality among social groups, that is, for hierarchy within a social system and group-based dominance in general. SDO stems from social dominance theory, which describes human society as consisting of oppressive group-based hierarchy structures and assumes that one's general inclination toward group dominance can be measured in terms of SDO (Pratto, Sidanius, Stallworth, & Malle, 1994).

It had been anticipated that engaging in these courses might lead to reductions in BJW and SDO, and the results supported such predictions. Paired *t*-tests showed that students had lower levels of BJW and SDO after the course than before ($ps < .01$). These results are statistically significant given that the overall sample was fairly small.[21] Because BJW and SDO are generally regarded as individual characteristics or personality traits, and not malleable learning outcomes, these results suggest that a single summer service-learning course, domestic or international, is associated with change in these deep worldviews. This finding is further supported because it was found that taking a one-credit service-learning course is *not* associated with such changes in BJW and SDO.[22] In addition, despite the presence of numerous possible significant predictors of incoming SDO, analyses predicting changes in BJW and SDO during the course found that no independent variable predicted changes in either of the two outcomes.[23] These results suggest that the educational efficacy of these courses is similar regardless of student demographics and their motivation for taking the course. The center's summer service-learning courses are responsible for these pre-post differences.

These changes in BJW and SDO in the students are important for this discussion because they indicate an outcome of greater openness in our students to social justice.[24] After all, it is logical to assume that a commitment to social justice corresponds to lower measures of BJW and SDO. Assuming that a high BJW means that an individual sees a great deal of suffering as somehow earned or deserving by those who suffer, a lower BJW suggests one sees that the world is in need of repair in a structural sense to lessen such suffering. Similarly, high SDO reflects people's orientation and acceptance for social hierarchy and domination that accepts a certain level of inequality for certain social groups, whereas people with low SDO are more concerned with others' well-being and prefer more egalitarian relationships among people. Instead of seeing one's lot in life as often deserved (high BJW) and inequality as predetermined or even desirable (high SDO), those committed to working for social justice tend to trace social issues such as ongoing poverty and lack of access to health care to causes that can and should be counteracted.

These findings have implications for service-learning more generally. A common critique states that students can be involved in many service-learning programs without conceptualizing the social issues beyond the direct one-on-one relationships that they form. However, the center's research suggests that there are rather significant changes in summer service-learners' orientations relevant to social justice and represents a significant finding about what needs to occur in service-learning courses, both domestic and international, for students to gain further insight into issues of social justice and inequality.

The changes that indicate transformation in ISSLP participants' perspectives signal the kind of worldview transformation that many proponents of ISL seek. They also indicate changes that a Catholic university is glad to see in its students. After all, Catholic social teaching presents structural injustice and oppression of social groups as appropriately requiring mitigation by human effort, linking a commitment to social justice to lived faith. Decreases in BJW and SDO among participants, therefore, suggest that one of the stated goals of the ISSLP, to instill perspectives from Catholic social teaching, in particular a commitment to social justice, seemingly is being achieved.

Tensions and Possibilities in Faith-Based International Service-Learning

These recent assessment results, which identify changing ethical worldviews among service-learning students, link the ISSLP and similar programs to a larger conversation and debate about the purposes of universities. This conversation has raised two different sorts of issues relevant to a discussion about service-learning and, by extension, ISL: first, the overall role of universities in society and, second, the specific task of university education in shaping students.[25] Though the conversation is multifaceted, at one end, educators like John Mearsheimer and Stanley Fish contend that universities should not aim to be social-service providers or aspire to a role in the moral, ethical, or civic education of their students.[26] To do so is to betray their role as universities. Instead, they should focus on the production of knowledge and the education of students in line with disciplinary expectations, regarding any other services offered to local communities, the larger world, or individual students as a by-product of those primary tasks. For their part, in their teaching of students, professors should offer their discipline-bound interpretations and invite students to grow in their own similar interpretive capacity, with any task beyond imparting interpretation considered beyond the university's role.[27] Others, however, believe that an institution of higher learning invariably affects the places and communities in which it operates and thus ought to do so responsibly. Also, higher education does not avoid imparting moral-ethical guidance to students. In light of such inevitability, higher education must be self-conscious about how it both serves its neighbors and other interlocutors and forms its students in ways beyond the strictly academic.

Faith-based universities that pursue ISL obviously have stakes in this debate, and a consideration of the experiences of the ISSLP and the recent assessment results from the Center for Social Concerns helps identify tensions arising at three different levels, with increasing degrees of complexity. First, service-learning in general, including ISL, has to face challenges from those like Stanley Fish who are suspicious of any universities that accept and embrace their twin role as moral-civic educators of students and as contributors to the well-being of local and larger communities. Second, ISL at faith-based universities in particular has to negotiate those suspicions while also accepting the university's distinctive religiously understood mission. Third and finally, the ISSLP, as a course in theology, has to also fulfill expectations of the academic discipline of theology, one that many service-learning theorists, like most academics, likely regard with considerable suspicion. Though the ISSLP at Notre Dame has not resolved tensions at these three levels fully, a discussion of each can illuminate some progress being made and also highlight ongoing questions. As will become clear, Catholic social teaching, while not solving these tensions, represents a valuable asset as programs like the ISSLP face them. Likely other religious traditions have similar resources to address such tensions.

International Service-Learning and the Role of Universities

In their efforts to protect the integrity of universities, critics like Fish do universities a service by forcing them to consider quite carefully their distinctive role and purpose. There is no doubt validity to warning universities not to embrace the status of social-service agencies and not to allow classrooms to become sites of ideological indoctrination. Yet, a cursory reading—and Fish's sometimes strident rhetoric (Butin, 2008)—can seemingly call into question all sorts of contemporary pedagogies and curricular innovations. These include "community-based pedagogies" (Butin, 2008, p. 68) like service-learning, which prioritize both the mutuality of the relationship between those served and the educational institutions providing the service—so that students do not simply use local communities for their own betterment— and the transformative nature of such undertakings for students themselves.

Universities in general and the service-learning community in particular have for some time anticipated and responded to such critiques. In the first place, led by Ernest Boyer, a number of commentators on higher education have sought to specify the university's role as a responsible local and global citizen, both embracing and yet simultaneously circumscribing that role so that the university's primary purposes are maintained (Bringle, Games, & Malloy, 1999).

In the area of service-learning in particular, there has been considerable development in addressing challenges like Fish's. Eyler and Giles's early work confidently (perhaps overconfidently?) described the broad goals of service-learning as both personal and intellectual: helping students acquire knowledge in understanding the world, developing critical thinking capacities, and even potentially leading students to identify their own commitments to improving the world. A successful service-learning program, they contended, would thus foster a deep perspective transformation that shapes students into lifelong learners and more productive citizens (Eyler & Giles, 1999). Recent commentators, however, have faced Fish's bracing critiques directly. The most incisive contributions from the perspective of service-learning have come from Dan Butin (2003, 2008, 2009), who differentiated the goals of service-learning by isolating four different perspectives or, "lenses," that are operative: technical ("better instruction for better academic outcomes"), cultural (referring to "imbued meanings" such as "tolerance and citizenship"), political ("about the empowerment of the dispossessed"), and antifoundational ("about the defamiliarization of the seemingly natural") (2008, p. 67).

In a review of Fish's (2008) *Save the World on Your Own Time*, Butin challenged the service-learning community to recall in particular the technical and antifoundational lenses of service-learning in giving rise and value to the field, which he believed can justify service-learning even in the eyes of someone like Fish. From a technical perspective, service-learning produces better learning and outcomes by generating an additional text that brings new sources of knowledge—real-world context and complexities—to the question under investigation, which Butin believed Fish should approve. From an antifoundationalist perspective, service-learning by its very character destabilizes and implodes fixed truths and narratives that students had previously constructed about the world (Butin, 2008).

In light of such goals, the BJW and SDO findings from the center's assessment suggest that transformations in worldview happen for summer service-learning students, which offer a powerful educational experience and deeper insight into contemporary global realities.[28] They also potentially lead students to identify and deepen their commitments *toward* improving the world in line with the goals set by Eyler and Giles and to question their previous assumptions in ways embraced by both Butin and Fish.

International Service-Learning in Faith-Based Universities

All institutions of higher education have to answer questions that arise from challenges to their larger social role and their particular educational aims. Yet by their very existence, faith-based universities are also obligated to follow the institution's founding and historical religious tradition, which distinguishes them both from other faith-based institutions of higher education and from secular universities. Faith-based institutions can be, and arguably should be, self-conscious about how they teach and the values they seek to cultivate in their students, while at the same time remain committed to the pursuit and sharing of truth and to full and free inquiry expected of all universities. Unsurprisingly, many faith-based universities embrace service-learning because of its outreach and contributions to local communities and its promise of more effective teaching and learning and their institutional aspirations to shape students' minds and hearts in social responsibility and critical awareness of social issues.

Most faith-based institutions have a long tradition of local and global service rooted in the institutions' founding and historical religious traditions and, judging from their mission statements, believe that moral education in some form should be part of higher education (Gunst Heffner & DeVries Beversluis, 2003, pp. xxviii–xxix). Notre Dame is no exception. As a Catholic university, it seeks to be a good citizen in its local community, as well as to serve the global common good. With regard to its educational philosophy, though it does not seek indoctrination of its students, and it welcomes faculty and students from a variety of religious orientations, including nonbelievers, it is nonetheless unapologetic about the formative role it seeks in shaping its students, embodied in the university's mission statement.[29] The ISSLP embodies this formative role and seeks to pursue the ideals of Notre Dame's mission in a global context.

Against educators who are dubious about universities' roles in moral formation, experience of the ISSLP supports those who emphasize its inevitability in educational processes, suggesting instead that it be as self-conscious as possible. In light of such inevitability, the program tries to help students honestly face questions arising from their experiences and to encourage habits of critical reflection on their deepest convictions—many of them faith convictions—that in turn can shape their commitments to social justice and their emerging global citizenship. The way the ISSLP affects students suggests that Fish's astringent approach to higher education represents what might be called a containment strategy that will never succeed, for service-learning—in this case ISL—has repercussions outside the strictly academic bounds within which he thinks universities ought to stay.

This is, however, admittedly difficult terrain to negotiate, for not all students and faculty are religious believers, and many who claim religious faith are non-Catholic. In the face of diverse beliefs among ISSLP participants, the program draws on Catholic social teaching to bridge social analysis and faith commitments, because many of its deepest principles have broader spiritual and humanistic appeal. As their ISL experience invites students to consider their worldviews, Catholic social teaching is a rich resource (O'Brien & Shannon, 1992), helping the program to meet students where they are while also exposing them to bodies of knowledge and traditions of inquiry to assist their interpretation and analysis. Some of these resources, like Catholic social teaching itself, are theological.

International Service-Learning as a Theological Pedagogy

The experience of ISL, which entails face-to-face encounters with the people and with the complexities behind classroom-dispensed statistics, naturally leads students to ask unsettling questions about themselves, about how they know what they know, and about their relationship to others (Braskamp, 2008). These are questions that emerge from service-learning experiences in communities where our students live and serve. They thus are propelled to consider their own responsibilities. In the ISSLP we try to help students address these questions honestly and in a sophisticated way and from many disciplinary perspectives. As a theology class, it also invites students to reflect on them in light of their religious convictions. That is to say, it strives to make their ISL part of the process of their "faith seeking understanding," as St. Anselm (1965) defined the task of *theology*.

Several facets of the ISSLP reflect its status as a theology class at a Catholic university like Notre Dame. First, in conceiving the program, the ISSLP intentionally chose institutional partnerships with organizations addressing poverty in developing countries,[30] modeling Catholic social teaching's principle of preferential option for the poor.[31] Second, ISSLP students work with many international Catholic development organizations and health, education, or social services provided by religious orders like the Congregation of Holy Cross, which founded Notre Dame. Working side by side with Catholic clergy and male and female members of Catholic religious orders, Catholic lay missioners, and others belonging to various religious traditions, students learn how faith commitments shape the action of these persons in inspiring ways and how it sustains them during difficult and challenging times in their work and personal lives.

Third, the ISSLP invites students to connect their own personal appropriations of their faith with the living faith of the people with whom they live, work, and worship during the summer. By encouraging theology in this way, the ISSLP helps students do theological reflection in the ways many contemporary theologians do theology, that is, from the ground up—in what Clemens Sedmak (2002) called local theology. Eschewing an approach to theology that simply applies unquestioned transcendental principles to existing situations, many theologians today prefer to have social experience be itself a profound source for theology (Bevans, 2004). In line with such a method, students are expected to do both social analysis and theological reflection together, integrating them rather than keeping them in distinct silos. This is in line with the self-understanding of the mission of the Department of Theology where the ISSLP is formally housed, which claims to pursue "the interpretation and articulation of the Catholic tradition and . . . the fostering of reflection and praxis concerning all aspects of Catholicism's various theological, doctrinal, liturgical, spiritual, historical, cultural, and canonical expressions and embodiments." Yet the department embraces ecumenical and interreligious understanding as well: "While the department's central core is the Catholic tradition, the department is deliberately ecumenical . . . [and] committed to dialogue with one another's traditions because theology can no longer be done adequately in a narrowly denominational manner."[32]

Fourth, ISSLP students are also invited to consider how their service-learning, along with other experiences, propels their own personal spiritual discernment so that it partakes in their lifelong spiritual journey. Religious faith has a variety of facets, but for the purposes of this discussion, one can helpfully consider such faith identity under the headings of *believing, belonging,* and *behaving*—that is, respectively, notional beliefs embodied in more-or-less propositional formulas adhered to by believers; liturgical and other ritual patterns that typify a given religious body's collective and individual worship; and ethical expectations and modes of reflective purposive behavior consonant with its moral expectations.[33] In light of such a classification, it is natural to assume that programs like the ISSLP invite students to consider the last, behaving, for the center concerns itself with the ethical formation of students by teaching Catholic social thought through service-learning pedagogies. New cultural contexts, intimate experiences of yawning economic disparity, and social displacement generate questions about students' moral identity. Unsurprisingly, many such questions implicate faith dimensions of moral identity in religiously inclined students. Economically disadvantaged settings lead many ISSLP participants to ask questions about their place and responsibility in the global order, their patterns of consumption and purchasing, and the distinctive features of their (usually U.S.) national identity as related to other places in the world. Their experiences of local communities that struggle together in the face of difficulties lead students to consider the justice at work in their own relationships, both intimate and more expansive. New considerations, fostered by the ISSLP, apparently lead to changes in students' BJW and SDO that are relevant to shaping their personal moral behavior.

Yet ISSLP students—and not only the Catholic students—regularly connect their summer service-learning not only to aspects of their personal code of behavior but also to their appropriations of belief and belonging. Contact with a different and vibrant religious tradition—Buddhists in Cambodia, Muslims in Senegal—can prompt reflection on long-held doctrinal convictions among our mostly Catholic students. Students who come to know Central American churches that have endured years of violent civil conflict gain new insights into the suffering Christ and his presence as claimed in the church or the consolation of the Virgin Mary. Vibrant African and Latin American liturgies place the staid Masses common in the United States in a new perspective. The meditative practices of Hindus in India inspire a hunger for stillness and a contemplative spirit among adventurous spiritual seekers.

In light of the transformative processes that ISSLP students undergo, the program offers resources to help them make sense of their new experiences. First, Catholic social teaching is a well-organized, accessible body of work that can appeal to non-Catholics and also coheres with the doctrinal and liturgical orientations of the world's largest single religious body. Such social teaching has the potential to ground the social commitments of non-believers and helps believing students connect their life of prayer and their social engagement (Bolan, 2005). Second, contemporary spiritual theology as articulated by theologians like John Dunne (1972, 2003) encourages students' close reflection on their experiences to discern their evolving insights into their vocation in the world. And third, other entities in the university—academic departments, research institutes, and student life units like Campus Ministry—also invite students to draw connections between their faith and their social commitments.

This theological orientation also raises a number of critical questions. First, not all Notre Dame students are Catholic or practicing Catholics, and one need not be a religious believer to participate in the ISSLP. Is it fair, therefore, for the ISSLP to ask them to do theological reflection? In the first place, the course is not required, and they choose to enroll. In addition, many of them—like many U.S. university students—profess their faith quite openly and self-consciously seek ways to integrate that faith with their education. Others struggle to articulate their convictions but come from religious backgrounds that they revere, even if inchoately. Others deeply question the religious traditions in which they were raised, for example, Catholics sometimes seeing a hypocritical and politicized church. Still others profess no faith at all and claim solely altruistic or humanitarian motives behind their ISSLP participation.

In any of these cases, the ISSLP can serve the students in question, as the changes in BJW and SDO indicate. In the first case, the ISSLP can make professed convictions more operative and coherent. In the second, it can encourage clearer articulation of and insight into underdeveloped faith convictions and their implications. In the third, it can encourage new perspectives on religious realities, questioning reflexive judgments with broader evidence. In the fourth case, the ISSLP can foster deeper understanding of how non-religious commitments to justice can resonate with religious commitments and of how religious convictions operate in peers and local communities elsewhere. At the same time, it must be admitted that ISL can also destabilize existing faith convictions—sometimes through discouraging encounters with local churches, sometimes through fascination with new religious forms and values, and sometimes through unavoidable disorientation that naturally occurs as faith evolves.

A second critical question raised by this theological orientation is: How do we acknowledge the ambivalent historical legacies of religious activities like Christian mission in many of the places where ISSLP students travel? Because some students have participated in international weeklong "mission" trips through either their church or their secondary schools, one session is devoted to contemporary understandings of mission in the postcolonial era and their implications for ISL undertaken by students at a Catholic university like Notre Dame. The students' own typical understandable reluctance to identify as "missionaries" is discussed, as are ways to think about how what they will do through the ISSLP nonetheless can partake in their often religiously defined sense of themselves (Tomas Morgan & Kollman, 2009).

In its programming, the ISSLP discusses good reasons to be suspicious of Christian mission and religious proselytism, which have served colonial and imperial purposes in the past and arguably still do today in some circumstances (Kollman, 2011). It considers how any type of "service," Christian or not, can reflect similar colonialist and paternalistic patterns of relationship. Practices and models of international development likewise fall prey to such power inequalities, which often operate in ISSLP settings, and our students often discover, painfully, their own unconscious assumptions of privilege.

In light of challenges like these, Catholic social teaching provides a formidable resource for the ISSLP. William Bolan helpfully outlined how *community-based learning* (a term he prefers to *service-learning*) practices like those embodied in the ISSLP parallel emphases within Catholic social teaching, so that service-learning "when practiced effectively and conscientiously . . . provides a way to realize both the pedagogy and the ends of Catholic social teaching" (2005, p. 116). Bolan identified several ways in which such synergy is achieved, each of which the ISSLP pursues. First, by bringing participants close to the marginalized, service-learning helps to promote the fact that those suffering from social injustice are real and that the "Other" is really a "neighbor" or a "brother or sister," something that ISSLP students often say. By putting a human face behind the social problems studied, the ISSLP creates learning that reduces stereotyping and enhances appreciation for diverse cultures, moving beyond tolerance to solidarity that is at the heart of Catholic social teaching. Second, by making students aware of the reality and extent of social problems, ISL encourages them to accept that they have a duty or obligation to do something about them. Third, beyond just helping students to see the reality of social problems, the ISSLP encourages awareness of the systemic nature of problems. Fourth, service-learning strives after reciprocity or mutuality with the partner organization and also strives to make sure that service-learning fills a community-identified need, something that resonates in the Catholic social teaching principle of subsidiarity.

Conclusion

In a review article on faith-based service-learning some years ago, Garry Hesser (2003) claimed that service-learning had helped religious universities recover the riches within their own faith traditions. "Service learning," he wrote, "has brought about a renewed interest in the social teachings that are grounded in, and evolving from, their respective faith traditions" (Hesser, 2003, p. 67). The same has been discovered at Notre Dame through programs like the ISSLP. At a time when many faith-based universities also seek to manifest their religious identity more fully while maintaining or increasing their academic standards, this experience suggests that ISL represents a potent resource both for individual students' aspirations and for the emerging missions of religiously affiliated institutions of higher education. Other traditions besides the Catholic Church have distinct social principles and spiritual insights to assist students to connect service and justice, as well as religious narratives to help make service-learning an ally in pursuit of greater institutional integrity at their universities.

Of course, further research on how ISL affects students at faith-based schools is needed, but categories like increased worship attendance are simplistic in capturing changes in students' faith commitments and insufficient indicators of spiritual transformation. Instead, faith-based universities interested in ISL need to assess the impacts of our programs on our students—impacts that reflect not only broader values associated with ISL but also the specifically religious values linked to our institutions' foundings.

In the same article, Hesser also contended that faith-based universities had the potential to serve the larger service-learning field because of their long experience of seeking to impart to their students a sense of social responsibility. Their religious resources, he believed, meant that they had a potentially deeper stake in moral formation than secular universities and thus perhaps more long-term viability in successful service-learning because of these foundational religious commitments.

Time will tell if Hesser's inkling about the comparative advantages of religious universities over their secular counterparts in fostering service-learning was well founded. The institutionalization of service-learning and ISL at Notre Dame and the interest in our faculty and students alike, however, lend support to his intuition. Certainly, the outcomes of the ISSLP suggest certain lessons for the broader ISL field. In the first place, communities of faith and the religious convictions of service-learning and ISL participants are an unacknowledged and overlooked resource for service-learning at all educational levels. This is unfortunate, and fear about proselytism and the place of moral education need not keep ISL pursued in secular settings from engaging the religious convictions of participants.

Those involved in postsecondary service-learning already know that religious institutions have often already served as significant entry points for students' service-learning engagement before their arrival at college or university, regardless of their particular religious tradition.[34] This is not surprising, because faith-based organizations have long been the largest providers of educational and health-related services in the United States and are also major players internationally in such service provision through nongovernmental organizations that offer humanitarian aid and development support. Congregations and communities of worship with elementary and secondary schools that provide education to the youth in their communities often shape curricula, linking an understanding of service to their religious traditions. Similar activities sponsored by religious bodies take place outside the classroom. Even certain federally funded organizations such as the National Corporation for Service and Learning include programs like Learn & Serve America's Inspired to Serve project,[35] which provides resources for youth-led interfaith service-learning.

In light of such realities, the religious sensibilities of most participants in ISL should not be ignored,[36] whether that ISL takes place in religiously affiliated or secular settings. Ignoring students' religious beliefs does little to integrate their education with their deepest convictions. ISL practitioners at religiously affiliated universities, therefore, have things to teach their colleagues at secular universities about how ISL can help forge integrated educational processes. Inviting students to utilize their own religious and spiritual narratives as they make sense of their service-learning experience provides a more holistic education for our students.

Experience of the ISSLP at Notre Dame suggests that ISL in faith-based contexts, especially when framed by Catholic social teaching, encourages students to connect their deepest convictions—often rooted in their personal religious identity—to their intellectual and moral education and places that educational process firmly in a global arena. In an era when many U.S. university students strive after such integration, we are grateful for the institutional support we receive, which helps our students achieve their educational goals. It is not surprising that at Notre Dame, the Center for Social Concerns currently provides impetus and leadership in a university-wide consultation designed to help our educational process encourage the values of global citizenship—often understood as a goal for secular educators as well (Lewin, 2009)—as a part of our Catholic mission.[37]

In these ethically challenging times, universities should have a sense of urgency to educate students with a deeply felt global responsibility to others. And faith-based institutions can and should play a leading role in pursuit of such a goal, at the same time reinforcing their own distinctive missions. ISL has considerable potential advancing such aims, making both faith-based universities and the students they serve better global citizens.

Authors' Note

The authors wish to acknowledge the significant contributions to this chapter by Jean Ann Sekerak and Nick Bowman. Sekerak assisted in the implementation of the ISSLP from 2008 to 2010 while a graduate student TA for the course, and Bowman was a postdoctoral research associate for the Center for Social Concerns from 2008 to 2011.

Endnotes

1. *Transformations at the edge of the world: Forming global Christians through the study abroad experience* (Morgan and Toms Smedley, 2010), an edited book that provides examples of global experiential learning courses and programs being carried out by Christian colleges and universities across the United States. Many of those included have been providing international experiences influenced by a Christian service ethic for their students for many years. This book is a resource for those interested in further investigating study abroad and cultural immersion currently being carried out by various Christian institutions of higher education.

2. For more information on these programs, see the following websites: www.augsburg.edu/global/; www.wheaton.edu/HNGR/; www.goshen.edu/sst/. The director of the ISSLP looked to these three study abroad programs and others when developing the ISSLP.

3. The term *faith-based* for these institutions does not mean to imply that each of them understands its mission in relation to the term *faith*, which has distinctly Christian overtones. The term instead has emerged in U.S. political contexts over the past several decades, in which sometimes contentious debates have raged about whether and how religiously affiliated institutions—Christian, Jewish, Muslim, Hindu, or connected to any other religious tradition—should receive government support. In this chapter we will use *religiously affiliated* and *faith-based* more or less interchangeably in order to distinguish such institutions from those that have no formal religious affiliation. Many of the most prominent private universities in the United States began with such an affiliation but have dropped it (Marsden, 1994).

4. Based on figures compiled by the U.S. Department of Education, National Center for Education Statistics (Knapp, Kelly-Reid, & Ginder, 2008), there are 4,000 degree-granting institutions of higher education in the United States: 1,600 are private, nonprofit campuses, of which 900 define themselves as "religiously affiliated." See also the same statistics organized in a helpful chart and compiled by Bob Andringa (2008), president of the Coalition of Christian Colleges & Universities. Because there has been no comprehensive study, one cannot say how many of the 900 carry out ISL programs or courses, but the authors of this chapter expect there are many. Given the numbers of religiously affiliated institutions of higher education, it is somewhat surprising that the literature on service-learning over the past 25 years, which has matured to include a breadth of theory, practice, study, and

research, has tended to overlook faith-based institutions (for exceptions, see sources at www.servicelearning.org/instant_info/bibs/cb_bibs/service-learning_faith-based). Even less has been written on the efforts of religious universities in ISL. For an overview and discussion of how Christian notions of mission intersect with ISL, see Tomas Morgan and Kollman (2009). For a recent study that considers some faith-based ISL programs, see Morgan and Toms Smedley (2010).

5. Both authors are involved in the ISSLP. Tomas Morgan developed the program and continues to oversee it. Kollman has served in a key advisory capacity and taught sections devoted to theology and mission. Both are coinstructors of the course.

6. For our purposes here, the authors use a framework for the term that is being developed by the Fostering Global Citizenship Learning Community at Notre Dame and includes the following components: (a) knowledgeable about the interdependence of the world, (b) competent to relate to others in empathy, and (c) committed to engaged social responsibility informed by Catholic values and concern for the common good. Authors acknowledge that there are tensions and potential with the concept of global citizenship. A survey by Lewin (2009) provides a comprehensive survey of the field of study abroad as a key strategy for global citizenship education. At Notre Dame, it is a concept that has secularist appeal but can also speak to characteristics of the Catholic character that is related to its social tradition.

7. See www.nd.edu/aboutnd/mission-statement for the full text of the Notre Dame mission statement.

8. See www.centerforsocialconcerns.nd.edu for more information about the Center for Social Concerns.

9. For purposes of this chapter, we employ *ISL* as defined by colleagues at the Center for Service and Learning at Indiana University–Purdue University in Indianapolis: "a structured academic experience in another country in which students (a) participate in an organized service activity that addresses identified community needs; (b) learn from direct interaction and cross-cultural dialogue with others; and (c) reflect on the experience in such a way as to gain a deeper understanding of global and intercultural issues, a broader appreciation of the host country and the discipline, and an enhanced sense of their own responsibilities as citizens, locally and globally" (Bringle, Hatcher, Jones, & Sutton, 2007). For one of the first collections highlighting 30 international service and service-learning program examples across 11 states in the United States, see North Carolina Campus Compact (2005). Tomas Morgan contributed to this collection.

10. Among those who developed those principles were the following: Eyler and Giles (1999); Honnet and Poulen (1989); Howard (1993); Jacoby & associates (1996); Schneider (1998).

11. These include the pioneering International Partnership for Service Learning, the HNGR program, and the three study abroad and international service programs mentioned in an earlier note. The ISSLP also drew on a definition of *academic service-learning* as the intersection of relevant and meaningful service with the community, purposeful civic learning, and enhanced academic learning (Howard, 2001) and later from the definition of *ISL* as developed by Bringle et al. (2007). The latter

definition further helps to distinguish the ISSLP from other international volunteer service initiatives or international internships across the university that may be somewhat carelessly referred to as ISL. The same *Michigan Journal of Community Service Learning* course-design workbook by Howard (2001) provides a helpful visual matrix that distinguishes ISL from internships and other forms of community service.

12. Effective ISL must be informed by multiple disciplinary and interdisciplinary fields. For an excellent overview of the theoretical foundations for ISL that makes this argument, see Crabtree (2008).

13. Students prepare for weekly class lectures with readings and a short written assignment or public reporting, often relating the topic at hand to their future host country. Such area-specific preparations sharpen students' understanding of social realities distinctive to their destinations. In addition to providing academic knowledge about global issues, the seminar aims to equip students in global competency by providing exercises, discussion, and reflection on notions of culture and the cross-cultural adaptation process. Finally, in accordance with wider university international travel guidelines, the seminar also provides students with practical advice related to gender, health, and safety abroad; travel logistics; and medical and emergency protocol and processes. Previous participants play an important leadership role in the preparation of the new cohort. They provide a series of site briefings that give the background and mission of the organization and also share personal experiences of the particular agency and host country. Involving past participants in the spring seminar also assists in their own ongoing reflection and reentry process. Additional area-specific facets include country or regional briefings given by faculty that aim to provide students with historical, social, economic, political, and cultural understanding of where they will be. The ISSLP also provides a bibliography of recommended resources for additional reading and research, and students are expected to complete a worksheet outlining various regional reading requirements, lectures, speakers, films, and local resource persons they have sought out over the course of the spring semester.

14. Evaluations in the ISSLP are collected from students and site partner organizations. Students evaluate the ISSLP in light of the program and course learning goals and objectives, interaction with their site mentors and others in the organization, and living logistics and complete a site description sheet that serves as a resource for information for future participants. Evaluations of the students and of the program are also asked of the site organization and the students' on-site mentor. Site partners are asked to give their impressions of the student and the attitudes, gifts, and weaknesses he or she brought to the service experience and to evaluate the relationship of the student with the organization and the people with whom he or she interacted, the quality of the work the student provided, the level of reflection and learning as demonstrated in regularly scheduled reflection sessions with the student, the extent to which the service provided was helpful to the organization and community, and if the service relationship was mutual or one-sided. The center assessment described in the chapter is the kind of assessment that is taking place more recently. In 2011, the ISSLP will employ the Global Perspectives Inventory.

For more information on the GPI, see https://gpi.central.edu/. Students submit copies of selected journal entries that demonstrate an engagement of their critical experiences with the weekly assigned readings and a final integrative paper or project from a variety of paper or project options.

15. Early on, the ISSLP program goals were lofty and inspirational in nature, including broad goals to "create bridges of understanding and solidarity." The following was the point of departure: "The lack of basic resources, access to health, education, and employment remains the challenge for developing and non-industrialized nations. In nations marred by political conflict and violence, efforts of peace, reconciliation, and democratization are slow and its affects are seen most clearly in the lives of the poor. As we continue to face these and other global concerns, the need to educate students about their responsibility in our global community becomes ever apparent. It becomes increasingly important to educate students willing to examine causes of poverty and to create links of solidarity across borders. The ISSLP seeks to provide ISL experiences in social concerns inspired by Gospel values and Catholic social teachings" (ISSLP Learning Agreement; http://socialconcerns.nd.edu/academic/summer/ISSLP .shtml).

16. Nick Bowman was very helpful in preparing this section of the chapter.

17. See Huba and Freed (2000). As another source wrote, "Assessment is the process of gathering and discussing information from multiple and diverse sources in order to develop a deep understanding of what students know, understand, and can do with their knowledge as a result of their educational experiences; the process culminates when assessment results are used to improve subsequent learning." See http:// tep.uoregon.edu/workshops/teachertraining/learnercentered/assessing/definition .html (accessed August 20, 2010).

18. The ISSLP also has typical ways whereby students seek to demonstrate what they have learned—oral presentations, writing assignments, journals, and a final paper or project—and in response a final grade is assigned to the students. Such means of grading have been collected. In fact, the ISSLP has archived all students' journals and final papers, numerous shorter assignments, notes from individual debriefing interviews, and pre- and postcourse assessment surveys given to each student with the aim to one day code and cull this qualitative data for analysis and research. Like many service-learning practitioners and faculty, often too consumed with the actual running of courses and programs, ISSLP directors have not yet undertaken the laborious task of collating all the data from such rich sources.

19. Principal investigators of the project are Nick Bowman and Jay Brandenberger. A presentation on the research, titled *Social Justice Outcomes on Service-Learning*, was given at the October 2010 International Association of Research on Service Learning and Civic Engagement Annual Conference in Indianapolis, IN. Presenters included Andrea Smith Shappell, Rachel Tomas Morgan, Nick Bowman, and Jay Brandenberger, all of the Center for Social Concerns (see Bowman, Brandenberger, Smith Shappell, & Tomas Morgan, 2010).

20. For more description of the measures used in the study, see Bowman, Brandenberger, Mick, and Toms Smedley (2010).

21. A total of 115 (approximately 50%) of the center's summer service-learning students (73% female, 20% students of color) completed a pretest survey late in the spring 2009 semester and a posttest survey after they returned from their extended immersions. Eighteen of these students were in the ISSLP. Learning gains did not differ significantly between domestic and international summer service-learning students.

22. See Bowman, Brandenberger, Mick, et al. (2010).

23. Multiple regression analyses were used to predict incoming levels of BJW and SDO. These showed that having a socially oriented motivation for taking the course was positively related to incoming SDO, whereas self-rated political conservatism, higher family income, and individually oriented motivation for taking the course were negatively related to SDO. Gender, race and ethnicity, and year in school were not significantly related to SDO, and no precourse variable was significantly associated with incoming BJW.

24. For a definition of *social justice* that shapes our use of it here, see the definition written by Jay Brandenberger (2008).

25. For a summary of this complex debate, see Kiss and Euben (2010).

26. These terms are not interchangeable, but they are often used interchangeably in the debate. For the purposes of this chapter, they can be used in a collective sense.

27. Fish, for example, proposed that the central question in curriculum building is as follows: "In saying or writing this, am I trying to get at the truth about some matter of intellectual concern or am I trying to advance my personal (no doubt deeply held and perhaps useful to society) views about character or about citizenship or about social justice or about anything (remembering always that anything, and certainly these, can legitimately be the topics of an academic discussion as long as that discussion is not politics in disguise)?" (Fish, 2010, p. 91). For Fish, if the answer is not no, then the professor oversteps his or her bounds.

28. See Kiely (2004) for an earlier study on perspective transformation and ISL.

29. For Notre Dame's mission statement, see http://nd.edu/aboutnd/missions-statement/.

30. Though *Open Doors* reports (2009 and 2010; www.iie.org/en/Research-and-Publications/Open-Doors; accessed August 10, 2010) suggest more students are heading to such places now than they were in the past, the ISSLP does seek to provide students the opportunity to learn from and within nontraditional study abroad contexts that were not offered through Notre Dame's traditional study abroad programming, which sends most students to Europe.

31. For more understanding of the Catholic social teaching's principle of "preferential option for the poor," see Henriot (2004) and Gutierrez (1973). Henriot defined the *option for the poor* as "an orientation in the life of a Christian" having the following interrelated elements: perspective, from the point of view of the poor; entry point to life and work, bringing the poor into life and work situations; a tool of evaluation, asking what does this mean to the poor; accompaniment, to be in solidarity; and advocacy that takes sides.

32. For the mission statement of the Department of Theology at Notre Dame, see www.theology.nd.edu.

33. For a discussion of other theories of religion, see Stausberg (2009).

34. According to UCLA's Higher Education Research Institute (2004) report, first-year students who participated in religious activities in secondary school are more likely to engage in volunteer activities generally and in service-learning specifically (57% compared to 43%) at university. The Higher Education Research Institute also reports that service-learning experience is high for first-year university students from a variety of religious traditions: Hindus (62.5%), Latter Day Saints (61.9%), Roman Catholic (59%), Muslim (57.6%), and Buddhist (56.9%). See www.spirituality.ucla.edu/docs/reports/A%20Summary%20of%20Initial%20 Findings%20(Survey%20Report).pdf (accessed August 28, 2010).

35. For more information, see www.inspiredtoserve.org/faith-based.

36. Today's U.S. college students for the most part show interest in spiritual matters. According to Astin, Astin, and Lindholm's (2003) *A Summary of Initial Findings From Pilot Survey 2000–2003* and the Higher Education Research Institute's (2004) *Spirituality in Higher Education: A National Study of College Students' Search for Meaning and Purpose*, only 27% report that the existence of God is a matter of indifference to them, 77% of college students pray, 78% discuss religious topics with friends, and 70% attended religious services in the past year.

37. For more information on Notre Dame's Fostering Global Citizenship Learning Community, see http://socialconcerns.nd.edu/faculty/SummitGlobal Citizenship.shtml.

References

Andringa, B. (2008). *Profile of US postsecondary education.* Washington, DC: Coalition of Christian Colleges & Universities. Retrieved November 10, 2010, from www.cccu.org/filefolder/Postsecondary.pdf

Anselm, St. (1965). *St. Anselm's proslogion.* Oxford, UK: Clarendon Press.

Astin, A. W., Astin, H. S., & Lindholm, J. A. (2003). *A summary of initial findings from pilot survey 2000–2003.* Los Angeles: Spirituality in Higher Education, UCLA. Retrieved August 28, 2010, from http://www.spirituality.ucla.edu/ docs/reports/A%20Summary%20of%20Initial%20Findings%20(Survey%20 Report).pdf

Bevans, S. (2004). *Models of contextual theology: Faith and cultures.* Maryknoll, NY: Orbis.

Bolan, W. (2005). Promoting social change: Theoretical and empirical arguments for using traditional community-based learning when teaching catholic social thought. In W. Mattison III (Ed.), *New wine, new wineskins: A generation reflects on key issues in Catholic moral theology* (pp. 103–118). Lanham, MD: Rowman and Littlefield.

Bowman, N., Brandenberger, J., Mick, C., & Toms Smedley, C. (2010). Sustained immersion experiences and student orientations toward equality, justice, and social responsibility: The role of short-term community-based learning. *Michigan Journal of Community Service Learning, 17*(1), 20–31.

Bowman, N., Brandenberger, J., Smith Shappell, A., & Tomas Morgan, R. (2010, October). *Social justice outcomes on service-learning.* Paper presented at the International Association of Research on Service Learning and Civic Engagement Annual Conference, Indianapolis, IN.

Brandenberger, J. W. (2008). Social justice. In F. C. Power, R. J. Nuzzi, D. Narvaez, D. K. Lapsley, & T. C. Hunt (Eds.), *Moral education: A handbook* (Vol. 2, pp. 420–421). Westport, CT: Praeger.

Braskamp, L. (2008). Developing global citizens. *Journal of College and Character, 10*(1). Retrieved from http://www.degruyter.com/view/j/jcc.2008.10.1/jcc.2008.10.1.1058/jcc.2008.10.1.1058.xml

Bringle, R. G., Games, R., & Malloy, E. A. (1999). Colleges and universities as citizens: Issues and perspectives. In R. G. Bringle, R. Games, & E. A. Malloy (Eds.), *Colleges and universities as citizens* (pp. 1–16). Needham Heights, MA: Allyn and Bacon.

Bringle, R., Hatcher, J., Jones, S., & Sutton, S. (2007). *Definition of international service-learning.* Retrieved August 3, 2010, from http://cservice-learning.iupui.edu/6c1.asp

Butin, D. W. (2003). Of what use is it? Multiple conceptualizations of service-learning in education. *Teachers College Record, 105*(9), 1674–1692.

Butin, D. W. (2008). Review essay: Saving the university on his own time; Stanley Fish, service-learning, and knowledge limitation in the academy. *Michigan Journal of Community Service Learning, 15*(1), 62–69.

Butin, D. W. (2009). *Rethinking service-learning: Embracing the scholarship of engagement in higher education.* Sterling, VA: Stylus.

Crabtree, R. (2008). Theoretical foundations for international service-learning. *Michigan Journal of Community Service Learning, 15*(1), 18–36.

Dalbert, C., Montada, L., & Schmitt, M. (1987). Glaube an die gerechte Welt als Motiv: Validnering Zweier Skalen. *Psychologische Beitrage, 29*, 596–615.

Dunne, J. S. (1972). *The way of all the earth.* New York, NY: Macmillan.

Dunne, J. S. (2003). *A journey with God in time: A spiritual quest.* Notre Dame, IN: University of Notre Dame Press.

Eyler, J., & Giles, D. E. (1999). *Where's the learning in service-learning?* San Francisco, CA: Jossey-Bass.

Fish, S. (2008). *Save the world on your own time.* New York, NY: Oxford University Press.

Fish, S. (2010). I know it when I see it: A reply to Kiss and Euben. In E. Kiss & J. Euben (Eds.), *Debating moral education: Rethinking the role of the modern university* (pp. 76–91). Durham, NC: Duke University Press.

Gunst Heffner, G., & DeVries Beversluis, C. (Eds.). (2003). *Commitment and connection: Service-learning and Christian higher education.* Lanham, MD: Rowman and Littlefield.

Gutierrez, G. (1973). *A theology of liberation.* Maryknoll, NY: Orbis.

Henriot, P. (2004). *Opting for the poor.* Washington, DC: Center of Concern.

Hesser, G. (2003). Faith-based service-learning: Back to the future. Review of the edited volume *Commitment and connection: Service-learning and Christian higher education. Michigan Journal of Community Service Learning, 10*(1), 59–69.

Higher Education Research Institute. (2004). *The spiritual life of college students: A national study of college students' search for meaning and purpose.* Los Angeles: University of California.

Honnet, E. P., & Poulen, S. J. (1989). *Principles of good practice for combining service and learning: A Wingspread special report.* Racine, WI: Johnson Foundation.

Howard, J. (1993). Community service learning in the curriculum. In J. Howard (Ed.), *Praxis 1: A faculty casebook on community service learning* (pp. 3–12). Ann Arbor, MI: OCSL Press.

Howard, J. (2001, Summer). Service-learning course design workbook. *Michigan Journal of Community Service Learning* [Companion volume].

Huba, M. E., & Freed, J. (2000). *Learner-centered assessment on college campuses: Shifting the focus from teaching to learning.* Needham Heights, MA: Allyn and Bacon.

Jacoby, B., & associates. (1996). *Service-learning in higher education.* San Franciso, CA: Jossey-Bass.

Kiely, R. (2004). Chameleon with a complex: Searching for transformation in international service-learning. *Michigan Journal of Community Service Learning, 10*(2), 5–20.

Kiss, E., & Euben, J. (Eds.). (2010). *Debating moral education: Rethinking the role of the modern university.* Durham, NC: Duke University Press.

Knapp, L. G., Kelly-Reid, J. E., & Ginder, S. A. (2008). *Postsecondary institutions in the United States: Fall 2007, degrees and other awards conferred: 2006–07, and 12-month enrollment: 2006-07* (NCES 2008-159). Washington, DC: National Center for Education Statistics, Institute of Education Sciences, U.S. Department of Education.

Kollman, P. (2011). At the origins of mission and missiology: A study in the dynamics of religious language. *Journal of the American Academy of Religion, 79*(2), 425–458.

Lerner, M. J., & Miller, D. T. (1978). Just world research and the attribution process: Looking back and ahead. *Psychological Bulletin, 85*, 1030–1051.

Lewin, R. (Ed.). (2009). *The handbook of practice and research in study abroad: Higher education and the quest for global citizenship.* New York, NY: Routledge.

Marsden, G. M. (1994). *The soul of the American university: From Protestant establishment to established nonbelief.* New York, NY: Oxford University Press.

Morgan, R., & Toms Smedley, C. (Eds.). (2010). *Transformations at the edge of the world: Forming global Christians through the study abroad experience.* Abilene, TX: ACU Press.

North Carolina Campus Compact. (2005). *Promising practices of international service and service learning.* Elon, NC: Author. Retrieved November 23, 2010, from http://org.elon.edu/nccc/resources/pub.html

O'Brien, D. J., & Shannon, T. A. (1992). *Catholic social thought: The documentary heritage.* Maryknoll, NY: Orbis.

Pratto, F., Sidanius, J., Stallworth, L. M., & Malle, B. F. (1994). Social dominance orientation: A personality variable predicting social and political attitudes. *Journal of Personality and Social Psychology, 67,* 741–763.

Schneider, M. K. (1998, June). *Models of good practice for service-learning programs: What can we learn from 1,000 faculty, 25,000 students, and 27 institutions involved in service. American Association of Higher Education Bulletin,* pp. 9–12.

Sedmak, C. (2002). *Doing local theology: A guide for artisans of a new humanity.* Maryknoll, NY: Orbis.

Stausberg, M. (2009). *Contemporary theories of religion: A critical companion.* London: Routledge.

Tomas Morgan, R., & Kollman, P. (2009). Service-learning at Catholic universities: Challenges and opportunities. *New Theology Review, 22*(1), 25–36.

12

A CRITICAL GLOBAL CITIZENSHIP

Eric Hartman
Kansas State University
Richard Kiely
Cornell University

We live in a globalized world, in which people are more connected and affect each other's lives more deeply (Lechner, 2009). Despite economic globalization, media globalization, and decreased costs of transportation and communication, we as a global public have yet to understand or precisely define our ethical relationships with one another (Singer, 2002). Higher education institutions in the United States have stepped into this gap, proclaiming their collective centrality to the mission of creating global citizens (Lewin, 2009; Nussbaum, 1997; Stoddard & Cornwell, 2003). In this chapter, we first problematize the existing literature on global citizenship, particularly in the context of service-learning and university-community engagement. Not content to examine theorizing alone, we consider the location of various global citizenship efforts academically and in relationship with community partners. We then consider diverse students' articulations of their own identity negotiations following exposure to global service-learning to suggest six empirically rooted dimensions of global citizenship. We combine these dimensions with critical theoretical accounts of global citizenship, service-learning, and study abroad to suggest a critical global citizenship as an alternative conceptual model. We advance this understanding of global citizenship as an applicable and empirically rooted goal for higher education.

Locating Global Service-Learning and Global Citizenship Education: Study Abroad

Attention to advancing global citizenship comes in the context of rapidly increasing study abroad participation among U.S. students, with rates more than tripling during the past two decades (Institute of International Education, 2010). Staggering increases in study abroad programming, regular highlighting of study abroad by university marketing offices, and increasing numbers of faculty involved with global service-learning absent substantial background in intercultural exchange or community development increase the possibility that global service-learning could be appropriated or misunderstood by stakeholders within the study abroad community. To call attention to the unique challenges presented to global-citizenship-building efforts within study abroad, we first examine recent scholarship in this area. Study abroad theorists have called attention to the contradiction between some study abroad rationales and purported global citizenship goals (Andreotti & de Souza, 2012; Ogden, 2007–2008; Plater, Jones, Bringle, & Clayton, 2009; Reilly & Senders, 2009; Tarc, 2013; Zemach-Bersin, 2012).

Study abroad by U.S. students has been justified in terms of producing an elite mobile social class and advancing U.S. interests abroad (Kiely, 2010; Plater et al., 2009). Current rhetoric is moving toward increasing the connection between national security and university exchange programming, making the rationale for study abroad programming "instrumental, prosaic, and nationalistic" (Reilly & Senders, 2009, p. 251) and privileging U.S. interests over discourse focusing on broader peace. Any study abroad program must carefully and systematically understand and create its place in geopolitics or risk being co-opted by nationalistic discourses (Reily & Senders, 2009).

Although program leaders must be proactive to avoid co-optation, Ogden called professors' attention to contemporary "colonial students" who want to be abroad to improve their career prospects and experience new cultures "in just the same way as new commodities are coveted, purchased, and owned" (Ogden, 2007–2008, p. 38). He urged the education abroad community to discover and embrace the pedagogies necessary to move students out of their comfort zones into transformative learning experiences. Ogden argued the increasing numbers of students abroad is causing universities to develop international structures that cater to U.S. students' wishes, in essence developing a bureaucratic higher education structure that mimics the earlier structures of colonialism. Students need not interact with dissimilar Others; they have all the comforts of home. There is on the one hand the profound need to avoid this, and on the other hand the risk that engaging students with overly challenging, new, and different situations will lead them to "retreat to the veranda and close themselves off to future encounters with cultural difference" (Ogden, 2007–2008, p. 44).

Fortunately, and despite this concern over rationales and neocolonial students, recent systematic studies of attitudinal change do demonstrate that students are learning in many desired ways in study abroad programs (Braskamp, Braskamp, & Merrill, 2009; Hartman, 2008), that the learning can be tracked, and that the study abroad field is responding to earlier calls (e.g., Jenkins & Skelly, 2004) to more systematically support desired learning outcomes. Yet study abroad does not necessarily lead to a heightened sense of global social responsibility or global citizenship.

After examining global perspectives of more than 200 students who participated in study abroad representing five different U.S. universities as sender-institutions, Braskamp et al. (2009) concluded that study abroad leaders and faculty must do more to intentionally foster global learning and development. Not surprisingly, increasing attention to critical reflective practice and questions of social concern are likely to lead to better integration of experience and academics and to further development of social responsibility (Braskamp et al., 2009). Similarly, Hartman (2008, 2014) demonstrated that targeted global citizenship outcomes do not develop absent clear, systematic curricula supporting their development, even in the case of study abroad programs exclusively using service-learning methodology.

Even as study abroad researchers clarify the need for systematic integration of academics, experience, reflection, and consideration of power and privilege, they are debating the nature of the study abroad experience in the context of postmodernism. Johnson asserted that so-called "rootless and cursory 'contact zones'" (2009, p. 181) such as bars and tourist traps are "some of the least-accessed teaching opportunities study abroad programs have historically utilized" (p. 181) and that "the proper application of post-structural, post-colonial, and postmodern theory is remarkably apropos and useful" (p. 181). She bemoaned what she sees as lack of engagement within the study abroad profession with the interrogation of terms such as *authentic, real, rural, indigenous,* and *traditional,* and she went on to assert, "To suggest the life of an urban native is any more or less 'real' than that of a rural citizen of the same culture is condescending and can indicate a disturbingly colonial nostalgia for a cultural experience laden with pre-development realities" (p. 184).

Reilly and Senders (2009, p. 252) recognized that many cities have created

middle-class oriented tourist "city centers" and pedestrian zones cleansed of threatening elements, and it is often these "theme park" cities that our students experience. If we are successfully to put study abroad to critical use, we will need to work with students to "see" and "read" such transformations of urban topography.

Reilly and Senders went on to recognize the importance of refusing essentialist dichotomizing language that forces people into modern, premodern, authentic, or Westernized categories, articulating the importance of sensitizing students to the dynamism of cultures and peoples.

It is in this reflective vein that Reilly and Senders (2009) offered a model of critical study abroad, suggesting "in place of class-reproduction it offers class-analysis; in place of self-development through accumulation it offers self-development through commitment; in place of internationalism it offers a critical and global perspective; in place of 'global competence' it offers global citizenship" (p. 242). They pointed out—through the example of Castilla and Spain—that we "encourage our students to accept uncritically and reproduce the nation-state system" (p. 251), even suggesting that we "reconsider our traditional rhetoric of 'international exchange' and replace it with one more precisely tailored to our condition" (p. 250) of inhabiting a single planet. "We recommend instead that students pay closer attention to 'borders,' 'contact-zones,' and liminal spaces. . . . Such work is particularly useful not only because it reminds us of the 'imagined' nature of nationalism, but also because it highlights the artificiality of responsibility's limits" (p. 251).

This deliberately brief review of recent study abroad theorizing explicitly tied to education for global citizenship, experiential education, and postmodern theorizing reveals several things. First, several rationales for study abroad programming risk co-opting the fledgling global citizenship discourse that has emerged in global service-learning, which offers an alternative rationale for traditional study abroad (Annette, 2002; Kiely, 2010; Kiely & Hartman, 2004, 2007; Plater et al., 2009). Second, neocolonial students may bring cultural expectations and a consumerist mind-set that reproduces colonial patterns in study abroad today. Third, more explicit integration of critical reflective practice, questions of social concern, and praxis through collaborative action are necessary in any effort to foster development of globally engaged students. Fourth, postmodern theorizing helps study abroad theorists understand the contingency of our knowledge and belief systems and the artificiality and continuously contested nature of our categories and borders.

Global Service-Learning and Global Citizenship Education

Global service-learning is in many ways a strong response to the critiques of traditional study abroad reviewed earlier. Yet the service-learning field has struggled to keep pace with the heightened interest in global service-learning and the development of global citizenship, partly because service-learning itself is largely situated within assumptions regarding the importance of national civic identity and national citizenship. Leading scholars of citizenship and service-learning Joel Westheimer and Joseph Kahne (2004) have articulated three primary models of citizens that are advanced within civic education in the United States and Canada: the personally responsible citizen, the participatory citizen, and the justice-oriented citizen. Of these three types, the first two are strongly dependent on existing legal and institutional structures (Westheimer & Kahne, 2004) and therefore have no real or potential connection to the notion of a global citizen, whose ethical concern and actions would presumably transcend existing state borders.

Westheimer and Kahne's (2004) theorizing reflects service-learning's position in two ways. First, much of K–12 service-learning takes place within and is funded by state institutions (schools) with an explicit interest in replicating statist identity and advancing national belonging at the expense of exploring universal human connection. Second, the service-learning field has developed with connections and interrelationships with the field of political science (as distinct from international relations), which still (though with increasing criticism; see Jacobson and Wang [2008]) takes the presence of states and the importance of borders as central operating assumptions.

Acknowledging the reality of state presence is sensible, yet higher education is attempting to rise to the challenge of preparing students to live in a world in which the collective population of international migrants (213 million) would compose the fifth-largest country in the world (United Nations, 2009), where environmental challenges and advocacy are definitively global in nature (Keck & Sikkink, 1998), and where as a moral and ethical community we continue to struggle to create a reality that reflects each individual's fundamental human rights (Singer, 2002; United Nations, 1948). Service-learning theorists are thus engaged in a predominantly national conversation vacillating between what has been, what is, and what may be. Westheimer and Kahne's (2004) research reflects past and present, while 15 essays by higher education faculty, staff, and administrators were written for a Campus Compact visioning effort on the topic of global citizenship (Holland & Meeropol, 2006). That effort, however, led to extraordinarily little consensus and surprisingly few clear conceptualizations or operationalizations of the construct and application of global citizenship in diverse contexts.

Although some of the Campus Compact visioning authors suggested national competitiveness as a driving rationale for global citizenship (Blanke & Dahlem, 2006), many global service-learning practitioners, students, and faculty leaders bring idealistic aspirations (Crabtree, 2008; Grusky, 2000). Despite the importance of these aspirations as ideals, global service-learning must contend with its position in the past half century of predominantly unsuccessful development history (Easterly, 2006; Escobar, 1994; Korten,

1990; Martinussen, 2005) and the long legacy of colonizing, Christianizing, and civilizing (Chasteen, 2001; Galeano, 1997) under the guise of building a better world. As if these historic patterns of oppression or, at least, inefficacy are not enough with which to grapple, the particular form of global service-learning brings challenges specific to working with university undergraduates, ranging from students' proclivity to leave old and dirty clothes as "gifts" for community members to the possibility that students—after having conducted their brief stint in poverty tourism—return unencumbered to their privileged courses of study and career tracks (Crabtree, 2008).

Global service-learning, furthermore, is arguably more susceptible to the critiques leveled at "traditional service-learning," including that it can be patronizing and that it can cement structures of power and privilege when, depoliticized, it serves simply as a "glorified welfare system" (Mitchell, 2008, p. 51). Many service-learning practitioners and researchers are profoundly concerned by simplistic, charity-focused versions of service-learning that focus on individual relationships only, with no attention to broader systemic pressures (Crabtree, 2008; Kiely, 2005). This situation is further complicated in the context of "community service-learning" and globalization, the former suggesting place and reciprocity and the latter indicating a rapid and incompletely understood process that is altering the dynamics of power, privilege, self, community, state, and market (Keith, 2005).

To contend with these criticisms, Mitchell (2008) traced the development of critical service-learning as an alternative to traditional service-learning. Critical service-learning is academic service-learning infused with a social change orientation, efforts to redistribute power, and a focus on developing alternative relationships. This kind of deep criticality is fundamentally necessary for responsible global service-learning and consideration of global citizenship, otherwise faculty members, program leaders, and students risk restrengthening and extending colonial structures through their practice (Mitchell, 2008).

Keith's (2005) careful consideration of community service-learning in the context of globalization, furthermore, calls attention to the need for university-community engagement scholars to understand and account for the role of neoliberalism. More broadly, Keith's (2005) article implies a need for scholars who wish to delve into university-community engagement to have a robust understanding of economic, political, and social theory as it relates to contemporary global processes, structures, and assumptions. This need refers not only to university scholars' understanding of social theories but also, and perhaps more important, to an understanding of one's own positionality in North-South relations (Keith, 2005). Working with community organizations and attempting to address social issues is best pursued through awareness of our interdependence and through acknowledgment of the profound role of the market and neoliberal ideology in our lives. Quoting respected development writers and sociologists, Keith (2005) pointed out that for many people the market has become more influential than the state in determining access (or lack thereof) to basic social justice in terms of opportunities for self-development and self-determination.

Keith's (2005) work may go furthest in the service-learning literature to articulate the moral and ethical role for service-learning in a continuously evolving, increasingly global environment. Keith did not offer a clear conceptualization of global citizenship, yet she did offer globalism as a theory grounded in difference working against the grand narrative status of neoliberalism. For Keith (2005), the essential components of globalism are (a) a dialogical and multivocal perspective; (b) clear acknowledgment of the perspective and struggles of others, as well as support for global peace, equity, and justice; and (c) emergence of nongovernmental organizations and growing global social movements.

Butin's (2007) articulation of service-learning as "antifoundational" is particularly apt here. Because of the breadth, distances, and complexity involved in global service-learning, our categories are arguably more likely to be clumsy and inappropriately rigid. Butin (2007, p. 5) wrote,

> What antifoundational service-learning does is open up the possibility that how we originally viewed the world and ourselves may be too simplistic and stereotypical. This condition of possibility for rethinking our taken for-granted world is what the educational philosopher Gert Biesta (1998) argues is a "radical undecidability" that cannot simply default into an either/or binary.

Although each of these writers has added considerably to conceptual approaches to service-learning practice, most global service-learning programs remain unclear about what the "global citizenship" is that they purport to advance (Hartman, 2008; Kiely & Hartman, 2004, 2007). Political theorists and others from diverse disciplines have, of course, contributed significantly to a robust set of theoretical approaches to global citizenship and cosmopolitanism (Carter, 2001; Falk, 2002; Nussbaum, 1997; Stoddard & Cornwell, 2003). In a dissertation on the everyday practice of cosmopolitanism, Wheatley (2010), drawing on Lu (2000), usefully summarized numerous cosmopolitan writers into moral, political, and economic cosmopolitan categories. We have narrowed this review of approaches to global citizenship and global university-community engagement by addressing only those writers with an explicit emphasis on empirical application in the context of global service-learning.

This review demonstrates the following: (a) citizenship theorizing in service-learning is premised on state-centric assumptions; (b) global citizenship conceptualizations advanced to date have been nonexistent or insufficient; (c) global service-learning must acknowledge its position in the frequently negative history of international development; (d) there is a deliberate effort within service-learning to move toward critical service-learning; (e) juxtaposing service-learning and neoliberalism calls attention to the question of ethical global engagement in the context of decreasing state and increasing market power; and (f) service-learning is at its core continuously reflective, questioning, and therefore antifoundational (Butin, 2007; Hartman, 2008; Kiely & Hartman, 2007). In addition, several compelling critiques of programmatically and methodologically weak versions of international service-learning have emerged from students (Zemach-Bersin, 2008), faculty (Madsen-Camacho, 2004), and development workers turned bloggers (Holligurl, 2008), explicitly targeting imbalances of power and privilege in global service-learning programming.

We have yet to point explicitly to a weakness attributable to the global service-learning field (and much of the academy) as a whole; conceptualizations have been foisted down from above rather than developed through grounded theory, ethnography, and practice (Crabtree, 2008; Hartman, 2008; Kiely, 2010; Plater et al., 2009). As a matter of theory and practice, community service-learning, community-university engagement, and popular educational models explicitly value knowledge developed through interaction and dialogue. Institutions of higher education that offer international service-learning opportunities purport to prepare students for engaged citizenship (Plater et al., 2009). Students are increasingly thrust into international contexts and expected to intellectually and socially navigate relationships that span traditional state borders (Kiely, 2002) and often return with a radically transformed worldview and without the knowledge, skills, and social and organizational mechanisms to transfer successfully their profound learning. Simultaneously, universities have ramped up institutional commitment to service-learning and community-based scholarship (Kenny, Simon, Kiely-Brabeck, & Lerner, 2001). These trends and associated challenges led to a research collaboration between the authors (Kiely & Hartman, 2004, 2007, 2010) and was further developed through the authors' teaching at a number of institutions and holding administrative roles designing and implementing global service-learning programs in a number of different contexts.

To better understand students' conceptions of global engagement, this comparative case study is informed by critical conceptions of global engagement cited previously and builds on previous empirical research (Kiely, 2002, 2004), which found that students who participated in global service-learning experienced transformational learning along moral, political, intellectual, personal, cultural, and spiritual dimensions. This chapter focuses on more recent collaborative research undertaken by the authors (Hartman, 2008; Kiely & Hartman, 2004, 2007, 2010) and focuses more specifically on how students experience global engagement after participating in two distinct global service-learning programs in Tanzania and Bolivia.

Methodology: Comparative Case Study

In this section, we provide a brief description of global service-learning programs that were the focus of our comparative case study and a larger program survey conducted with students enrolled in a number of programs coordinated through a nonprofit organization that offers global service-learning opportunities in various countries. A comparative case study design provided a useful approach for exploring the meaning students attributed to their learning experience before, during, and after participation in international service-learning.

The purpose of this comparative case study was to understand how participation in international service-learning affects students' understanding of social responsibility and civic engagement and the actions associated with their understandings. To address the overall intent of the study, this research focused on two central questions:

1. How does international service-learning impact students' understanding of global engagement?
2. In what ways and to what extent do students engage in socially responsible behavior upon return to the United States?

We draw on data from three distinct sources (Hartman, 2008; Kiely & Hartman, 2004, 2007). First we have a set of semistructured, ongoing, qualitative interviews conducted with a set of students who self-initiated a service-learning partnership between a Tanzanian community and a large Research I university in the American South. Second, we have a set of semistructured interviews conducted with a group of students representing a large Research I university in the Northeast following their participation in a global service-learning course in Bolivia. Third, we draw on a multimethods study of global service-learning programming with more than 160 students in diverse courses at diverse locations (Kiely & Hartman, 2004, 2007).

All of our research and analysis are influenced by our roles as research practitioners. Our data point in a direction parallel to those in the literature reviewed earlier. That is, working with students involved with global service-learning reveals a substantial identity struggle in which concepts of citizenship seem dated, irrelevant, or misappropriated (Hartman, 2008; Kiely, 2004; Kiely & Hartman, 2007). Although our initial research on global service-learning focused on how students understand the meanings and actions related to global citizenship, analysis of data indicates that participants do not understand or act in ways that are consistent with the construct of global citizenship. On the basis of our ongoing research (Hartman, 2008; Kiely, 2002, 2004; Kiely & Hartman, 2004, 2007), we found that students, their mentors, and community partners are engaged in an ongoing struggle to define and understand the dimensions and ethical practice of what we call a critical approach to global citizenship, which we believe more accurately depicts participants' understanding, intentions, and actions in global service-learning.

We utilized a "multimethod triangulation approach" (Patton, 2002) that included diverse data-gathering sources and methods including on-site participant observation, document analysis, focus groups, and semistructured interviews. We utilized a constant comparative method of analysis (Glaser & Strauss, 1967) to identify categories and themes generated by study participants that gave more robust meaning to their understanding of global citizenship and engagement after participation in global distinct service-learning programs. Finally, we focused our analysis within each case and across the two cases. Analysis of a set of pre- and postsurvey data from a third case further corroborated themes that emerged from the two case studies.

Case 1: Student-Initiated Service-Learning Program in Tanzania

The Tanzania global service-learning program was initiated during the 2004 Maymester. The program was largely designed and developed by three undergraduate students and one graduate student working with a faculty adviser—who did not participate in the on-site experience. The students and faculty member cocreated the syllabus and course design. Students did a noncredit pre-service-learning seminar with their faculty adviser, focusing on action research, project planning, communication, community collaboration, safety, logistics, planning, and reporting. Students conducted action research with community partners and, on the basis of their collaborative study, engaged in the design and implementation of four service-learning projects in the township of Moshi. The projects included the creation of an adult learning community center, a women's support group, a tutoring program, and a youth soccer league.

To better understand students' learning and action before, during, and after participation in the Tanzania program, the case study utilized a variety of methods for collecting data. Data collected and analyzed for the Tanzania case study included participant journals, a final report and manual, ongoing interviews, and focus groups with participants before and for 2 years after the program. In addition, students documented and provided evidence of the learning that resulted from their global service-learning experience by generating a number of documents (i.e., proposals, papers, PowerPoint presentations, posters, and websites) for various peer-reviewed presentations made at local and national conferences.

Case 2: Students Who Participated in Global Service-Learning in Bolivia

Five students participated in a global service-learning program in Bolivia. All of the students attended a large Research I university in the Northeast. The service-learning course took place during the summer and was focused on the topic of global citizenship. Students read texts on global citizenship and considered various approaches to global ethical engagement while they worked with an indigenous community on a school-building project. Data collected and analyzed included field notes from on-site observations, journals, and postprogram semistructured interviews.

Case 3: A University-Nonprofit Global Service-Learning Partnership

Hartman (2008, 2014) conducted an evaluation of a university-nonprofit partnership to support global service-learning. The evaluation featured a quantitative global civic engagement index based on domestic civic engagement measures, as well as some qualitative interviews and extensive observation and practice. More than 150 students completed the pre- and postsurveys regarding quantitative civic engagement measures. Roughly half of the population was exposed to a deliberately reflective global engagement curriculum tied to global citizenship learning. The curriculum was similar to the curricula examined by Peterson (2002) and suggested by Lutterman-Aguilar and Gingerich (2002). The other half of the sample was simply exposed to academic global service-learning absent a targeted civic development curriculum.

Findings: A Critical Global Citizenship

The students with whom we worked did not uniformly identify with existing theories of global citizenship, though numerous students mentioned profound personal struggles and shifts in their thinking and behavior as they worked to integrate their global service-learning experiences with their lives at home. Numerous other scholars have documented the struggle students experience following global service-learning (Kiely, 2002; Peterson, 2002; Porter, 2000; Tonkin & Quiroga, 2004), but in the past this observation frequently led to the conclusion that the field needed a better conceptualization of global citizenship (Hartman, 2008; Holland & Meeropol, 2006). Findings from this comparative case study, which confirm and expand on previous research (Kiely, 2004; Kiely & Hartman, 2004, 2007) and address the shortcomings of global citizenship theorizing reviewed previously, lead us to suggest a model for critical global citizenship that contains six learning outcomes and associated actions.

The negotiations consistently mentioned by students undertaking a critical global citizenship fall along the following dimensions: intellectual, political, moral, social, cultural, and personal (see table 12.1).

Intellectual Dimension
Study findings indicate that students in both groups focused on the need for critical reflection on their own and others' assumptions regarding their education, the source and solution to problems in the communities with which they work, and the importance of learning how to conduct collaborative research with their peers, faculty, and community members to create knowledge to better understand and address local and global problems. For example, in their project report, the students in the Tanzania program described their reflection process as a "journey" and stressed the importance of engaging in critical reflection before, during, and after the global service-learning program.

> Active reflection on what one sees, experiences, and observes is an integral part of the S-L [service-learning] experience. It allows students to understand the connection between their academic learning, their field experiences, and their service programs. Our reflection model presents a method of digesting the material, issues, and feelings experienced while immersed in diverse and dynamic settings. This reflective process leads students to think critically and holistically about issues that impact our world, fostering new and creative solutions to those problems. (Final Reflective Report, Tanzania GSL Program)

The students in our study consistently emphasized the importance of valuing local knowledge and engaging in various reflection activities to better understand and address local and global issues and problems. Students returning from Tanzania stressed that critical reflection means combining "academic learning and community engagement through interactions with

TABLE 12.1
Dimensions of Critical Global Citizenships

Learning Outcome	Understanding	Actions
Intellectual	Critical reflection, collaborative research, interdisciplinary	Read a global service-learning manual; create action research projects; develop conference proposals
Political	Rights and responsibilities on multiple levels (personal, interpersonal, institutional, community, policy) and unrelated to citizenship status	Organize and create student organizations; develop and implement university-community-based projects aimed at direct and indirect service; provide policy and institutional support for service-learning
Moral	Empathy, solidarity, reciprocity, collaboration	Organize fund-raisers and events that raise awareness and build allies to address social problems; promote service-learning to solve local and global community-based problems
Social	Communication (i.e., verbal and nonverbal), dialogue, connection	Develop social networks, websites, presentations, papers, reports, and manuals; listen to diverse perspectives; provide an encouraging voice
Cultural	Engage in cross-cultural interaction, embrace diversity, dismantle cultural myths	Resist dominant norms related to privilege, power, race, class, gender, nationality, consumption, and education; value and learn to navigate local norms and beliefs
Personal	Lifestyle change, academic pursuits, professional development	Be aware of impact of personal and professional decisions and actions; reduce ecological footprint

community members, the scholarly literature, faculty members, and multiple research methods."

Key to the Tanzanian participants' approach to global service-learning is to think about the generation and application of knowledge to solve community-based problems as *interdisciplinary teams*. They illustrated the importance of an interdisciplinary team approach in their final report:

> Interdisciplinary Teams are crucial when it comes to planning a success-ful Service-Learning [S-L] program. The problems facing communities are multifaceted and persistent. These types of problems cannot be understood or addressed fully from a "unidisciplinary" standpoint. While the ability to integrate S-L into some fields of study is more apparent than in others, it is true that nearly anyone can integrate their course of study into a S-L project. . . . On our program there was a geneticist, an educator, and a geographer. We worked with a Tanzanian activist, village leaders, farmers, and community mothers. Utilizing the comparative advantage each team member has in their past experience not only increases the effectiveness and overall success of the S-L program, but also gives each team member a chance to put his/her knowledge into practice. (Final Reflective Report, Tanzania GSL Program)

Political Dimension

Students emphasized increased interest in and engagement with local, national, and international politics, specifically in relation to the communi-ties where they've served and the issues about which they've learned more. They demonstrated substantially more interest in global civil society mecha-nisms and responded positively when given "start lists" of diverse global civil society organizations—representing varied political and religious perspec-tives—that all seek to build a better world more consistent with an assump-tion of common human dignity. They focused their understanding on their own and others' rights and responsibilities and how rights and responsibili-ties entail multiple roles on a variety of levels (i.e., personal, interpersonal, institutional, community, policy) depending on the context.

Once Tanzania students returned home, they connected their roles and responsibilities to engaging in activities that fostered individual, community, and institutional change. They wrote a comprehensive service-learning report and guide and sent it to the university president and a variety of campus administrators whom they identified as persons responsible for making deci-sions related to study abroad and service-learning efforts at the institution. In the report the students were very clear about their role and the responsibil-ity of various university stakeholders in creating structures and policies that might further service-learning opportunities on campus. They stated,

> To encourage service learning [S-L] at both a local and global level, there is a need to create a center at [the university] committed to the ideals of service-learning and educating students to become ethical inhabitants of

the world. Students and faculty are interested in these ideas, but do not currently have a knowledge base or institutional process for creating effective S-L programs. The University needs to provide a means to encourage creative and interdisciplinary solutions to issues. Students need a way to receive credit for S-L activities, professors need guidance in how to create effective S-L opportunities, and there needs to be money available for S-L programs. A center for S-L would facilitate [the university] becoming leaders in a global movement. Only through establishing dialogue between communities abroad and those in our local community can a difference be made in the world. Together we can work towards a common goal of open cross-cultural communication and equality. These are the steps that we are committed to changing; we anxiously await the university's reply. (Final Reflective Report, Tanzania GSL Program)

Students in both the Tanzania and Bolivia programs organized fundraisers and events to generate support and educate students on how they might become more involved in solving local and global problems in the community through service-learning and greater engagement. Tanzania students created a student organization called "globally aware and active people" (GAAP) that they hoped would serve as an umbrella organization aimed at supporting other student groups' efforts to engage in social action projects locally and globally. They sponsored a local poverty initiative, wrote articles in departmental newsletters, and gave presentations on how to get involved in local and global initiatives aimed at solving problems related to poverty. In the end, students were less concerned with their roles and responsibilities as citizens and more concerned with their various roles and responsibilities in addressing local and global problems. Responding to a question regarding their understanding of their role as it relates to global citizenship, Jed stated,

It's (global citizenship) beyond politics, it's more in the realm of the idea of what democracy is and having a choice in something and what it means to have a choice is also knowing what your options [are]. . . . The more you talk to people from around the world the more you realize that democratic and republican doesn't help you to communicate with people in the world you know. It's just being associated with that idea of what democracy might be, on a larger scale. Not U.S. based, overall. That's the global aspect.

One of the Bolivia students represents the diverse manifestations of his political (and personal) engagement and specifically attributed it to his global service-learning experience:

I worked for over a year as a political organizer, which relates to Cochabamba to me in that economic hardship (lack of health care, low wages, etc.) knows no national borders. Part of Global Citizenship, as we learned in Cochabamba, is that every person in the world has certain rights, no matter what country they are from. I believe that everyone has a right to adequate health care, a good education, etc. So for me, working for these rights in the U.S. is part of the larger job of working for them on a global level. As for the future, I am going to be a volunteer with WorldTeach starting in about a month. I will teach English for around a year, will live with a host family, and so on. This is most definitely connected to my experience in Cochabamba. Indeed, had it not been for that experience, I probably would not be doing this at all.

When asked to explain how their global service-learning experience impacted their understanding and enactment of global citizenship, students consistently found it difficult to define *global citizenship* and downplayed the term as reflective of the cumulative experience. Jeff's comments seem indicative of students' overall impression of global citizenship as something that didn't quite capture the meaning of their experience:

Global citizenry is such a relative term in my mind. But for me, S-L [service-learning] has helped me to realize how big the world truly is. I mean, 4 million people in Atlanta Metro alone, 350 million in the United States, 6+ billion in the world. . . . One can't really wrap their mind around these numbers. The only way to even come close to understanding how many differences this translates into, with regard to cultures, values, religions, viewpoints, etc. . . . . is to travel and to befriend people and truly experience how they live, day to day. It isn't feasible for someone to do this with every society on the planet, but if you can do it with a few, and really become part of their community, especially if they are less affluent, basically less lucky, then perhaps you can project what you've learned on a broader scale. Being a global citizen then, to me, is to be understanding and accepting of the fact that the world does not revolve around an individual, a culture, a society, a country, but around the pantheon of these that exist in our world. Ultimately, having the mind-set that no one way to live is the right way, and then allowing or desiring equal opportunity for those who choose to live differently, is the crux of being a global citizen.

Moral Dimension

Students renegotiated assumptions regarding right and wrong. They both moved beyond nationalized conceptions of ethics and reconsidered the possibilities for plural, diverse bases for ethical assumptions. They better understood the plausibility of diverse, legitimate truth streams simultaneously approaching a conception of the good that recognizes fundamental human dignity. For example, the Tanzania students summarized the key value of reciprocity in sustaining global service-learning partnerships:

> Without a foundation of reciprocal partnerships between local people and those from [the university] there can be no sustainability. These partnerships must start long before traveling to the host country, grow while the student is immersed in the culture of the host country, and continue long after the student is back at home. (Final Reflective Report, Tanzania GSL Program)

Another student completing a final reflective essay on the topic of global citizenship for a global service-learning course through the university-nonprofit partnership expressed her new frustration and sense of nuance in hearing others' assumptions regarding right, wrong, and African development. She also offered an expanded comprehension of the challenges of development, with an implicit call for better and more holistic development efforts:

> On the flight from Amsterdam to Detroit, I sat next to a 16-year-old girl making her way home from a mission in Kenya. At first I was stoked for the girl and even jealous that she was beginning her path as a global citizen as early as I would have liked to. After she began talking about her experience, I could not help but become critical. Although I never thought I could criticize anyone who went to Africa with the best intentions, I was so frustrated by what this girl told me. She told me she accompanied a woman who had built a school in Kenya and that they were bringing clothes because "all the little kids just run around naked." . . . Before the trip, I thought that we would be treated as liberators, freeing the people from their poverty. In the back of my mind, I thought that it could not be that hard. I thought the poverty trap could be overcome with just a water harvesting tank, some preventative medicine, and an education. But when people have water, but not enough nutritious foods, or bed nets, but not enough beds, or schools, but not enough teachers, books, or desks, they cannot escape the poverty trap. After experiencing Tanzania for a month, I know that our skills were useful and that we did make a difference over there, but I know what's more important. I am so honored that we were able to work with the NGOs WOMEDA and FADECO.

Social Dimension

The social-learning dimension of students' critical global citizenship meant communicating their global service-learning experience more effectively (i.e., both nonverbally and verbally) with a variety of stakeholders, including community members, peers, faculty, university administrators, and a broader audience. This meant learning how to listen intently, dialogue, ask questions, participate in nonverbal activities (e.g., dance, drumming, religious ceremonies, meals, service work), and observe. Many of the students we interviewed participated in a variety of community activities described earlier in order to connect with people in ways that did not require fluency in language. Other students created blogs to communicate the value of their experience but also created theme-based and programmatic websites meant to educate their peers and others who might visit their site online on important social issues specific to the country where they conducted their service work. For example, Alice, who went to Bolivia, created a site devoted to global citizenship and later spoke about citizenship as "more about common humanity" rather than one's national affiliation and said "to be conscious of how your actions might help or hurt others" in the world.

The Tanzania students also communicated their learning by developing a website that described their projects in Tanzania, the different types of issues affecting Tanzanians in the region where they worked, and how others might get involved with and/or support their work. Many of the students described the importance of building social networks with other students and the local community. The Tanzanian group created a student organization and joined university-wide committees as a way to build social networks meant to work together to solve social problems locally and globally.

Cultural Dimension

Findings suggest that the cultural dimension of students' learning experience represented two primary dimensions: to engage with and respect diverse cultural perspectives and to recognize and challenge cultural norms, rituals, practices, and roles that are harmful to themselves and others. For students, the cultural learning entailed in critical global engagement meant developing the ability to reflect critically on and deconstruct sometimes difficult and deeply held cultural assumptions. For example, upon return all of the students questioned dominant materialistic and individualistic tendencies of their American peers and institutions and policies that promote it. Tanzanian and Bolivian students questioned the value of assumptions embedded in traditional study abroad and classroom learning in their institutions and called for more service-learning opportunities. The Tanzania students explained this dimension in their service-learning philosophy:

> As the world becomes increasingly interconnected, no country is isolated from the global community. To have any hope for future understanding across broad cultural differences in the world, people must gain a respect for and ability to work with diverse peoples. This commitment is made at

both a local and global level. As mentioned on our philosophy page, the quagmire of traditional study abroad is that it simply mimics a classroom situation. However, the objective of Global S-L [service-learning] programs is to discover creative learning opportunities for students that work toward solving real world problems. The challenge presented to educators and students when working outside of the classroom is that real world problems are not contained in semesters, they do not fit into one edition of a textbook, and their effects extend far beyond a grade. There is a far greater responsibility and accountability put upon professors and students due to the community component of S-L. For this reason, there must be an institutionalized structure in place based around a philosophy that ensures that S-L programs are sustainable and capable of evolving as needed. (Final Reflective Report, Tanzania GSL Program)

Personal Dimension

The personal dimension clearly has many connections to the other dimensions mentioned, yet we chose to include it as a distinct category because we noted the highly personal nature of identity negotiation following global service-learning experiences. Perhaps because a superstructure of governance or authority is nonexistent, students responded to global service-learning in highly personalized ways often related to lifestyle and consumption habits. They reported thinking about children in developing countries while they shopped at the grocery store or washed their clothing and used the dryer. They chose to shrink their environmental footprints or to completely change their career paths. For example, the Tanzania students expressed their unified conception of the personal dimension of their global service-learning philosophy as *global personhood*:

Global Personhood is a fundamental aspect of our philosophy. It challenges people to be aware of the global impact of their everyday choices. For example, when one drinks coffee that is not fair trade or shade grown, they indirectly support deforestation and perpetuate the poverty of coffee farmers in the developing world. Service-Learning introduces students to global experiences that change how they interact with people of the world. Students learn to critically look at the world locally, nationally, and ecologically. Students develop a consciousness of the interdependent and interconnected nature of the world. They begin to understand how their daily decisions affect a wide range of people and environments. By understanding your global personhood, you can begin to make better decisions that affect the world in a positive way. (Final Reflective Report, Tanzania GSL Program)

A Critical Global Citizenship: Combining Thought and Intention With Action

In interviews and experiences with students, the desire to take action and make a difference has been a central concern. Students engage in actions, particularly along the political and personal dimensions. In the final analysis of students' understanding, intention, and action, a critical global citizenship emerges as an alternative to study abroad's traditional emphasis on intercultural competency and service-learning's traditional emphasis on civic education (see table 12.2).

A Critical Global Citizenship: Possibility, Challenges, and Limitations

Findings from this study emerged through conversation with students struggling to acknowledge distant individuals' full humanity, the diversity of belief systems in the world, and their roles relating to others' human experiences. Our understanding of global citizenship, then, takes as a contingent yet firmly held truth that all humans are equally deserving of common dignity. It recognizes the vast diversity of truth systems that exist in the world and the possibility—indeed the certainty—that we will continue to more deeply understand and revise our sense of what it means to be fully human. *Critical global citizen pioneers* (we borrow this terminology from Richard Falk [2000], who recognized global citizens as being on a journey to an as-yet-unimagined tomorrow) understand the arrogance involved in "global thinking" (Esteva & Prakash, 1997) and therefore approach knowledge and action with deep humility. As pioneers committed to the notion of equal human dignity, however, they will move to action in ways consistent with affirmative postmodernists (Yappa, 1996), who recognize possibility for just action in specific situations and commitments.

We are deeply aware of Nussbaum's recognized work on global citizenship (1992, 1997, 2002) and understand her characterization of a global citizen as a person who recognizes common human dignity, develops his or her narrative imagination (or empathy) for other humans, and who cultivates critical distance from one's culture and traditions. Yet we do not believe Nussbaum and her acolytes go far enough in their cultivation of criticality. Our work around the world, in diverse contexts, cultures, and communities, along with our knowledge of various truth systems, the literature reviewed previously, our students' suggestions and articulations, and the many harms done in the name of development, leads us to advance a critical understanding of global citizenship as an approach that is substantially more conscious of the continuously evolving and

TABLE 12.2

Intercultural Competency, Civic Education, and a Critical Global Citizenship

	Intercultural Competency	Civic Engagement	Critical Global Citizenship
Purpose	Competent functioning for nationals in another nation for whatever means	Educate citizens to fulfill civic obligations and build a more just national society	Draws attention to the notion of fundamental human equality and tentatively building a more just world.
Core learning goal	Informational and skill competency	Responsible citizens with the knowledge, skills, and efficacy necessary to participate in national politics	Uses transformative education to connect people who work toward a world that more clearly recognizes fundamental human equality.
Knowledge	Utilized to learn customs, norms, and language and to adapt to habits of host culture	Focus on institutional arrangements, citizen rights and responsibilities, rules, laws, and possibly pressing social issues	Emphasizes collaborative research to generate knowledge of sources and solutions to social problems and focuses on identifying and examining cultural assumptions in order to navigate diverse cultures. Through immersion, reflection, and service work, students engage with local and global realities.
Questioning	Typically confined to consideration of home and host cultures' differing assumptions and how to navigate and adapt to those differences	Frequently not included; if included, often confined to justice-seeking within recognized state borders	Engages critical reflective tradition to foster analysis of how educational, social, institutional, cultural, political, and economic structures do or do not promote the ethic of fundamental human equality.

(Continues)

TABLE 12.2

Intercultural Competency, Civic Education, and a Critical Global Citizenship (Continued)

	Intercultural Competency	Civic Engagement	Critical Global Citizenship
Culture shock and reverse culture shock	To be processed to permit adaptation abroad and at home	Typically not included	Provides vital learning moments and opportunity to address observed truths and work (an ongoing struggle) against unjust global realities.
Emotion	Not typically included; emphasis is rather on cognitive understanding and communication skills	Visceral connection with other citizens is emphasized and considered in light of civic responsibilities, duties, and national health	Emphasizes and considers visceral connections with other individuals in light of concepts related to empathy, human equality, and how existing institutions recognize it.
Institutions and policies	Accepted for facility of travel, logistics, and exchange	Government institutions central as mechanisms to allow "our" public voice and governance	Questions and considers institutions and policies in respect to their relevance to human equality.
Spirituality	Typically not included	Typically not included	Engages spirituality as component of participant's meaning-making, supporting and changing through transformative journey.

temporally and culturally contingent nature of concepts such as rights (Donnelly, 2003) and citizenship. Our study recognizes that a critical global citizenship necessarily entails an ongoing struggle aimed at disrupting, decolonizing, and transforming historical, linguistic, structural, cultural, and institutional arrangements that cause harm. This is an ongoing, principled negotiation that current conceptions of global citizenship learning do not address.

As our research suggests, a critical approach to global citizenship, carried out in global service-learning programs, means focusing on intellectual, political, moral, social, cultural, and personal learning outcomes. Although this model confirms previous research (Kiely, 2002),[1] it articulates more clearly the complex and patterned ways in which students combine their understanding, intentions, and actions. In addition, it adds a social dimension as a learning outcome that is necessary for communicating more effectively with diverse stakeholders in global service-learning contexts and for creating more substantial social networks necessary for supporting long-term and sustainable campus-community partnerships.

Study abroad and service-learning theorists, as indicated previously, have been moving continuously toward more critical models of engagement that acknowledge our postmodern position and allow for ongoing efforts to build a better world. Simultaneously, students have struggled to re-create and renegotiate their identities following exposure to global service-learning. They have not always found global citizenship theory relevant to their experiences. Our understanding of a critical global citizenship follows from student articulations of their experiences, accepts our postmodern positions, and allows for diverse, currently unknown or unknowable efforts toward building a better world. This kind of global citizenship therefore admits that we do not have precise answers but calls us to humble, careful, and ongoing action to better acknowledge common human dignity. It continuously reminds us of the possibility of our own, perhaps unintentional or unwitting, complicity in perpetuating structures of exclusion (such as states) and patterns of oppression.

Although a strength of our definition of *global citizenship* is that it was developed through dialogue with students and is therefore an en vivo account of such global participation, its roots hardly extend beyond theorists, practitioners, and the student population. In the future, theorists should develop an account of global citizenship rooted in university, public, student, community member, and faculty member dialogue and exchange. A broader base of en vivo accounts may help us better understand how diverse global actors wish (or wish not) to work together to understand and build a better world.

Future directions relating to critically approaching global citizenship should undertake research such as that mentioned in this chapter, consideration of institutional limitations and institution building, and deeper investigation of personal practices. By institutional limitations and institution building, we are referring to the often-repeated lament that global service-learning programs are the work of a small number of individuals on campuses who are prepared to overlook their institutional incentives regarding tenure and promotion. There will be no transformation—only tension—if institutions continue to treat "global citizenship education" as merely a nominal goal absent critical analysis of existing societal structures. If faculty members are recognized for deep university-community engagement efforts, for community-based participatory research, and for facilitating new knowledge development through cooperative dialogue on building a better world with community partners and with students, then more faculty members will take part in such activities. What are the structures that could support this kind of effort and still ensure universities meet their other goals?

Finally, more research and development of practice is needed to understand how individuals and organizations can continue to undertake positive actions to build a better world. As more actions are documented, others interested in critical global citizenship will become more aware and have more possibilities for cooperating to build a better world. Without being prescriptive, theorists have an opportunity to help facilitate growth and movement toward growing global identity and concern for others around the world. Furthermore, admitting to the possibility of an imaginative, critical global connectedness without relying heavily on the prescribed roles of citizens or states calls attention to better understanding the numerous other important and legitimate ways in which people self-organize, handle disputes, and arrange things such as "civility" to one another (Werbner & Ranger, 1996). We are all—consciously or otherwise—bound up with imagining, identifying, and naming other possibilities that might exist to organize better in the future (Falk, 2002; Reilly & Senders, 2009; Stout, 2010).

Endnote

1. The "spiritual" dimension found in Kiely's (2002) study did not emerge as a salient pattern in this study. This does not mean that it isn't an important dimension of critical global citizenship. There is a need for further study to uncover the deeper spiritual dimension underpinning critical global citizenship.

References

Annette, J. (2002, Winter). Service learning in an international context. *Frontiers: The Interdisciplinary Journal of Study Abroad, VIII*, 83–93.

Biesta, G. (1998). The right to philosophy of education: From critique to deconstruction. In S. Tozer (Ed.), *Philosophy of education yearbook* (pp. 476–484). Urbana-Champaign, IL: Philosophy of Education Society.

Blanke, D., & Dahlem, K. (2006). Educating for a global citizenship. In B. Holland & J. Meeropol (Eds.), *A more perfect vision: The future of campus engagement*. Providence, RI: Campus Compact. Retrieved from http://www.compact.org/20th/papers

Braskamp, L. A., Braskamp, D. C., & Merrill, K. (2009, Fall). Assessing progress in global learning and development of students with education abroad experiences. *Frontiers: The Interdisciplinary Journal of Study Abroad, XVIII,* 101–118.

Butin, D. (2007). Justice learning: Service-learning as justice oriented education. *Equity and Excellence in Education, 40,* 1–7.

Carter, A. (2001). *The political theory of global citizenship.* New York, NY: Routledge.

Chasteen, J. C. (2001). *Born in blood and fire: A concise history of Latin America.* New York, NY: W. W. Norton.

Crabtree, R. (2008). Theoretical foundations for international service-learning. *Michigan Journal of Community Service, 15*(1), 18–36.

Donnelly, J. (2003). *Universal human rights in theory and practice.* Ithaca, NY: Cornell University Press.

Easterly, W. (2006). *The White man's burden: Why the West's efforts to aid the rest have done so much ill and so little good.* New York, NY: Penguin Press.

Escobar, A. (1994). *Encountering development: The making and unmaking of the third world.* Princeton, NJ: Princeton University Press.

Esteva, G., & Prakash, M. S. (1997). From global thinking to local thinking. In M. Rahnema & V. Bawtree (Eds.), *The post-development reader.* New York, NY: Zed Books.

Falk, R. A. (2000). *Human rights horizons: The pursuit of justice in a globalizing world.* New York, NY: Routledge.

Falk, R. (2002). An emergent matrix of citizenship: Complex, uneven, and fluid. In N. Dower (Ed.), *Global citizenship: A critical introduction.* New York, NY: Routledge.

Galeano, E. (1997). *Open veins of Latin America.* New York, NY: Monthly Review Press.

Glaser, B., & Strauss, A. (1967). *The discovery of grounded theory: Strategies for qualitative research.* Chicago, IL: Aldine.

Grusky, S. (2000). International service-learning: A critical guide from an impassioned advocate. *American Behavioral Scientist, 43*(5), 858–867.

Hartman, E. (2008). *Educating for global citizenship through service-learning: A theoretical account and curricular evaluation* (Doctoral dissertation). Retrieved from http://etd.library.pitt.edu/ETD/available/etd-11132008-094725/unrestricted/HartmanEM2008etd_final.pdf

Hartman, E. (2014, March). Educating for global citizenship: A theoretical account and quantitative analysis. *eJournal of Public Affairs.*

Holland, B., & Meeropol, J. (Eds.). (2006). *A more perfect vision: The future of campus engagement.* Providence, RI: Campus Compact. Retrieved from http://www.compact.org/20th/papers

Holligurl. (2008). *Giving back: The volunteers descend on Ghana.* Retrieved from http://www.aidworkers.net/?q=node/1603

Institute of International Education. (2010). *Open doors 2010 fast facts*. Retrieved from http://www.iie.org/en/research-and-publications/~/media/Files/Corporate/Open-Doors/Fast-Facts/Fast%20Facts%202010.ashx

Jacobson, D., & Wang, N. (2008). What if the model does not tell the whole story? The clock, the natural forest, and the new global studies. *New Global Studies*, *2*(3), 1035–1059.

Jenkins, K., & Skelly, J. (2004, Winter). Education abroad is not enough. *International Educator: The Magazine of NAFSA: International Educators, XII*(1), 6–12.

Johnson, M. (2009, Fall). Post-reciprocity: In defense of the "post" perspective. *Frontiers: The Interdisciplinary Journal of Study Abroad, XVIII*, 181–186.

Keck, M. E., & Sikkink, K. (1998). Environmental advocacy networks. In *Activists beyond borders: Advocacy networks in international politics* (pp. 121–164). Ithaca, NY: Cornell University Press.

Keith, N. (2005). Community service-learning in the face of globalization: Rethinking theory and practice. *Michigan Journal of Community Service-Learning, 11*(2), 5–24.

Kenny, M. E., Simon, L. A. K., Kiley-Brabeck, K., & Lerner, R. M. (2001). *Learning to serve: Promoting civil society through service-learning*. New York, NY: Springer.

Kiely, R. (2002). *Toward an expanded conceptualization of transformational learning: A case study of international service-learning in Nicaragua* (Doctoral dissertation). Retrieved from *Dissertation Abstracts International*. (63 (09A), 3083)

Kiely, R. (2004). A chameleon with a complex: Searching for transformation in international service-learning. *Michigan Journal of Community Service Learning, 10*(2), 5–20.

Kiely, R. (2005). A transformative learning model for service-learning: A longitudinal case study. *Michigan Journal of Community Service Learning, 12*(1), 5–22.

Kiely, R. (2010). Study abroad, intercultural learning and international service-learning. In R. Bringle, J. Hatcher, & S. Jones (Eds.), *Research perspectives in international service-learning* (Vol. 1, pp. 243–274). Sterling, VA: Stylus.

Kiely, R., & Hartman, E. (2004, October). *Developing a framework for assessing learning for global citizenship: A comparative case study analysis of three international service-learning programs*. Proceedings of the 4th Annual International Service-Learning Research Conference, Clemson University, SC.

Kiely, R., & Hartman, E. (2007, October). *The relationship among context, program factors and learning in global service-learning: A comparative case study of three programs in Nicaragua, Bolivia and Tanzania*. Paper presented at the 7th International Research Conference on Service-Learning and Community Engagement, Florida Campus Compact, Tampa Bay, FL.

Kiely, R., & Hartman, E. (2010). Qualitative research in international service-learning. In R. Bringle, J. Hatcher, & S. Jones (Eds.), *Research perspectives in international service-learning* (Vol. 1, pp. 291–318). Sterling, VA: Stylus.

Korten, D. (1990). *Getting to the 21st century: Voluntary action and the global agenda*. Bloomfield, CT: Kumarian Press.

Lechner, F. J. (2009). *Globalization: The making of world society*. Singapore: Utopia Press.

Lewin, R. (2009). *The handbook of practice and research in study abroad: Higher education and the quest for global citizenship*. New York, NY: Routledge.

Lu, C. (2000). The one and many faces of cosmopolitanism. *Journal of Political Philosophy, 8*(2), 244–267.

Lutterman-Aguilar, A., & Gingerich, O. (2002, Winter). Experiential pedagogy for study abroad: Educating for global citizenship. *Frontiers: The Interdisciplinary Journal of Study Abroad, VIII*, 41–82.

Madsen-Camacho, M. (2004). Power and privilege: Community service learning in Tijuana. *Michigan Journal of Community-Service-Learning, 10*(3), 31–42.

Martinussen, J. (2005). *State, society, and market: A guide to competing theories of development*. New York, NY: St. Martin's Press.

Mitchell, T. (2008). Traditional vs. critical service-learning: Engaging the literature to differentiate two models. *Michigan Journal of Community Service-Learning, 14*(2), 50–65.

Nussbaum, M. (1992). Human functioning and social justice: In defense of Aristotelian essentialism. *Political Theory, 20*(2), 202–246.

Nussbaum, M. (1997). *Cultivating humanity: A classical defense of reform in liberal education*. Cambridge, MA: Harvard University Press.

Nussbaum, M. (2002). *For love of country?* Boston, MA: Beacon Press.

Ogden, A. (2007–2008, Fall–Winter). The view from the veranda: Understanding today's colonial student. *Frontiers: The Interdisciplinary Journal of Study Abroad, XV*, 35–56.

Andreotti, V., & de Souza, L. M. (2012). *Postcolonial perspectives on global citizenship education*. New York, NY: Routledge.

Patton, M. Q. (2002). *Qualitative research and evaluation methods* (3rd ed.). Thousand Oaks, CA: Sage.

Peterson, C. F. (2002, Winter). Preparing engaged citizens: Three models of experiential education for social justice. *Frontiers: The Interdisciplinary Journal of Study Abroad, VIII*, 165–206.

Plater, W. M., Jones, S. G., Bringle, R. G., & Clayton, P. H. (2009). Educating globally competent citizens through international service learning. In R. Lewin (Ed.), *The handbook of practice and research in study abroad* (pp. 62–74). Florence, KY: Taylor and Francis Books.

Porter, M. (2000). "Ayni" in the global village: Building relationships of reciprocity through global service-learning. *Michigan Journal of Community Service-Learning, 8*(1), 5–17.

Reilly, D., & Senders, S. (2009, Fall). Becoming the change we want to see: Critical study abroad for a tumultuous world. *Frontiers: The Interdisciplinary Journal of Study Abroad, XVIII*, 241–267.

Singer, P. (2002). *One world*. New Haven, CT: Yale University Press.

Stoddard, E. W., & Cornwell, G. H. (2003). Peripheral visions: Toward a geoethics of citizenship. *Liberal Education, 89*(3), 44–51.

Stout, M. (2010). Back to the future: Toward a political economy of love and abundance. *Administration and Society, 42*(1), 3–37.

Tarc, P. (2013). *International education in global times: Engaging the pedagogic*. New York, NY: Peter Lang.

Tonkin, H., & Quiroga, D. (2004, Fall). A qualitative approach to the assessment of international service-learning. *Frontiers: The Interdisciplinary Journal of Study Abroad, X*, 131–149.

United Nations. (1948). *The universal declaration of human rights*. Retrieved from http://www.un.org/en/documents/udhr/

United Nations. (2009). *International migration 2009: Graphs and maps from the 2009 wall chart*. Retrieved from http://www.un.org/esa/population/publications/2009Migration_Chart/IttMig_maps.pdf

Werbner, R., & Ranger, T. (Eds.). (1996). *Postcolonial identities in Africa*. New York, NY: Zed Books.

Westheimer, J., & Kahne, J. (2004). Educating the "good" citizen: Political choices and pedagogical goals. *PS: Political Science and Politics, 37*(2), 241–247.

Wheatley, E. S. (2010). *"Everyday" cosmopolitical practices in contested spaces: Moving beyond the state of cosmopolitanism* (Doctoral dissertation, Arizona State University).

Yappa, L. (1996). What causes poverty? A postmodern view. *Annals of the Association of American Geographers, 86*(4), 707–728.

Zemach-Bersin, T. (2008, March 7). A student's excursion into "global citizenship." *Chronicle of Higher Education*.

Zemach-Bersin, T. (2012). Entitled to the world: The rhetoric of U.S. global citizenship education and study abroad. In V. Oliveira Andreotti & L. M. de Souza (Eds.), *Postcolonial perspectives on global citizenship education*. New York, NY: Routledge.

CONCLUSION

Does Tension in International Service-Learning
Lead to Transformation?

Patrick M. Green
Loyola University Chicago

I nternational service-learning (ISL) is rife with tensions, as indicated in the chapters of this edited volume. Each chapter framed ISL uniquely based on the institutional type and mission, the global context of the service, and the context of the learning. From questions of power and privilege to the complexities of language, culture, and customs, there is ripe opportunity for tension to emerge in ISL. The previous chapters serve as case studies demonstrating the tensions that arise when implementing ISL. Does this tension, sparked by language barriers and demanding cultural competencies, fueled by institutional mandates and faculty-framed experiences, and inflamed by the expectations of international community partners, as well as students and faculty, lead to transformation?

The transformative experiences discussed in the context of ISL and often referred to in the literature of ISL crosses many dimensions of learning (Kiely, 2004). Inherent within the attempts of many faculty and universities to create ISL opportunities is the desire to create these transformative learning experiences, exposing students to an international context, global issues, and conceptual foundations of global citizenship. On the basis of the practice of ISL shared in these chapters, perhaps I should address basic principles of ISL implementation to leverage the tension and to foster transformative learning.

The *Principles of Good Practice for Combining Service and Learning* (Honnet & Poulsen, 1989) and the adapted *Principles of Good Practice for Service-Learning Pedagogy* (Howard, 1993) provide powerful guidelines for implementing service-learning. Yet the tensions presented when implementing ISL, such as those in the chapters of this edited volume, add layers of complexity. The essential elements of culture, language, and social context are shifted, and the dimensions of learning and service are altered. How can these foundational principles be adapted to establish principles for ISL that respect the pedagogical foundations of service-learning and the complex context of the international community? How can the tension that inherently exists be leveraged to enhance all dimensions of learning?

Principles of Good Practice for International Service-Learning Pedagogy

Adapting the lessons learned in the chapters highlighted here and building on the traditional principles to guide service-learning, the following principles are variations specific to ISL. Although not exhaustive, this list of principles invites us to apply basic service-learning principles to ISL, while honoring the complexities of the international contexts with which we work. In essence, the principles challenge us to uncover tensions, name them, and operate intentionally with such tensions in mind.

Principle 1: Establish Learning Goals for the ISL Program or Experience

Why is the ISL program or experience being facilitated? How is learning enhanced through this ISL program? How is facilitating it in an international context essential to a domestic or even local context? Why does this program or experience exist? Establishing the learning goals or outcomes may be an essential exercise in framing an ISL program, articulating expected outcomes, and preparing for assessment and evaluation.

As the chapters in this text reveal, there are many dimensions of learning and conceptual frameworks from which to operate. Identifying learning goals in the context of the following concepts may provide a guideline:

- Power
- Privilege
- Otherness
- Culture
- Language
- Teaching and learning
- Awareness of American context and society
- Community development and capacity development
- Critical consciousness
- Faith and spirituality
- Justice
- Social change
- Social responsibility and social enterprise
- Professional skill development
- Global citizenship

Principle 2: Establish Criteria for the International Organization and for the Service Work to Be Done, as Related to the Learning Goals of ISL

Outlining the essential characteristics of the international community partner and the service work with which students are engaged is essential to framing ISL. This basic step may be the difference between students participating in an educational pilgrimage or global site visit, where they observe work and increase awareness, and students participating in actual work. Setting specific criteria for both organizations and service work encourages the latter. Sample criteria may include the following:

- Established number of hours worked per week or day
- Organization provides clear orientation and training
- On-site mentor or supervisor
- Clearly detailed project with set outcome, deadline, or conclusion
- Regularly scheduled interaction with community members
- Opportunity for on-site visits to other organizations or communities
- Family homestays
- Conversational interaction to enhance language skills

Principle 3: Communicate With the International Community Partner to Establish a Service or Project Based on Community Priorities

The onset of ISL must reside not in the desire of an institution to provide this opportunity but in the agreement by the international partner to receive a group of students and faculty to meet community-defined priorities. The priorities of the international community partner must be clearly established, recognizing community assets, needs, and essential goals of the service. Through clear communication, the criteria for the international partners and for the service work may be established and articulated. Identifying priorities with international partners may emerge from encouraging international partners to respond to questions, such as the following:

- What strengths or assets currently exist in your community?
- How can a group of volunteers support those assets?
- What are some needs in your community?
- How can a group of volunteers support the community in addressing those needs?
- Is language fluency a requirement for volunteers to provide such support?

Principle 4: Establish Learning Objectives for the International Experience With the International Partner

The learning objectives are essential to any course construction, but they hold significant weight in an international course because the dimensions of learning are multiplied. Students are learning across multiple contexts, such as culture and language. The insight of international partners in framing the learning objectives not only invites them in as a coeducator of the students but also honors their experience and knowledge as essential in this partnership. Develop the learning objectives in collaboration with the international community partner by asking key questions, such as, What do you hope the students learn from this experience?

Principle 5: Intentionally Design Learning Activities Connecting International Service Work to Course Content as Related to Learning Objectives

Organizing the learning activities in a global context means connecting the service work to the course content so students can achieve the desired learning outcomes. The international service work may be the core experience, but facilitators of ISL must also craft learning strategies around the service work to foster the learning objectives. Course assignments and class dialogue integrally connect the service work to course content. In addition, presentations on experience create accountability and an opportunity for students to document and articulate their learning. For example, Doll et al. in chapter 10 discussed the China immersion program, in which students return to campus for a reflection debriefing session and a presentation of their experience to faculty and staff.

Principle 6: Intentionally Design Reflection Activities Connecting International Service Work to Course Content as Related to Learning Objectives

Crafting reflection assignments is equally important as designing learning activities. It is essential for students to have space to reflect on their international experience, and designing reflection through multiple modes of expression (verbal, written, multimedia) is important. With the added layers of complexity in ISL (language, culture, etc.), students may require more space to process their experiences, and intentional, critical reflection assignments may provide this. For example, in chapter 7, Stokamer, Hall, and Morgan discussed the reflection seminar created for students to process their experience through written and dialogical reflection.

Principle 7: Prioritize Orientation With the International Community Partner Site

An important aspect of leveraging the learning in ISL is orienting students to the international community. An orientation introduces students to the cultural expectations and norms, addresses issues of safety and personal responsibility, and frames the learning environment in which the students are operating. Coordinating an orientation with international partners also invites them into the coeducation of students and represents the partnership. In chapter 8, Ong and Green emphasized combining the common practice of study abroad initiatives with the development of ISL initiatives, such as predeparture orientation and on-site orientation with the community partner.

Principle 8: Integrate the Classroom Learning and International Community Learning

ISL provides ample opportunity for integrative learning, as students are in an international setting. The learning objectives may be met by blending the service with core concepts from the course through a variety of activities, assignments, reflections, and other educational strategies. In chapter 1, Mellom and Herrera discussed a "framework of integration" in which students "see the larger social, economic, and political frames." In chapter 12, Hartman and Kiely provided an extensive framework of learning in the context of critical global engagement that integrates such learning.

Principle 9: Let the International Experience Guide the Learning

There are many dimensions of the learning that facilitators may not plan for in ISL. Students may enhance their language skills, develop cultural competencies, improve interpersonal skills, or develop leadership skills. The course learning objectives will be the facilitator's articulated set of learning goals, but the students and international partners may have others as well. For example, students who "want to see if they can survive this experience" may improve their self-efficacy, and community partners who "want to educate others about an issue" may increase students' awareness about complex global issues. The unscripted learning outcomes from ISL are potentially at the intersection of transformative learning and tensions that arise from such learning. Facilitators of ISL must be prepared to address such unscripted learning as students make meaning of the international experiences in an ongoing process during and after the experience.

Principle 10: Plan for Students' Reentry

A consistent programming issue in study abroad tends to be preparing students for reentry into their home country. The challenge with ISL, whether it is a short weeklong excursion or a semester- or yearlong excursion, is students return struggling to articulate their "transformative learning":

> Participation in international service-learning programs can trigger extremely powerful visceral, emotional, cognitive reactions from students who begin to critically reflect on long-held and taken-for-granted assumptions about themselves, their lifestyle, career, relationships, social problems, and unjust hegemonic dimensions of the world around them. (Kiely, 2004, p. 18)

Students often desire to share their stories but often struggle to communicate their shift in thinking since traveling. Facilitators of ISL may need to prepare students for reentry with scheduled meetings to continue facilitating group dialogue and common experience. Providing opportunities for shared experiences among participants of ISL in the home country allows for continued reflection and processing of the transformative learning. In chapter 5, Halverson-Wente and Halverson-Wente discussed the "before, during, and after" approach of the program. They also noted the important role of students as "returnees" who continue working with the program and even return to the international partner site to engage in other contexts (internships, etc.).

Conclusion

ISL provides transformative learning opportunities for students through complex, tension-filled programming and implementation. As educators, why do we facilitate such difficult, time-consuming, resource-heavy ISL programs that are tension-filled and complicated to implement? The answer lies within the very tension and transformative educational experience it provides our students, specifically a "change in one's frame of reference" (Mezirow, 1991). ISL changes the minds of students, and such learning is worth the tension.

References

Honnet, E. P., & Poulsen, S. J. (1989). *Principles of good practice for combining service and learning* (Wingspread Special Report). Racine, WI: The Johnson Foundation.

Howard, J. (1993). Community service learning in the curriculum. In J. Howard (Ed.), *Praxis I: A faculty casebook on community service learning* (pp. 3–12). Ann Arbor, MI: OCSL Press.

Kiely, R. (2004). A chameleon with a complex: Searching for transformation in international service-learning. *Michigan Journal of Community Service Learning, 10*(2), 5–20.

Mezirow, J. (1991). *Transformative dimensions of adult learning.* San Francisco, CA: Jossey-Bass.

EDITORS AND CONTRIBUTORS

Editors

Patrick M. Green serves as the founding director of the Center for Experiential Learning at Loyola University Chicago, overseeing the service-learning, academic internships, undergraduate research, and electronic portfolio programs. In addition, Green is the clinical instructor of experiential learning and teaches a variety of general elective experiential learning courses, engaging students in service-learning, community-based research, international service-learning, internship experiences, and undergraduate research. Green received his BA from Loras College (Dubuque, IA), MA in history from Marquette University (Milwaukee, WI), and PhD in education from Roosevelt University (Chicago, IL), specializing in leadership in higher education. He has focused his research on the impact of experiential learning, especially reflection, skill development and career development, and the intersection of electronic portfolios with experiential learning. He has engaged with students and international service-learning in Italy, Peru, El Salvador, and Ghana. He has launched numerous experiential learning programs including social justice research fellowships, internship programs, and service-learning partnerships. He serves as an Engaged Scholar with National Campus Compact and as the chair-elect on the board of directors of the International Association for Research on Service-Learning and Community Engagement.

Mathew Johnson is an associate professor of sociology and environmental studies and director of academic community engagement at Siena College. He is also the codirector of the National High Impact Initiative of the Bonner Foundation and cofounder and director of the National Assessment of Service and Community Engagement. He serves as a commissioner on the New York State Commission on National and Community Service and as an officer of the board of several local and regional nonprofits. Johnson is the cofounder (with Dr. Don Levy) of the largest national study of service and community engagement in the United States. The National Assessment of Service and Community Engagement includes more than 50 institutions and more than 20,000 student respondents. For more than 10 years, Johnson has taken students all over the world to study community development, including India, Bolivia, and the Zapatista Autonomous Region of Chiapas, Mexico.

Contributors

Arturo Caballero Barrón is a research professor at the Marist University of Mérida. He has a degree in economics from the National Autonomous University of Mexico, a master's in education from Marist College, and a diploma in legal anthropology from the National Institute of Anthropology and History. He is an active member of the Ashoka International Organization for Social Entrepreneurs and coordinator of Social Development for the Yucatan Strategic Plan Foundation. He has served as a consultant to various UN agencies in southeastern Mexico, such as the United Nations High Commission for Refugees for Guatemalan refugees; Food and Agricultural Organization programs to support the modernization of coastal fisheries; the United Nations Development Programs' Small Grants Program to preserve the environment and provide natural disasters risk management; and UNICEF's evaluation of the Escuela Amiga program. He has published book chapters and articles on topics of community development, education, and human development.

Robert G. Bringle is professor emeritus of psychology at Indiana University-Purdue University Indianapolis, and Kulynych/Cline Visiting Distinguished Professor at Appalachian State University. He was formerly director of the IUPUI Center for Service and Learning, and chancellor's professor of psychology and philanthropic studies at Indiana University-Purdue University Indianapolis. For his numerous publications, accomplishments, and scholarship on service-learning, Dr. Bringle was awarded the Ehrlich Faculty Award for Service Learning and he was recognized at the International Service-Learning Research Conference for his outstanding contributions.

Joy Doll graduated from the University of South Alabama with a bachelor's of science in occupational therapy and from Creighton University with her doctor of occupational therapy (OTD). After receiving her doctorate, Doll completed a VISTA with AmeriCorp. After her VISTA, she acted as the coordinator for the Office of Interprofessional Scholarship, Service, and Education, designing and implementing community engagement activities for students across Creighton University's School of Pharmacy and Health Professions. Currently, Doll is an assistant professor in the Department of

Occupational Therapy at Creighton University and the director of the Post Professional OTD Program. Doll has passion for service and grant writing. She has written over 20 grants and is the author of the text *Grant Writing and Program Development in Occupational Therapy: Making the Connection* (Jones and Bartlett, 2009). Her research interests include service-learning, Native American health, and international occupational therapy.

Amanda L. Espenschied-Reilly is currently dean of general education and online learning at the Aultman College of Nursing and Health Sciences and is a doctoral candidate in the Higher Education Leadership program at Kent State University in Kent, Ohio. Her dissertation is a critical qualitative study of the experiences of low socioeconomic status students in service-learning courses. She completed her BS and MS in biological sciences at Wright State University (Ohio) and her MA in educational leadership at West Virginia University.

Carlton D. Floyd is a professor of English and ethnic studies at the University of San Diego (USD) and has been on the faculty since 2000. Floyd specializes in African American literature, mixed-race and ethnic studies, identity and community, and representations of children and childhood. He was a founding faculty member of USD's Jamaica study abroad program, where he taught Black Caribbean literature from 2006 to 2009. From 2010 to 2012, he also served as the associate provost for inclusion and diversity at USD. He has recently written for and edited a special volume on August Wilson in *College Literature*.

Lori Gardinier is the director of human services at Northeastern University in Boston, Massachusetts. She holds an MA in social work from Boston University and a PhD from Northeastern University. She has practiced in the area of antipoverty and social justice work in community-based settings and as a counselor in organizations addressing intimate partner violence. In her role at Northeastern, she is a leader in experiential education practice in both local and global settings. Over the past 10 years, Gardinier has established project-based service-learning capacity-building programs with nonprofits in Benin, Costa Rica, India, Mexico, and Zambia. In this role she and her students collaborate with local leaders to identify creative solutions to organizational challenges. Her research spans social movement studies, sexual violence, and best practice in experiential education.

Caroline Goulet is founding dean and professor, School of Physical Therapy, University of the Incarnate Word in San Antonio, Texas. Prior to that appointment, she was an associate professor in physical therapy, director of the Transitional Doctor of Physical Therapy Program, and codirector of the Office of Interprofessional Scholarship, Service, and Education in the School of Pharmacy and Health Professions at Creighton University in Omaha, Nebraska. She grew up in Montreal, Quebec, where she obtained a BSc in physical therapy (1986) from McGill University, an MSc in applied biomedical engineering (1989), and a PhD in biomedical sciences (1995) from the Université de Montréal. Prior to coming to Omaha, she held assistant professor positions at the University of Ottawa, Ontario, Canada; the University of Iowa; and the Hong Kong Polytechnic University. She is licensed to practice physical therapy in both Texas and Nebraska.

Shpresa Halimi is the director of the Vietnam-USA Professional Fellows Program in the Center for Public Service at Portland State University. Prior to joining the Center for Public Service, she was affiliated with the Institute for Sustainable Solutions at Portland State University. Her research interests include multilevel environmental governance, community-based environmental management, and sustainability in higher education. Halimi has broad-based experience in program management, teaching, research, training, and consulting work with institutions of higher education, public sector organizations, NGOs, and community groups in the United States, Southeast Europe, and Southeast Asia. For over a decade she has designed and implemented capacity-building programs for the Vietnamese institutions of higher education and for mid- and senior-level professionals from the public and private sectors. Halimi holds a PhD in public administration and policy from Portland State University.

Jennifer Hall has over 35 years of experience in instruction and administration. She has spent the past 22 years employed at the University of Technology, Jamaica (UTech), where her positions have been vice dean, Faculty of Education and Liberal Studies; program leader, master's of science in Workforce Training and Education; head, Department of Liberal Studies; and head, Communication Division. She was the program director for the International Partnership for Service Learning and Leadership program at UTech for 3 years. She holds a PhD in education with an emphasis on curriculum and instruction from Northern Caribbean University, Mandeville, Jamaica; a master's of science in workforce education and development from Southern Illinois University, United States; and a bachelor's of arts (Hons) from the University of the West Indies, Mona. Her research profile includes action and applied research in teaching and learning, diversity, and communication.

Lori Halverson-Wente an instructor of communication at Rochester Community and Technical College, was named MN Educator of the Year by the

Minnesota Colleges and Universities Chancellor's Office. She served as a Fulbright Scholar to Denmark and as a fellow at the American University of Phnom Penh. Recently she and Mark Halverson-Wente lived in Cambodia to further develop Cambodian and American educational communities' international service-learning programming, faculty development, and intercultural communication programs.

Mark Halverson-Wente is an adjunct instructor of political science. Since 2006, along with his cofounder and facilitator, he has been involved with Rochester Community and Technical College's International Service-Learning/Travel Study course in intercultural communication, which has won national and international awards and recognition. His interests include political philosophy, Cambodian culture and history, music, and spending time with his border collie.

Eric Hartman is cofounder and editor of criticalservicelearning.org. He recently received the Early Career Research Award from the International Association for Research on Service-learning and Community Engagement. He was also awarded the 4 Under 40 Impact Prize from the University of Pittsburgh's Graduate School of Public and International Affairs, recognizing his work developing evidence-based curricula to advance global citizenship and his leadership as executive director of Amizade Global Service-Learning from 2007 to 2010. Through Amizade, where he currently serves on the board of directors, he has been fortunate to support community-driven development in Bolivia, Jamaica, the Navajo Nation, Tanzania, and several other locations around the world. This work has led his research to focus on fair trade learning, a conceptualization of educational exchange that prioritizes partnership, reciprocity, and transparency.

Socorro Herrera serves as a professor of elementary education at Kansas State University and is the executive director for the Center for Intercultural and Multilingual Advocacy in the College of Education. Her K–12 teaching experience includes an emphasis on literacy development. Her research focuses on literacy opportunities with culturally and linguistically diverse students, reading strategies, and teacher preparation for diversity in the classroom. Herrera has authored several books, including *Assessment Accommodations for Classroom Teachers of Culturally and Linguistically Diverse Students* (Pearson, 2007, 2013) and *Crossing the Vocabulary Bridge: Differentiated Strategies for Diverse Secondary Classrooms* (Teachers College Press 2011). Herrera serves as a KSU faculty adviser for the College of Education preservice teacher training study abroad trips to China,

Guatemala, Mexico, and Paraguay where the students are placed with host families and spend time in local classrooms to observe, assist, and co-teach with local classroom teachers in addition to completing course assignments.

Julie Hoffman is an assistant professor in the Department of Physical Therapy at Creighton University. She received her master of physical therapy degree from Hahnemann University and transitional doctor of physical therapy degree from Creighton University. She practiced as a physical therapist at Madonna Rehabilitation hospital prior to joining the PT faculty where she teaches cardiovascular and pulmonary physical therapy. In addition to her teaching responsibilities, Hoffman is the director of physical therapy in the Institute for Latin American Concern (ILAC) program that provides students with clinical experience while providing needed physical therapy for the underserved in the Dominican Republic. Her research interests include clinical reasoning with professional students, cardiopulmonary PT interventions, and global health.

Marcus Ingle is a professor of public administration and director of international public service in the Center of Public Service, Mark O. Hatfield School of Government at Portland State University in Oregon. He earned a BA from the University of California, Riverside; an MPA from the University of Washington; and a PhD from the Maxwell School of Syracuse University in 1977. He has more than 35 years of experience in more than 80 countries. His career spans local to multinational assignments in the government, nonprofit, and corporate sectors, including for the U.S. Agency for International Development, The World Bank Group, and the University of Maryland. From 1997 to 2003, he worked with Booz Allen Hamilton, the worldwide strategy and technology consulting firm, in Colombia, Vietnam, Hungary, and the Balkans. He serves as a public leadership and management facilitator for many coproduced programs and initiatives domestically and globally.

Susan V. Iverson is associate professor of higher education administration and student personnel at Kent State University and holds affiliate faculty status with both women's studies and LGBT studies. Iverson's research interests focus on equity and diversity, status of women in higher education, the use of feminist poststructural perspectives in research, and feminist pedagogy, and she is currently coediting a volume on *Feminist Community Engagement* (Palgrave). Prior to becoming faculty, Iverson worked in student affairs administration for more than 10 years. Iverson earned her doctorate in higher educational leadership, with a concentration in women's studies, from the University of Maine; she also holds a BA in English from Keene State College (New Hampshire), an MA in higher education administration from Boston College, and an MEd in counseling from Bridgewater State College (Massachusetts).

Lou Jensen is an assistant professor in the Department of Occupational Therapy at Creighton University. Jensen earned a bachelor's of science in occupational therapy and psychology from St. Ambrose University and a professional doctorate degree in occupational therapy from Creighton University. She teaches courses related to neurology and professional practice. In addition to her teaching responsibilities, Jensen is the coordinator of the Greater Omaha Pathway, a distance entry-level pathway for occupational therapy students at Creighton. Jensen's research interests include issues related to clinical education, best practices in stroke rehabilitation, and the outcomes of international and interprofessional education. She has been a faculty member in the China Honors Interprofessional Program at Creighton University.

Kevin Kecskes is associate professor of public administration in the Mark O. Hatfield School of Government at Portland State University. He teaches graduate courses in the master's of public administration program on the global roles of NGOs, strategic planning, and ethics, as well as undergraduate courses focused on community engagement. For over a decade, Kecskes provided university-wide leadership in various positions at PSU, including associate vice provost for engagement and director for community-university partnerships. From 1997 to 2002, he was regional program director of the Western Region Campus Compact Consortium. Kecskes is on the editorial board of the *Journal of Public Scholarship in Higher Education* and has advised numerous college and university campuses in the United States and globally for over 15 years. He edited *Engaging Departments: Moving Faculty Culture From Private to Public, Individual to Collective Focus for the Common Good* (Wiley, 2006).

Richard Kiely currently serves as the director of Engaged Learning + Research at Cornell University. In 2002, he received his PhD from Cornell University, and in 2005 he was recognized nationally as a John Glenn Scholar in Service-Learning for his longitudinal research that led to the development of a transformative global service-learning model. He has taught at and has served as an adviser to numerous (global) service-learning programs and was the cofounder of a global service-learning partnership in Puerto Cabezas, Nicaragua, which will be entering its 20th year in 2014. He continues to be an active scholar in the area of global service-learning and engagement in higher education and regularly conducts seminars and workshops on course design, (global) service-learning, community development, participatory action research, and program evaluation. He is currently working on a coauthored book, *Building a Better World: The Pedagogy and Practice of Global Service-Learning* (Stylus, forthcoming).

Paul Kollman is an associate professor of theology at the University of Notre Dame, where he has been on faculty since 2001. He became the third director of Notre Dame's Center for Social Concerns in July 2012. Kollman is a fellow of the Kellogg Institute for International Studies, the Kroc Institute for International Peace Studies, and the Nanovic Institute for European Studies, all at Notre Dame. His academic interests include African Christianity, world Christianity, and international service-learning, and he has taught in eastern Africa and pursued research there and in Nigeria, South Africa, and in archives in Europe and the United States. Kollman received his BA and MDiv degrees from the University of Notre Dame and his PhD from the University of Chicago Divinity School.

John Loggins is the associate director for the Center for Community Service-Learning at the University of San Diego. He is an alumnus of USD's College of Arts and Sciences and also earned his master's degree in leadership studies from USD. Loggins joined USD's community service-learning leadership team in 2002 after serving 2 years in the Peace Corps, Jamaica, where his work focused on community building and development. Prior to his arrival at USD, Loggins also worked in the nonprofit field with the Leukemia and Lymphoma Society as a program manager overseeing a $2 million fundraising campaign. Since 2006, he has coordinated the community service-learning component of a study abroad program in Jamaica, West Indies, and he has also led service-immersion programs in Uganda, Guatemala, and New Orleans. His current work-related efforts are trained on identifying innovative pathways to further connect students to the community in meaningful and sustainable ways.

Paula J. Mellom has a PhD in linguistics and serves as the associate director of the Center for Latino Achievement and Success in Education (CLASE) at the University of Georgia. As such, she is responsible for seeking funding for CLASE's array of programs, as well as conducting qualitative research on their impacts. In addition, Dr. Mellom leads CLASE's "SALSA" program, a summer science enrichment course for English-language-learning high school students and a study abroad course in Costa Rica, "Language and Culture

Service Learning." Dr. Mellom lived in Costa Rica for 10 years, where she was an elementary classroom teacher at a bilingual school, the director of the English-language program for the graduate school at CATIE, and that center's official translator. Her research interests include code-switching in the classroom and the ways in which globalization and issues of identity construction impact language acquisition and use.

A. Rafik Mohamed is a sociology professor and the chairperson of social sciences at Clayton State University. From 1999 to 2009, Mohamed was a professor at the University of San Diego, where he also served as the chairperson of the Department of Sociology. He earned his BA from the George Washington University and his MA and PhD from the University of California at Irvine. Since 2006, he has served as the director of a summer study abroad and community service-learning program in Jamaica, West Indies. He is the coauthor of *Dorm Room Dealers: Drugs and the Privileges of Race and Class*, (Lynne Rienner, 2011), a monograph exploring the world of college drug dealers, and he has also published works and presented conference papers on the benefits and challenges of studies abroad. Currently, he is completing work on *Lords of the Blacktop*, a book exploring issues of race, sports, masculinity, and class in the United States.

Marisol Morales is the founding director of the Office of Civic and Community Engagement at the University of La Verne in Southern California. Prior to joining the University of La Verne in 2013, she served as the associate director (2007–2013) and assistant director for community development (2005–2007) of the Steans Center for Community-based Service Learning and Community Service Studies at DePaul University in Chicago. Morales has been in higher education and service-learning for more than 8 years and community development for more than 15 years. She has led or developed international service-learning programs in over six different countries and has a special emphasis on community engagement with students of color. Morales holds a BA in Latin American/Latino Studies and a MA/MS in International Public Service Management from DePaul University.

Rachel Tomas Morgan is assistant director of the Center for Social Concerns and director of International Service Learning and Justice Education. She oversees the international engagement efforts of the center and the center's justice education programming. Tomas Morgan designed, implemented, and directs the International Summer Service Learning Program and works with other center colleagues on international service-learning and community-based learning abroad. She also works with faculty across the university interested in developing courses that include an international experiential or community-based learning component and consults on international-related initiatives across the university. Tomas Morgan received her MA in the area of systematic theology from the University of Notre Dame. She has previously worked in the fields of international development and natural disaster assistance, religious studies in secondary education, and faith-based social outreach.

Thomas Winston Morgan is president of International Partnership for Service-learning and Leadership with nearly 20 years of experience in intercultural education and international management for profit-based and non-profit organizations. Morgan has held leadership positions in intercultural educational operations such as AFS Intercultural Programs, headquartered in New York; AHA Study Abroad/University of Oregon in Portland, Oregon; and international tech companies like MusicMatch in San Diego. Morgan is also an AFS Returnee (Honduras, 1980–1981). His firsthand experience living and working in a variety of intercultural settings has provided him with an understanding of, and commitment to, service, community involvement, social justice, and accessibility in intercultural education. His educational background includes advanced degrees in Germanic languages and literatures, Spanish, and international business. He speaks fluent German, Spanish, and French and is learning Italian and Thai. He and his partner own a guesthouse in Portland, Oregon.

Keli Mu is an associate professor and chair in the Department of Occupational Therapy at Creighton University. Mu received his occupational therapy degree from Creighton University and his doctoral degree from University of Nebraska–Lincoln. In addition to his teaching and administrative responsibilities, he has been actively participating in various research studies and grant projects. His research interests include evidence-based practice, experiential learning, outcomes research, occupational therapy practice errors and client safety, and issues related to international and interprofessional education. He is the recipient of the James S. Todd Memorial Award for patient safety research. He has published over 40 peer-reviewed research articles in professional journals and is a frequent presenter at national and international professional conferences. He currently serves on editorial boards for three professional journals. He also directs the China Honors Interprofessional Program at Creighton University.

Amye Day Ong holds an MA in religion from Yale University and is an MFA creative writing–nonfiction candidate at Columbia College Chicago.

She worked as a study abroad adviser at both Loyola University Chicago and Northern Kentucky University. While at Loyola University Chicago, she specialized in developing faculty-led and service-learning study abroad programs for the university. Specifically, she worked in collaboration with Dr. Patrick Green and Loyola's Center for Experiential Learning to create new short-term and semester-long service-learning programs in both Peru and Vietnam.

Phung Thuy Phuong is a senior lecturer at the University of Science in Ho Chi Minh City (a member of Vietnam National University) and the cofounder of the Center for Educational Excellence. She received her bachelor's degree in biology (1982) from the University of Ho Chi Minh City, Vietnam; her master's degree in environmental management (1994) from the Asian Institute of Technology, Thailand; and her doctoral degree in environmental management (2002) from Wageningen University, the Netherlands. She was a Fulbright Visiting Scholar at Portland State University (Oregon) (2005–2006).

Stephanie Stokamer is the director of the Center for Civic Engagement and an assistant professor in peace and social justice at Pacific University in Forest Grove, Oregon. She has taught and administered community-based learning courses in both undergraduate and graduate programs since 2005 and was the program director for the International Partnership for Service Learning and Leadership program at Portland State University for 3 years. She has a doctorate in educational leadership and master's degrees in postsecondary education and social science. Stokamer's areas of scholarship include service-learning and civic engagement, particularly with respect to pedagogical practices and faculty development. Her service and scholarship have been recognized with awards from both local and international organizations, including the International Association for Research on Service-Learning and Community Engagement. She is a published author and owns a small business with her husband in Portland, Oregon.

Honnet, E. P., 243
hospitals, 178–80
host community
    ecotourists and ambivalence by, 21
    people's behavior differences in, 22
    students lacking respect from, 22–23
    students' views as romanticized of,
        19–20
host family, 156
hostility phase
    student's desire to retreat in, 24–25
    student's flight of fight response in,
        21–22
    in U-curve hypothesis, 21–25
housing, 148, 155–56
Howard, J., 243
humanity, common, 232
human rights, 237
humor phase, 25–27
hybrid classes, 81n1

IDEAS. *See* Innovative Development
    and Engagement Across Sectors
IDI. *See* Intercultural Developmental
    Inventory
IHD. *See* integral human development
ILAC. *See* Institute for Latin American
    Concern
Illich, Ivan, 117
imperialism, 4
"In Bondage" (McKay), 167
India, 201
Indiana University-Purdue, 207n9
indigenous autonomy, 4–5
indigenous community, 4–5
indoctrination, 197, 199
Innovative Development and Engage-
    ment Across Sectors (IDEAS),
    49–50
"Inspired to Serve Project," 205
Institute for Latin American Concern
    (ILAC), 184–86
    administration supporting programs
        of, 177

collaborative health care mission of,
    176
at Creighton University, 175–77
faculty programs of, 176, 177,
    181–83
Institutional Baseline Assessment, 50
institutions. *See also specific institutions*
    community liaisons with partnership,
        130
    global impact and responsibility of,
        154–56
    Ireland's research on, 35–36, 43n5
    ISL globally located, 145–47
    ISL partnership complexities with,
        132
    ISL program design and responsibility
        of, 154
    ISL served by partnerships of host, 130
    service-learning resistance by, 37–38,
        40
    USD identity as Catholic, 166
instructors, 92–93, 118–19
integral human development (IHD),
    68–69, 76–80
integration, 77–78
integrative learning, 247
intellectual dimensions, 226–28
Intel Vietnam Scholar (IVS) Program,
    62–63
intercultural competency, 235–36
Intercultural Developmental Inventory
    (IDI), 101–2
interdisciplinary teams, 228
international communities, 245, 247
international exchange, 218
international partner objectives, 246
International Partnership for Service-
    Learning and Leadership (IPSL),
    86, 127–31
    challenges of, 131, 135
    community needs first in placements
        by, 133
    Concordia University-Portland's new
        partnership with, 141–42

collaboration across campus units to develop institutional capacity for ISL; and the role that community constituencies should assume as cocreators of the curriculum, coeducators in the delivery of the curriculum, and coinvestigators in the evaluation of and study of ISL. The contributors demonstrate sensitivity to ethical implications of ISL, issues of power and privilege, the integrity of partnerships, reflection, reciprocity, and community benefits.

Sty/us

22883 Quicksilver Drive
Sterling, VA 20166-2102   Subscribe to our e-mail alerts: www.Styluspub.com

Also available from Stylus

A Guide for Students Planning to Engage in College-Level Study Abroad and International Service-Learning.

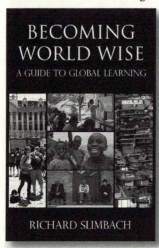

Becoming World Wise

A Guide to Global Learning

Richard Slimbach

This book draws on the author's extensive travel and many years of guiding college students' global learning. Richard Slimbach offers a comprehensive framework for pre-field preparation that includes, but goes beyond, discussions of packing lists and assorted "do's and don'ts" to consider the ultimate purposes and practical learning strategies needed to enter deeply into a host culture. It also features an in-depth look at the post-sojourn process, helping the reader integrate the experiences and insights from the field into her or his studies and personal life. This book constitutes a vital road map for anyone intent on having their whole being—body, mind, and heart—stretched through the intercultural experience.

Becoming World Wise offers an integrated approach to cross-cultural learning aimed at transforming our consciousness while also contributing to the flourishing of the communities that host us.

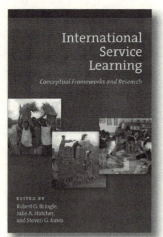

International Service Learning

Conceptual Frameworks and Research

Edited by Robert G. Bringle, Julie A. Hatcher, and Steven G. Jones

The book argues that rigorous research is essential to improving the quality of ISL's implementation and delivery, and providing the evidence that will lead to wider support and adoption by the academy, funders, and partners. It is intended for both practitioners and scholars, providing guidance and commentary on good practice. The volume provides pioneering analysis and understanding of why and under what conditions ISL is an effective pedagogy.

Individual chapters discuss conceptual frameworks, research design issues, and measurement strategies related to student learning outcomes; the importance of ISL course and program design; the need for faculty development activities to familiarize faculty with the component pedagogical strategies; the need for resources and